PREFACE

This edition of Book III of Propertius is similar in scope and intention to those of Books I and IV which have preceded it (Cambridge University Press, 1961 and 1965). It will, I hope, be followed shortly by an edition of Book II on the same lines. There is in general no need to repeat or amplify here what has been said in earlier prefaces; but it must be emphasized that in this book, as in all Propertius, there are fairly numerous uncertainties of text and interpretation. I have tried neither to obscure nor to exaggerate this fact in the notes below.

Only three transpositions have been adopted, affecting xi, 6 -8, xiv, 15–16 and xx, 13–14. Perhaps Postgate's transposition of xix, 15–16 to follow xix, 20 should have been adopted too. Divisions not made by the MSS have been made here in the pieces traditionally numbered viii and xx.

To the lists which I gave earlier of the books which I have principally consulted must be added now the text and translation by Professor Luck which appeared (Zurich, Artemis Verlag) in 1964. Among other friends I have again to thank especially Mr Sandbach, Mr Wilkinson, Mr Lee and Sir Roger Mynors, for help not less generous nor less indispensable than in the past.

With the permission of the Delegates of the Clarendon Press the Latin text of this edition is based, as before, on the Oxford text, in this case the Oxford text of 1960. Divergences are listed on pp. 9–10. Most of the *apparatus* also has been excerpted from the Oxford edition. I am glad to acknowledge gratefully, and with emphasis, this particular debt of my own to the Oxford editor, the late Mr E. A. Barber, as well as the wider obligation to him which I share with all students of Propertius.

W. A. C.

Cambridge

PREFACE TO 1985 EDITION

This edition of Propertius III reprints that published in 1966 by the Cambridge University Press, without change except for the correction of some erring references and the addition of a few items to the *apparatus criticus*. There then are added (pp. 173ff.) a number of supplementary notes, intended to clarify or amend those of the 1966 edition, mostly in response to the suggestions of reviewers: these notes should also enable the above-mentioned additions to the *apparatus* to be identified. Asterisks set in the margin against the original notes will tell the reader where reference to the supplement is invited. It will be found that in several places the editor's preference in respect of a reading or interpretation has changed since 1966: for example he now believes that the MSS tradition's *tingere* in 3.42 is established by Professor Suits' observation cited on p. 173; and he would follow Professor Richardson in transposing 19.15–16 and not transposing 20.11–12; and would read *spatiis* with the Leipzig Teubner in 21.25. These are examples only. The text of 1966 has not been altered to reflect such changes of judgement, for stability's as well as simplicity's sake. Suggestions enclosed in square brackets are reported, more or less tentatively, for consideration.

In addition to Professor Richardson's Commentary on all four books of the Elegies (University of Oklahoma Press 1977), and W.R. Smyth's splendid and instructive *Thesaurus criticus ad Sexti Propertii textum* (Leyden 1970), there have also appeared in recent years new Teubner texts edited by R. Hanslik (Leipzig 1979) and P. Fedeli (Stuttgart 1984). A list is appended (p. 172) of readings in the more recent of these which differ from the text printed here. More recently still has appeared a full-scale Commentary by Dr. Fedeli, richly annotated (*Properzio, Il Libro Terzio delle Elegie*: Bari 1985).

Thanks are due to John H. Betts, the General Editor of Bristol Classical Press, for enabling this commentary on the third book of the Elegies to remain available and for seeing the various corrigenda and addenda noted above through the press.

W.A.C.

Cambridge, 1985

PROPERTIUS
ELEGIES
BOOK III

PROPERTIUS
ELEGIES

BOOK III

EDITED BY W. A. CAMPS

*Fellow of Pembroke College and
Lecturer in Classics in the University of
Cambridge*

Published by Bristol Classical Press
General Editor: John H. Betts
(by arrangement with the Syndicate of
the Cambridge University Press)

First published in 1966 by Cambridge University Press

This edition published in 1985, by arrangement with the
Syndicate of the Cambridge University Press, by
Bristol Classical Press
an imprint of
Gerald Duckworth & Co. Ltd
61 Frith Street
London W1D 3JL
e-mail: inquiries@duckworth-publishers.co.uk
Website: www.ducknet.co.uk

Reprinted 1993, 2001

A catalogue record for this book is available
from the British Library

ISBN 0-86292-116-3

Printed in Great Britain by
Antony Rowe Ltd, Eastbourne

CONTENTS

INTRODUCTION

Book III belongs almost exactly to the middle of Propertius' poetical career, if the comparatively few datable references in his works are a fair guide. For Elegy xviii appears (see note below on line 32 of the poem) to have been written at the very time of the death of Marcellus, which occurred late in 23 B.C. Elegy xi may have been suggested by the quadrennial celebration of the victory of Actium held (Dio C. LIII, 2) in 24 B.C.; and the emphasis in Elegy iv on military preparation against the Parthians suits the period about 22 B.C. Datable references in Book I point to the year 30 and thereabouts; those in Book IV to the year 16. Book III is thus a mid-point. We can suppose with probability that it was begun not earlier than 25, because Elegy x of the preceding Book II mentions as impending an expedition against Arabia which set out in that year. On the other hand Elegy xii of this book and Elegy iii of Book IV both imply a time before the settlement reached with Parthia in 20 B.C. but later than the first preparations. It seems therefore safe to fix the limits of Book III as not wider than 25–20, perhaps 24–21.

In Books I and II Propertius had presented what in appearance at least is the record of a personal experience of love in various phases and aspects; this is 'subjective love-elegy' in the natural sense of the term. In Book III a curious development occurs. The poet insists firmly and repeatedly (see for instance III, i, 9, III, ii, 2, III, iii, 47, III, v, 21 ff., III, ix, 45) that love-elegy is and must be his sphere; and of the twenty-five elegies that compose the Book all but two (the *epicedia* vii and xviii) are in fact related somehow or other to the love-theme. But in nine of these (i, ii, iii, v, ix on the poet's literary views and intentions, and iv, xi, xiii, xxii on national and patriotic topics)

I

this relation is either indirect, as in the literary elegies, or tenuous and artificial, as for instance in Elegy xi where four lines on the poet's subjection to a woman lead to a review in eighteen lines of legendary female tyrants and thus to a declamation in thirty-four lines on Rome's escape from Cleopatra. Moreover, of the fourteen poems to which, in virtue of their professed subjects, the term 'love-elegy' would more naturally apply, nearly half (xii, xiv, xv, xvii, xix, xxi) are impersonal in character (e.g. the 'essays' xiv and xix) or composed substantially of matter extraneous to the subject of love (e.g. xv consists chiefly of the tale of Dirce and Antiope, xvii chiefly of a recital of the attributes of Bacchus, etc., xxi chiefly of a traveller's tour recounted in anticipation). And in the remainder, love-elegies proper (vi, viii, x, xvi, xx, xxiii, xxiv, xxv), the tone is light, varying from the cynical to the mildly sentimental, and the sense of involvement is correspondingly small, except in the last two, which purport to say an angry farewell to Cynthia. This heroine and inspiration of Book I is in the present book named only three times, and then in a context of dismissal (xxiv and xxv) or escape (xxi). Hence it is clear that in this Book the author is no lover in search of a means of expression, but a poet in search of subjects. He seems to feel the need of an identified department of poetry within which to work, and the need of the love-theme to provide the identifying label, and so he persists in presenting himself as a 'love-elegist'. But he proceeds to extend the limits of the department 'love-elegy' in such a way as to make it no longer meaningful. It is thus no surprise to us to find (in Book IV) that the farewell to Cynthia in Elegies xxiv and xxv of this Book is also a farewell to the role of love-elegist, despite the protestations of Elegies i–v.

The reader of Book III may be struck from time to time with the feeling that here is an elegiac counterpart to Horatian lyric; and indeed we find here many of the same poem-types, subjects and leading motives: the dramatic monologue (in Horace a dramatic dialogue also), the hymn to a god, the birthday poem, the appeal to a friend to return from abroad (in Horace it is welcome to a friend returning), the boast of the poet's achievement, the forecast of his immortality; the declamations on the fall of Cleopatra, on the evils of mounting extravagance, on the praises of Italy, on the poet's comparative poverty not regretted, etc. Another feature of the book which everyone will remark is the strongly rhetorical character of some of the poems: especially the essay-form (corresponding to known rhetorical exercises) of Elegies xi, xiii, xiv, xix and xxii, and the methodical enumeration of instances to illustrate a point, both in these elegies and in others (e.g. iii, i, 25 ff. Homeric subjects, iii, v, 25 ff. subjects of didactic poetry, iii, ix, 9 ff. sculptors and painters, iii, xii, 23 ff. Ulysses' adventures, iii, xvii, 21 ff. attributes of Bacchus and his worship, iii, xxii, 7 ff. wonders of Greek legend and 29 ff. horrors of Greek legend). It will be noticed that the thought of these and of many other elegies in this Book is organized in a very simple and almost prosaically business-like way. Thus in Elegy xxii the thought is 'Abroad you may see many legendary marvels: but the marvels of Italy are better: and in Italy there are no marvels of evil as there were in Greek legend'; these propositions, few, simple and consequent, are then each supported with a stock of parallel illustrative instances. This methodical simplicity of the layout is sometimes accompanied by a quantitative balance in the component parts. For instance Elegy ii, after an introductory couplet, falls into line-groups of $8+8+8$; Elegy iii into $26+26$; Elegy xvi into $10+10+10$; Elegy xviii into $10+10+10(+4)$. Sometimes there is balance about an unbalanced central section, as in Elegy vi, where the pattern is $8+26$ (the Report) $+8$, or in Elegy xxi, where the pattern is $10+14$ (the Journey) $+10$. There seems no doubt that this was intended by the poet, or at least corresponded to some instinctive inclination on his part. But it does not seem to have been a general principle of composition with him, for in some elegies (e.g. xiv and xix) no system of balance is apparent, at least to me. In others again (and these a good many) it is hard to determine with certainty the exact limits of the parts into which an elegy appears to fall; and the reader is therefore asked to treat with critical reserve the analyses offered in some of the notes below.

The order of the elegies in the book is evidently considered, but not in any important sense significant. The first five elegies (i–v) stand apart (as in a different way do the first six odes of Horace's third book), being concerned with the poet's literary views and ambitions. In the following eight elegies (vi–xiii) erotic and non-erotic pieces appear to be set in alternation (with the result that the whole first half of the book contains only three examples of love-elegy in the normal sense of the term); but this alternation does not continue after Elegy xiv. The last five pieces of the book (xxi–xxv), though they show no sign of having been composed to form a group, have probably been selected to stand together because they all can be read as pointing to the end of Propertius' career as a lover and love-poet: in xxi he is setting out for Athens in the hope of forgetting Cynthia; in xxii he looks forward to the return from abroad of Tullus, whom we know from Book I as a representative of the conventional Roman virtues; in xxiii the tablets used for love-letters have been lost; and xxiv and xxv profess to dismiss Cynthia for good. The two *epicedia* (vii and xviii) are set apart from one another in roughly corresponding positions. The lack here of any clearer principle of arrangement, such as we find in Books I and IV, may be due to the diversity of the matter which this book comprises.

The diversity of subject-matter is matched by the diversity of the diction. In elegies such as vi and xxiii, which might be speeches from comedy, the language is a metrical version of

4

crisply styled conversation: e.g. III, vi, 21–2 *ille potest nullo miseram me linquere facto, et qualem nolo dicere habere domi?* Consider, on the other hand, III, xi, 9–12 *Colchis flagrantis adamantina sub iuga tauros egit et armigera proelia seuit humo, custodisque feros clausit serpentis hiatus, iret ut Aesonias aurea lana domos*; here, while almost every word is from the vocabulary of prose, the application in almost every case is unprosaic. But on their different levels the two passages both exhibit properties of style which are characteristically Propertian: firmness of texture, organized sound, and a high degree of expressiveness. These are independent qualities of style *per se*; but the first two are often found contributing to one another and to the third.

Firmness of texture is achieved both by avoiding idle words and by extracting as much effect[1] as possible from those which are at work. One means to it is the suppression of terms of syntax or of sense which can be supplied by the imagination. Thus in the example III, vi, 22 above, a term of *syntax* is omitted, the antecedent to *qualem*; in III, xi, 55 *tanto...ciue* is an ablative absolute, with ellipse of a participle of the verb 'to be'; in III, xxi, 33 *seu moriar, fato* there is ellipse of a second *moriar* with *fato*. These ellipses are syntactical. But there may also be ellipse of terms of *meaning*; thus in the example from III, xi, 9–10 quoted above Medea is said to have yoked the bulls, when what is understood is that she enabled Jason to yoke them; and she is said to have sowed battles, when what is understood is that she emboldened Jason to sow the dragon's teeth from which then sprang the armed men who engaged in battle together. In III, ix, 41 the Wooden Horse is said to plough the site of fallen Troy because it brings about

---

[1] The effect desired is usually one of meaning. But sometimes it may be purely stylistic. Hence in a passage such as II, i, 63–4 *Mysus et Haemonia iuuenis qua cuspide uulnus senserat, hac ipsa cuspide sensit opem* the repeated words are not idle. One does not want too much of this, of course, and from Propertius one does not get too much.

the victory which in turn brings about this result. Both these forms of ellipse are common in Propertius in numerous variations.[1] But firmness of texture is achieved in other ways than by ellipse. For instance, the value of significant words may be enhanced by packing them closely together, as in III, vi, 33 *putris et in uacuo texetur aranea lecto*; III, xi, 39 *incesti meretrix regina Canopi*; III, xviii, 24 *torui publica cumba senis*. Or the length of words as well as their juxtaposition may be exploited to make them yield more meaning, as in III, xxb, 11–12 *tu quoque, qui aestiuos spatiosius exigis ignis, Phoebe, moraturae contrahe lucis iter*; or their order as well as their juxtaposition, as in III, xvii, 25–6 *curuaque Tyrrhenos delphinum corpora nautas in uada pampinea desiluisse rate.*

In the last example quoted the nimble dactylic movement of the pentameter accompanies appropriately, if it does not express, the springing of the sailors overboard. The sonority of III, ii, 21 *nec Mausolei diues fortuna sepulcri* assists the statement that it contains about the splendour of the monument.[2] A similar intention is evident in III, xxii, 21–2 *nam quantum ferro tantum pietate potentes stamus*, in which as well as sonority there is a very obvious alliterative pattern. Alliterative patterning in Propertius is seldom of this obvious kind, but as a phenomenon it is ubiquitous;[3] see for instance

---

[1] Some more examples: III, xvi, 6 *ut timeam audaces in mea membra manus*; III, xvii, 21 *maternos Aetnaeo fulmine partus*; III, vi, 26 *staminea* (i.e. *spun by its thread*) *rota*; III, xvii, 26 *pampinea* (i.e. *overgrown* with vine) *rate*; III, v, 44 (*num*) *Tityo iugera pauca nouem* (i.e. whether the story is true of a giant so huge that nine acres are too small a space for his outstretched body). In III, xv, 18 *uilem ieiunae saepe negauit aquam* the epithet *ieiunae* has the value of a separate statement: 'she starved her, and...'. In III, i, 28 *Hectora per campos ter maculasse rotas* a brief and in itself cryptic phrase acquires and conveys an abundance of meaning through recall of two passages in the *Iliad*.

[2] The whole passage III, ii, 19–26 illustrates admirably the value of sound in relation to sense.

[3] It is produced of course by the poet's ear guiding his choice of words in quest of a total sound effect that will satisfy it; not by his mind searching for combinations of particular vowels and consonants, though such combinations in fact are the basis of the sound effect and are (as the sound effect is

III, i, 26 *fluminaque Haemonio comminus isse uiro*; III, xiii, 15 *felix Eois lex funeris una maritis*; III, xvi, 2 *Tibure me missa iussit adesse mora*; III, xvi, 15 *luna ministrat iter, demonstrant astra salebras*; III, xxB, 25–6 *ergo, qui pactas in foedera ruperit aras, pollueritque nouo sacra marita toro*; III, xxiv, 8 *cum tibi quaesitus candor in ore foret.* In these instances the patterning is simply a quality of style. In others, as in the first example above (from III, ii, 21), it assists the sense; e.g. III, xxiv, 13 *correptus saeuo Veneris torrebar aeno*; or is positively expressive, as in III, xvii, 33–4 *mollia Dircaeae pulsabunt tympana Thebae, capripedes calamo Panes hiante canent*, or in the sigmatic hissing of the snake in III, xi, 11.

These qualities of texture and sound are general properties of Propertius' style. Sometimes, as has been seen, they contribute to its expressiveness. The basic constituent, however, of this expressiveness is the poet's feeling for the strongly significant word, whether in metaphor or in direct statement. See, for instance, III, xv, 9 *sepeliuit*, III, xvii, 9 *custodit*, III, xiii, 64 *serpere* (*dixit equum*), III, xv, 14 *fixit* (*in ora manus*), III, xviii, 1 *ludit* (*pontus*), III, xiii, 31 *uestitas* (*frondibus uuas*), III, xvi, 5 *obductis* (*tenebris*), III, xi, 5 *praesagit*, III, xiv, 11 (*gyrum*) *pulsat*, III, xiv, 29 *uadit*, III, xvii, 18 *inquinet*, III, xv, 41 *cruentantur*, III, xv, 33 (*sonitus*) *rarescit*, III, ii, 8 *rorantis* (*equos*), III, vi, 27 *turgentis* (*ranae*), III, v, 36 (*Pleiadum*) *spisso* (*cur coit*) *igne chorus.* In most of these examples the word chosen communicates something very clearly and exactly recognizable by the mind's eye. And in fact the poet's control of language is

not) demonstrable on paper. The patterning found in Propertius resembles in kind and degree that found in Virgil and Horace, though each has his individual character; by contrast, the patterns in Lucretius are much more pronounced (tending to be based on initial letters), those in the hendecasyllables of Catullus more delicate. On the subject in general and its importance for the appreciation of much Latin poetry see L. P. Wilkinson, *Golden Latin Artistry* (Cambridge, 1963).

co-operating with a characteristic property of his imagination, which tends to work through particular visible or audible images. When Propertius thinks of the wine-harvest, he sees the juice staining the legs of the pressers. When he thinks of the defeat of the Suevi, he sees the mangled bodies of the dead swept along in the blood-dyed waters of the Rhine. This tendency is nowhere more apparent than in Elegy vii, the *epicedion* for Paetus lost at sea, in which Propertius' sensibility, responsive always to the thought of death, is excited especially by the horror of the circumstances. This prompts a succession of images: the fishes nibbling curiously at the floating corpse, the sea-birds perched on it (or on the skeleton on the beach), the nails torn from his hands, the choking water, the sharp rocks on to which he sees himself swept, the swirl of the sea as he goes under for the last time.

The above does not profess to be a complete account even of the limited aspect of Propertius' poetry which it discusses. But it may help to explain some judgements in the text and notes which follow; for instance those in favour of *delinisse* in III, ii, 3, of *cane* in III, xi, 49, of *cumulus* in III, xvi, 29, of *utroque toro* in III, xvii, 12, of *rapta* in III, xvii, 24, and of *tuae* in III, xviii, 32.

VARIANTS FROM THE
OXFORD TEXT (1960)

ii, 2 gaudeat ut   3 delinisse   16 nec defessa

iii, 17 hinc   42 cingere

iv, 3 magna uiris merces

v, 2 sat mihi   8 caute   14 ab inferna...rate   18 Parcae
(*and remove obeli*)

vi, 9 sicin eam   22 ...domi?   23 ...lecto?   28 exuctis
30 cinctaque...toro

vii, 21–4 *no square brackets*   22 Athamantiadae   29 curuate
et   47 non tulit hic Paetus   49 sed   50 ecfultum
52 ...aquam?   53 ...ligno?   54 ...mala?

viii, 13 seu   16 *colon at end of line*   26 tua   27 quos
29 grata   35 ff. *separate and print as* viii b

ix, 9 ecfingere   38 Cadmi, nec semper   55 claustraque
57 mollis   59 *comma at end of line*

x, 6 minax   13 at primum   26 perstrepat   28 grauius

xi, 5 uentorum...motus   29 nexerit   49 cane   55 non
haec, Roma, fuit   58 femineas...minas?   65–8 *after*
58   59 *remove obeli*

xii, 12 armato   25 et Ciconum mors Ismara capta

xiii, 2 ...opes?   39 Arcadii

xiv, 10 and 16 *semi-colons at end*   15–16 *after* 12 (*with Scaliger*)

xv, 3 praetexti pudor est releuatus amictus   10–11 *division,
not lacuna*   11 sero   33 litore sub tacito   42–3 *division*

xvi, 29 cumulus

xvii, 2 pacato   3 flatus   12 utroque toro   16 carpent
(*and comma at end of line*)   17 tumeant   18 *full stop
at end of line*   24 rapta   38 libabit

xviii, 8–9 *no lacuna*   29–30 *no square brackets*   32 huc...
portant...tuae   33 qua...qua

xix, 21–2 teque, o...tondens...coma?   25–6 *no brackets; and colon at end of* 25   27–8 *no transposition*

xx, *print* 1–10 *as* xxa *and* 11–30 *as* xxb

xxb, *transpose* 13–14 *before* 11–12, *do not transpose* 19–20

xxi, 6 possit   32 situ

xxii, 3 fabricata in uite (*and no obeli*)   6 at desiderio (*and full stop at end of line*)   38 curtatas

xxiii, 20 diras

xxiv, 8 *full stop at end of line*   11 haec ego   12 fatebar (*and no parenthesis*)

SIGLA

N = codex Neapolitanus, nunc Guelferbytanus Gudianus 224.
    circa annum 1200 scriptus

F = codex Laurentianus plut. 36.49. circa annum 1380
    scriptus

L = codex Holkhamicus 333. anno 1421 scriptus

P = codex Parisinus 7989. anno 1423 scriptus

D = codex Dauentriensis 1.82 (olim 1792). saec. XV

V = codex Ottoboniano-Vaticanus 1514. saec. XV

$Vo.$ = codex Leidensis Vossianus 117. saec. XV

Δ = consensus codd. $DVVo.$

O = consensus codd. $NFLPDVVo.$

ς = codices deteriores

scito, lector, ex multis quae exstant codicum lectionibus et
uirorum doctorum coniecturis paucas admodum in apparatu
ostendi.

SEXTI PROPERTI ELEGIARVM
LIBER TERTIVS

I

Callimachi Manes et Coi sacra Philitae,
    in uestrum, quaeso, me sinite ire nemus.
primus ego ingredior puro de fonte sacerdos
    Itala per Graios orgia ferre choros.
dicite, quo pariter carmen tenuastis in antro?   5
    quoue pede ingressi? quamue bibistis aquam?
a ualeat, Phoebum quicumque moratur in armis!
    exactus tenui pumice uersus eat,—
quo me Fama leuat terra sublimis, et a me
    nata coronatis Musa triumphat equis,   10
et mecum in curru parui uectantur Amores,
    scriptorumque meas turba secuta rotas.
quid frustra missis in me certatis habenis?
    non datur ad Musas currere lata uia.
multi, Roma, tuas laudes annalibus addent,   15
    qui finem imperii Bactra futura canent.
sed, quod pace legas, opus hoc de monte Sororum
    detulit intacta pagina nostra uia.
mollia, Pegasides, date uestro serta poetae:
    non faciet capiti dura corona meo.   20
at mihi quod uiuo detraxerit inuida turba,
    post obitum duplici faenore reddet Honos;
omnia post obitum fingit maiora uetustas:
    maius ab exsequiis nomen in ora uenit.

---

5 tenuastis *NF4*: tenuistis *cett.*   22 reddet *F4V2Vo.*: reddit *cett.*   **onus**
O, corr. ς   23 omnia] Fame *N*   uetustẹ *N*

nam quis equo pulsas abiegno nosceret arces,   25
   fluminaque Haemonio comminus isse uiro,
Idaeum Simoenta Iouis cum prole Scamandro,
   Hectora per campos ter maculasse rotas?
Deiphobumque Helenumque et Pulydamanta et in armis
   qualemcumque Parim uix sua nosset humus.   30
exiguo sermone fores nunc, Ilion, et tu
   Troia bis Oetaei numine capta dei.
nec non ille tui casus memorator Homerus
   posteritate suum crescere sensit opus.
meque inter seros laudabit Roma nepotes: 35
   illum post cineres auguror ipse diem.
ne mea contempto lapis indicet ossa sepulcro
   prouisum est Lycio uota probante deo.

II

Carminis interea nostri redeamus in orbem,
   gaudeat ut solito tacta puella sono.
Orphea delinisse feras et concita dicunt
   flumina Threicia sustinuisse lyra;
saxa Cithaeronis Thebas agitata per artem   5
   sponte sua in muri membra coisse ferunt;
quin etiam, Polypheme, fera Galatea sub Aetna
   ad tua rorantis carmina flexit equos:
miremur, nobis et Baccho et Apolline dextro,
   turba puellarum si mea uerba colit?   10

---

25 arces *N2, ς*: artes *O*   26 esse uiro *ND*: ille raro *F1*   27 cum prole
Scamandro *G. Wolff*: cunabula (can- *L*) parui *FLPΔ*: om. *N*   29 Puly-
damanta (Polyd.) et *Lachmann*: poli(puli(y) *F1LPVo.*)led(laed *Vo.*)amantes
NF1LPVo.: Pulydamantos (-tis *Phillimore*) *Postgate*   32 oetaei *F4DV*:
oete I *N*: oete *F1LPVo.*   36 augur..ipse deae *N*
II *priori coniungunt Muretus, Scaliger, alii*   1–2 *priori coniunx. multi*
2 ut *V2Vo.*: in *cett.*   3 delinisse (= delenisse) *Ayrmann*: detinuisse
NLPV2Vo.: detenuisse *F1V1*   6 in muri *DV*: in numeri *LVo.*:
innumeri *NP*: imineri *F1*

quod non Taenariis domus est mihi fulta columnis,
    nec camera auratas inter eburna trabes,
nec mea Phaeacas aequant pomaria siluas,
    non operosa rigat Marcius antra liquor;
at Musae comites et carmina cara legenti,   15
    nec defessa choris Calliopea meis.
fortunata, meo si qua es celebrata libello!
    carmina erunt formae tot monumenta tuae.
nam neque Pyramidum sumptus ad sidera ducti,
    nec Iouis Elei caelum imitata domus,   20
nec Mausolei diues fortuna sepulcri
    mortis ab extrema condicione uacant.
aut illis flamma aut imber subducet honores,
    annorum aut ictu, pondere uicta, ruent.
at non ingenio quaesitum nomen ab aeuo   25
    excidet: ingenio stat sine morte decus.

III

Visus eram molli recubans Heliconis in umbra,
    Bellerophontei qua fluit umor equi,
reges, Alba, tuos et regum facta tuorum,
    tantum operis, neruis hiscere posse meis;
paruaque tam magnis admoram fontibus ora,   5
    unde pater sitiens Ennius ante bibit;
et cecinit Curios fratres et Horatia pila,
    regiaque Aemilia uecta tropaea rate,
uictricesque moras Fabii pugnamque sinistram
    Cannensem et uersos ad pia uota deos,   10

---

13 ph(a)eacias *et similia* O, *corr. edd.*   15 comites *F4V2*: comitis
NDV1Vo.: comiti *F1LP*   16 nec *Baehrens*: uerbum *om.* N: Et *cett.*
17 es 𝒮: est O: *om.* V1   23 subducit N   24 ictus *D, Housman*
pondera *F, Housman*
III 5 iam *Guyet, Heinsius*   7 cecini 𝒮   8 *et* 12 *inter se mut.* Polster

Hannibalemque Lares Romana sede fugantis,
    anseris et tutum uoce fuisse Iouem:
cum me Castalia speculans ex arbore Phoebus
    sic ait aurata nixus ad antra lyra:
'Quid tibi cum tali, demens, est flumine? quis te   15
    carminis heroi tangere iussit opus?
non hinc ulla tibi speranda est fama, Properti:
    mollia sunt paruis prata terenda rotis;
ut tuus in scamno iactetur saepe libellus,
    quem legat exspectans sola puella uirum.   20
cur tua praescriptos euecta est pagina gyros?
    non est ingenii cumba grauanda tui.
alter remus aquas alter tibi radat harenas,
    tutus eris: medio maxima turba mari est.'
dixerat, et plectro sedem mihi monstrat eburno,   25
    quo noua muscoso semita facta solo est.
hic erat affixis uiridis spelunca lapillis,
    pendebantque cauis tympana pumicibus,
orgia Musarum et Sileni patris imago
    fictilis et calami, Pan Tegeaee, tui;   30
et Veneris dominae uolucres, mea turba, columbae
    tingunt Gorgoneo punica rostra lacu;
diuersaeque nouem sortitae iura Puellae
    exercent teneras in sua dona manus:
haec hederas legit in thyrsos, haec carmina neruis   35
    aptat, at illa manu texit utraque rosam.
e quarum numero me contigit una dearum
    (ut reor a facie, Calliopea fuit):
'Contentus niueis semper uectabere cycnis,
    nec te fortis equi ducet ad arma sonus.   40

11 lares *F*: lacres *LP*, ? *V1*: lacies *N*   17 hinc *Volscus, Fruter*: hic *codd.*
21 pr(a)escripto (perscr. *N*) seuecta est (*om. FL*) pagina giro *O*: *corr.*
Lipsius, Guellius   26 Quo *N*: Qua *cett.*   29 orgia *Heinsius*: Ergo
O: organa *Eldik*   30 pan tegeee *V2*: patege(a)e *NL2P*: *uarie cett.*
32 rostra *F4*, *P corr.*, *VVo.*: nostra *NF1L*, *P primo*, *D*   33 rura *O*,
corr. ς, *Scaliger*

nil tibi sit rauco praeconia classica cornu
    flare, nec Aonium cingere Marte nemus;
aut quibus in campis Mariano proelia signo
    stent et Teutonicas Roma refringat opes,
barbarus aut Sueuo perfusus sanguine Rhenus   45
    saucia maerenti corpora uectet aqua.
quippe coronatos alienum ad limen amantis
    nocturnaeque canes ebria signa fugae,
ut per te clausas sciat excantare puellas,
    qui uolet austeros arte ferire uiros.'   50
talia Calliope, lymphisque a fonte petitis
    ora Philitea nostra rigauit aqua.

IV

Arma deus Caesar dites meditatur ad Indos,
    et freta gemmiferi findere classe maris.
magna uiris merces: parat ultima terra triumphos;
    Tigris et Euphrates sub tua iura fluent;
sera, sed Ausoniis ueniet prouincia uirgis;   5
    assuescent Latio Partha tropaea Ioui.
ite agite, expertae bello date lintea prorae
    et solitum armigeri ducite munus equi!
omina fausta cano. Crassos clademque piate!
    ite et Romanae consulite historiae!   10
Mars pater, et sacrae fatalia lumina Vestae,
    ante meos obitus sit precor illa dies,
qua uideam spoliis oneratos Caesaris axis,
    ad uulgi plausus saepe resistere equos,

41 nil] nec *Fruter*   42 Flere *O, corr. Fruter*   cingere *VVo.*: tingere *cett.*
45 s(a)euo *O, corr.* ς
IV 3 uiris *uel* uiae *Heinsius*: uiri *O*: datur *Barber*   4 tua *O*: noua *Heinsius*
iuga uestra *Postgate*: iuga nostra *Barber*   5 Seres et...uenient *Heinsius*
11 sanctae *Postgate*   13 onerato...axe *Muretus*   14 ac...plausu
Barth   14 *post hunc u. duo uu. excidisse putat Bailey, post* 16 *Richmond*

inque sinu carae nixus spectare puellae   15
   incipiam et titulis oppida capta legam,
tela fugacis equi et bracati militis arcus,
   et subter captos arma sedere duces!
ipsa tuam serua prolem, Venus: hoc sit in aeuum,
   cernis ab Aenea quod superesse caput.   20
praeda sit haec illis, quorum meruere labores:
   me sat erit Sacra plaudere posse Via.

V

Pacis Amor deus est, pacem ueneramur amantes:
   sat mihi cum domina proelia dura mea.
nec tamen inuiso pectus mihi carpitur auro,
   nec bibit e gemma diuite nostra sitis,
nec mihi mille iugis Campania pinguis aratur,   5
   nec miser aera paro clade, Corinthe, tua.
o prima infelix fingenti terra Prometheo!
   ille parum caute pectoris egit opus.
corpora disponens mentem non uidit in arte:
   recta animi primum debuit esse uia.   10
nunc maris in tantum uento iactamur, et hostem
   quaerimus, atque armis nectimus arma noua.
haud ullas portabis opes Acherontis ad undas:
   nudus ab inferna, stulte, uehere rate.
uictor cum uictis pariter miscebitur umbris: 15
   consule cum Mario, capte Iugurtha, sedes.

17–18 *post* 14 *Keil*   19 serua pr. *NV2Vo.*: pr. serua *cett.*   22 Mi ⲋ
sacra *NVVo.*: media *FPD*: om. *L*
V *priori coniungunt Muretus, Scaliger, alii*   2 sat *Liuineius*: Stant *O*
6 (a)era *F4*, ⲋ: aere *N*: ire *F1LP*Δ   clade *NF4*: classe *LP*Δ: pace *F1*
7 fingenti *F3LP*Δ: frangenti *N*: frugenti *F1*   8 caute *O*: cauti *in mg. pro*
u.l. P2, ⲋ   12 nectimus *NF4P2VVo.*: qu(a)erimus *F1L*, ? *P1, D*   14 ab
inferna...rate ⲋ: at inferna *Schrader*: in inferna *Barber*: ad infernas...
rates *O*

Lydus Dulichio non distat Croesus ab Iro:
  optima mors Parcae quae uenit acta die.
me iuuat in prima coluisse Helicona iuuenta
  Musarumque choris implicuisse manus: 20
me iuuat et multo mentem uincire Lyaeo,
  et caput in uerna semper habere rosa.
atque ubi iam Venerem grauis interceperit aetas,
  sparserit et nigras alba senecta comas,
tum mihi naturae libeat perdiscere mores,   25
  quis deus hanc mundi temperet arte domum,
qua uenit exoriens, qua deficit, unde coactis
  cornibus in plenum menstrua luna redit,
unde salo superant uenti, quid flamine captet
  Eurus, et in nubes unde perennis aqua;   30
sit uentura dies mundi quae subruat arces,
  purpureus pluuias cur bibit arcus aquas,
aut cur Perrhaebi tremuere cacumina Pindi,
  solis et atratis luxerit orbis equis,
cur serus uersare boues et plaustra Bootes,   35
  Pleiadum spisso cur coit igne chorus,
curue suos finis altum non exeat aequor,
  plenus et in partis quattuor annus eat;
sub terris sint iura deum et tormenta gigantum,
  Tisiphones atro si furit angue caput,   40
aut Alcmaeoniae furiae aut ieiunia Phinei,
  num rota, num scopuli, num sitis inter aquas,
num tribus infernum custodit faucibus antrum
  Cerberus, et Tityo iugera pauca nouem,

---

18 Parcae *Lachmann*: parca *NF4LPΔ*: carpta *Baehrens*   acta *NL, P primo*:
apta *F, P corr.*, Δ   per te...acta, dies *Nencini*   21 iuuat *PΔ*: iuuet *NFL*
24 Sparserit et *N*: Sparsit et *FLP1*   nigras *ς*: integras *O*   35 seros *N*
plaustra bootes *DV*: pl. boet(h)es *P in ras., Vo.*: flamma boon *N*: flamma
palustra *F1* (flamma *deleuit et* boothes *ad fin. uersus scripsit F4*), *L*: cur seros
uersare boues it flamma Bootae *Rothstein*   39 gigantum *om. N*:
reorum *Housman*: nocentum *Lobeck*   40 *et* 42 *inter se mut. Housman*
42-3 *non* quater *NL, sed primum illud non ex* num *corr. L, ut uidetur*

19

an ficta in miseras descendit fabula gentis,   45
  et timor haud ultra quam rogus esse potest.
exitus hic uitae superest mihi: uos, quibus arma
  grata magis, Crassi signa referte domum.

VI

Dic mihi de nostra, quae sentis, uera puella:
  sic tibi sint dominae, Lygdame, dempta iuga.
num me laetitia tumefactum fallis inani,
  haec referens, quae me credere uelle putas?
omnis enim debet sine uano nuntius esse,   5
  maioremque timens seruus habere fidem.
nunc mihi, si qua tenes, ab origine dicere prima
  incipe: suspensis auribus ista bibam.
sicin eam incomptis uidisti flere capillis?
  illius ex oculis multa cadebat aqua?   10
nec speculum strato uidisti, Lygdame, lecto?
  ornabat niueas nullane gemma manus?
ac maestam teneris uestem pendere lacertis,
  scriniaque ad lecti clausa iacere pedes?
tristis erat domus, et tristes sua pensa ministrae   15
  carpebant, medio nebat et ipsa loco,
umidaque impressa siccabat lumina lana,
  rettulit et querulo iurgia nostra sono?
'Haec te teste mihi promissa est, Lygdame, merces?
  est poenae seruo rumpere teste fidem.   20

---

46 haut *N*: aut *cett.*
VI 3–4 *post* 8 *Housman*   3 Num ς: Non *N*: Dum *cett.*   5 sine uano
NF4D1V2Vo.: siue uanus *F1*: sine uanus *L1, ut uid.*: sine uanis *PL2D2V1*
nuntius *om. F1 (in mg. add. F4), et L1* (relator *post* esse *add. L2*)   esse
relator *PD2V*   7 Non *N*   9 sic(c)in(e) eam *uulgo*: sicin (ς) (h)eram,
Damsté: Sicut eam *FLPΔ*: Si eâ (e *ex* c) *N*   11 in strato *Heinsius*   12 *et* 14 *inter se mut. Suringar*
20 poena et *Bailey*

ille potest nullo miseram me linquere facto,
  et qualem nolo dicere habere domi?
gaudet me uacuo solam tabescere lecto?
  si placet, insultet, Lygdame, morte mea.
non me moribus illa, sed herbis improba uicit: 25
  staminea rhombi ducitur ille rota.
illum turgentis ranae portenta rubetae
  et lecta exuctis anguibus ossa trahunt,
et strigis inuentae per busta iacentia plumae,
  cinctaque funesto lanea uitta toro.   30
si non uana canunt mea somnia, Lygdame, testor,
  poena erit ante meos sera sed ampla pedes;
putris et in uacuo texetur aranea lecto:
  noctibus illorum dormiet ipsa Venus.'
quae tibi si ueris animis est questa puella,   35
  hac eadem rursus, Lygdame, curre uia,
et mea cum multis lacrimis mandata reporta,
  iram, non fraudes esse in amore meo,
me quoque consimili impositum torquerier igni:
  iurabo bis sex integer esse dies.   40
quod mihi si e tanto felix concordia bello
  exstiterit, per me, Lygdame, liber eris.

---

22 Et qualem nullo *N*: (A)Equalem nulla *cett.*: *corr. Palmer*   domi *cod.
Vat.-Pal. 910, Heinsius*: domo *O*   26 rhombi *V2Vo.*: rumbi *FLPDV1*:
bombi *N*   28 exuctis *Housman*: exsectis *F4*, ʒ: exectis *NLΔ*: exactis
F1: ex sectis *P*   29 tacentia *Palmier*   30 Cin(c)taq; *O* (*sed* -q; *postea
add. N*): tinctaque *Barber*   uitta *PDV*: uicta *FVo.*: uita *NL*   toro (*siue
rogo) Heinsius*: uiro *O*   31 cadunt *DV2Vo.*   39 consuli *N*   torrerier
Palmier   41 mihi si] nisi *N*   e *Lachmann*: et *N*: *om. cett.*: quod mihi
si tanto *uulgo*

21

VII

Ergo sollicitae tu causa, pecunia, uitae!
　　per te immaturum mortis adimus iter;
tu uitiis hominum crudelia pabula praebes;
　　semina curarum de capite orta tuo.
tu Paetum ad Pharios tendentem lintea portus　　　5
　　obruis insano terque quaterque mari.
nam dum te sequitur, primo miser excidit aeuo
　　et noua longinquis piscibus esca natat;
et mater non iusta piae dare debita terrae
　　nec pote cognatos inter humare rogos,　　　10
sed tua nunc uolucres astant super ossa marinae,
　　nunc tibi pro tumulo Carpathium omne mare est.
infelix Aquilo, raptae timor Orithyiae,
　　quae spolia ex illo tanta fuere tibi?
aut quidnam fracta gaudes, Neptune, carina?　　　15
　　portabat sanctos alueus ille uiros.
Paete, quid aetatem numeras? quid cara natanti
　　mater in ore tibi est? non habet unda deos.
nam tibi nocturnis ad saxa ligata procellis
　　omnia detrito uincula fune cadunt.　　　20
sunt Agamemnonias testantia litora curas,
　　quae notat Argynni poena Athamantiadae:
hoc iuuene amisso classem non soluit Atrides,
　　pro qua mactata est Iphigenia mora.
reddite corpus humo, posita est in gurgite uita;　　　25
　　Paetum sponte tua, uilis harena, tegas;
et quotiens Paeti transibit nauta sepulcrum,
　　dicat 'Et audaci tu timor esse potes.'

VII *priori continuant* F₁L₁: *uersuum ordinem multifariam mutauerunt edd.*
13–16 *post* 24 *Otto*　　17–18 *post* 64 *Vivona*　　21–24 *post* 36 *Scaliger*
22 Qu(a)e *FV*: Qua *cett.*　　nota ς　argynni *V₂Vo.*: arginni *LP*: argiuni *F*:
agynni *N*　p. Athamantiadae *Hertzberg*: p. minantis aquae *O*　　23 Hoc
NF₄V₂Vo.: Nec *F₁LPDV₁*: hic *Lachmann*　　25 humo] aquae (*uoc.*)
Damsté, Alton posita est *N*: positaque *cett.*

22

ite, rates curuate et leti texite causas:
  ista per humanas mors uenit acta manus.   30
terra parum fuerat, fatis adiecimus undas:
  fortunae miseras auximus arte uias.
ancora te teneat, quem non tenuere penates?
  quid meritum dicas, cui sua terra parum est?
uentorum est, quodcumque paras: haud ulla carina   35
  consenuit, fallit portus et ipse fidem.
natura insidians pontum substrauit auaris:
  ut tibi succedat, uix semel esse potest.
saxa triumphalis fregere Capharea puppis,
  naufraga cum uasto Graecia tracta salo est.   40
paulatim socium iacturam fleuit Vlixes,
  in mare cui soliti non ualuere doli.
quod si contentus patrio boue uerteret agros,
  uerbaque duxisset pondus habere mea,
uiueret ante suos dulcis conuiua Penatis,   45
  pauper, at in terra nil nisi fleret opes.
non tulit hic Paetus stridorem audire procellae
  et duro teneras laedere fune manus;
sed thyio thalamo aut Oricia terebintho
  ecfultum pluma uersicolore caput.   50
huic fluctus uiuo radicitus abstulit unguis,
  et miser inuisam traxit hiatus aquam?
hunc paruo ferri uidit nox improba ligno?
  Paetus ut occideret, tot coiere mala?

---

29 curuate *Peskett, Lendrum*: curuas *Passerat*: curu(a)e *O*   42 soliti (*et
solum*) ς: soli *O*   45 ante suos biberet *Phillimore*   46 nil nisi *F3DV*: nil
ubi *N, F1 et F3 corr., LPVo.*   flere potest *O, corr. Baehrens*   47 Non
O: nunc *Barber*: noluit *O. Skutsch*   hic ς: ħ (? = haec) *N*: hoc *F*: hunc
LPΔ   48 *post hunc u. lacunam statuit Canter, post* 49 *Keil*   49 Sed
O: seu *Barber*   chi(y)o *O, corr. Santen* (thyiae *iam Itali*)   calamo
F1LPVo.   oricia ς: orythia, corythia *et similia O*   50 ecfultum *Jones*:
Et fultum *O, nisi quod* Furtum *F1*: est fultum *Palmer*: effultum *Guellius, Ast*
(effultus *iam Puccius*)   51-2 et 53-4 *inter se mut. Smyth*, 51 et 53
Fischer   51 uiuos *Palmier*

23

flens tamen extremis dedit haec mandata querelis,   55
   cum moribunda niger clauderet ora liquor:
'Di maris Aegaei quos sunt penes aequora, uenti,
   et quaecumque meum degrauat unda caput,
quo rapitis miseros primae lanuginis annos?
   attulimus longas in freta uestra manus.   60
a miser alcyonum scopulis affligar acutis!
   in me caeruleo fuscina sumpta deo est.
at saltem Italiae regionibus euehat aestus:
   hoc de me sat erit si modo matris erit.'
subtrahit haec fantem torta uertigine fluctus;   65
   ultima quae Paeto uoxque diesque fuit.
o centum aequoreae Nereo genitore puellae,
   et tu materno tracta dolore Theti;
uos decuit lasso supponere bracchia mento:
   non poterat uestras ille grauare manus.   70
at tu, saeue Aquilo, numquam mea uela uidebis:
   ante fores dominae condar oportet iners.

VIII A

Dulcis ad hesternas fuerat mihi rixa lucernas,
   uocis et insanae tot maledicta tuae,
cum furibunda mero mensam propellis et in me
   proicis insana cymbia plena manu.
tu uero nostros audax inuade capillos   5
   et mea formosis unguibus ora nota,
tu minitare oculos subiecta exurere flamma,
   fac mea rescisso pectora nuda sinu!

---

57 et quos *J. H. Voss*   60 an tulimus *Arntzen*   sanctas *Waardenburg*:
nocuas *Housman*: longas...comas *Oudendorp*   66 noxque *FLPDV1*
68 tacta *V2Vo.*: fracta *Heinsius*   thetis *NF4, P corr., V in ras.: corr. Itali*
VIII A *priori continuant FLDV*   3 Cur *O, corr. Beroaldus*   4 irata
Burman: alii alia

nimirum ueri dantur mihi signa caloris:
  nam sine amore graui femina nulla dolet.   10
quae mulier rabida iactat conuicia lingua,
  haec Veneris magnae uoluitur ante pedes—
custodum gregibus circa seu stipat euntem,
  seu sequitur medias, Maenas ut icta, uias,
seu timidam crebro dementia somnia terrent,   15
  seu miseram in tabula picta puella mouet:
his ego tormentis animi sum uerus haruspex,
  has didici certo saepe in amore notas.
non est certa fides, quam non in iurgia uertas:
  hostibus eueniat lenta puella meis.   20
in morso aequales uideant mea uulnera collo:
  me doceat liuor mecum habuisse meam.
aut in amore dolere uolo aut audire dolentem,
  siue meas lacrimas siue uidere tuas,
tecta superciliis si quando uerba remittis,   25
  aut tua cum digitis scripta silenda notas.
odi ego quos numquam pungunt suspiria somnos:
  semper in irata pallidus esse uelim.
dulcior ignis erat Paridi, cum grata per arma
  Tyndaridi poterat gaudia ferre suae: 30
dum uincunt Danai, dum restat barbarus Hector,
  ille Helenae in gremio maxima bella gerit.
aut tecum aut pro te mihi cum riualibus arma
  semper erunt: in te pax mihi nulla placet.

---

11 grauida *O, corr. Scaliger* 12 Et *O, corr. Liuineius* 13 seu
Lachmann: se *O* 18 Nam *F1LPDV1* certas *ς* 19 iniurgia *N*:
iniuria *LPΔ*: iuria *F1 (in superscr. F2)* uersat *O, nisi quod* uertat *F*: *corr.*
Vahlen quae non in iurgia uertat *Phillimore* 24 *post hunc u. lacunam statuit*
Mueller 25–6 *hic alienos esse putant multi* 26 tua *O*: mea *Barber*
27 quos *in mg. pro u.l. F2*: qu(a)e *O*: cui *Palmer* 29 grata *O*: Graia
Fruter

VIIIB

Gaude, quod nulla est aeque formosa: doleres,   35
    si qua foret: nunc sis iure superba licet.
at tibi, qui nostro nexisti retia lecto,
    sit socer aeternum nec sine matre domus!
cui nunc si qua data est furandae copia noctis,
    offensa illa mihi, non tibi amica, dedit.   40

IX

Maecenas, eques Etrusco de sanguine regum,
    intra fortunam qui cupis esse tuam,
quid me scribendi tam uastum mittis in aequor?
    non sunt apta meae grandia uela rati.
turpe est, quod nequeas, capiti committere pondus   5
    et pressum inflexo mox dare terga genu.
omnia non pariter rerum sunt omnibus apta,
    palma nec ex aequo ducitur una iugo.
gloria Lysippo est animosa ecfingere signa;
    exactis Calamis se mihi iactat equis;   10
in Veneris tabula summam sibi poscit Apelles;
    Parrhasius parua uindicat arte locum;
argumenta magis sunt Mentoris addita formae;
    at Myos exiguum flectit acanthus iter;
Phidiacus signo se Iuppiter ornat eburno;   15
    Praxitelen propria uendit ab urbe lapis.

35-40 *priori continuant codd., aliunde intrusos putabat Postgate*   37 nexisti
P2 (m. rec.) et apud Priscianum (GLK 2.536. 8) *et Diomedem (GLK* 1.369. 21):
tendisti *O*   40 Offensam *O, corr.* ς
IX 8 Palma (*et* Fama) ς: Flamma (Flamina *LD*) *O*   ulla *O, corr.* ς
9 ecfingere *Jones:* effingere *N:* fingere *cett.*   10 calamus *O, corr.* ς
14 Ad *O, corr.* ς   Myos *Volscus, Beroaldus:* muros *et sim. O*   16 uendit
ab *Barber:* uindicat *O* (uendicat *P, sicut in* 12)

est quibus Eleae concurrit palma quadrigae,
    est quibus in celeres gloria nata pedes;
hic satus ad pacem, hic castrensibus utilis armis:
    naturae sequitur semina quisque suae.   20
at tua, Maecenas, uitae praecepta recepi,
    cogor et exemplis te superare tuis.
cum tibi Romano dominas in honore securis
    et liceat medio ponere iura foro;
uel tibi Medorum pugnaces ire per hastas,   25
    atque onerare tuam fixa per arma domum;
et tibi ad effectum uires det Caesar, et omni
    tempore tam faciles insinuentur opes;
parcis et in tenuis humilem te colligis umbras:
    uelorum plenos subtrahis ipse sinus.   30
crede mihi, magnos aequabunt ista Camillos
    iudicia, et uenies tu quoque in ora uirum,
Caesaris et famae uestigia iuncta tenebis:
    Maecenatis erunt uera tropaea fides.
non ego uelifera tumidum mare findo carina: 35
    tota sub exiguo flumine nostra mora est.
non flebo in cineres arcem sedisse paternos
    Cadmi, nec semper proelia clade pari;
nec referam Scaeas et Pergama Apollinis arces,
    et Danaum decimo uere redisse ratis,   40
moenia cum Graio Neptunia pressit aratro
    uictor Palladiae ligneus artis equus.
inter Callimachi sat erit placuisse libellos
    et cecinisse modis, Coe poeta, tuis.
haec urant pueros, haec urant scripta puellas,   45
    meque deum clament et mihi sacra ferant!

22 conor *Broekhuyzen, Heinsius*   25 hastas *Markland*: hostes *O*: astus *Lachmann*: arcus *Helvetius*   26 ornare *Dempster*   35 *om. N*   36 Tuta 5   flumine *NV2Vo.*: e (*sive* est) flumine *FLPD*   37 sidisse paternam *Heinsius*   38 semper *O*: septem *Lipsius*   44 Coe *Beroaldus*: dure *O*: Dore *Scriuerius*   45 curant (*bis*) *O, corr. Itali*

te duce uel Iouis arma canam caeloque minantem
    Coeum et Phlegraeis Oromedonta iugis;
celsaque Romanis decerpta palatia tauris
    ordiar et caeso moenia firma Remo,   50
eductosque pares siluestri ex ubere reges,
    crescet et ingenium sub tua iussa meum;
prosequar et currus utroque ab litore ouantis,
    Parthorum astutae tela remissa fugae,
claustraque Pelusi Romano subruta ferro,   55
    Antonique grauis in sua fata manus.
mollis tu coeptae fautor cape lora iuuentae,
    dexteraque immissis da mihi signa rotis.
hoc mihi, Maecenas, laudis concedis, et a te est,
    quod ferar in partis ipse fuisse tuas.   60

X

Mirabar, quidnam uisissent mane Camenae,
    ante meum stantes sole rubente torum.
natalis nostrae signum misere puellae
    et manibus faustos ter crepuere sonos.
transeat hic sine nube dies, stent aere uenti,   5
    ponat et in sicco molliter unda minax.
aspiciam nullos hodierna luce dolentis;
    et Niobae lacrimas supprimat ipse lapis;
alcyonum positis requiescant ora querelis;
    increpet absumptum nec sua mater Itym.   10
tuque, o cara mihi, felicibus edita pennis,
    surge et poscentis iusta precare deos.

47–56 *post* 20 *Hetzel*   48 Oromedonta *edd.*: oromod(dom *F*)onta
(unta *N*) *O*: Eurymedonta *Huschke*   49 *et* 51 *inter se mut. Peiper*
55 claustraque *Palmier, Lipsius*: Castraque *O*   57 Mollis *O*: mollia
Broekhuyzen   fautor *pro u.l. F2*, Δ: factor *N*: faustor *F1LP*   59–60 *post*
46 *Lachmann*
X 1 misissent *O, corr. Heinsius*   6 Ponat *F3PDV*: Ponet *NF1LVo.*
minax *NF1LPDV1*: minas *F3V2Vo.*

at primum pura somnum tibi discute lympha,
 et nitidas presso pollice finge comas:
dein qua primum oculos cepisti ueste Properti   15
 indue, nec uacuum flore relinque caput;
et pete, qua polles, ut sit tibi forma perennis,
 inque meum semper stent tua regna caput.
inde coronatas ubi ture piaueris aras,
 luxerit et tota flamma secunda domo,   20
sit mensae ratio, noxque inter pocula currat,
 et crocino naris murreus ungat onyx.
tibia nocturnis succumbat rauca choreis,
 et sint nequitiae libera uerba tuae,
dulciaque ingratos adimant conuiuia somnos;   25
 publica uicinae perstrepat aura uiae:
sit sors et nobis talorum interprete iactu,
 quem grauius pennis uerberet ille puer.
cum fuerit multis exacta trientibus hora,
 noctis et instituet sacra ministra Venus,   30
annua soluamus thalamo sollemnia nostro,
 natalisque tui sic peragamus iter.

XI

Quid mirare, meam si uersat femina uitam
 et trahit addictum sub sua iura uirum,
criminaque ignaui capitis mihi turpia fingis,
 quod nequeam fracto rumpere uincla iugo?
uentorum melius praesagit nauita motus,   5
 uulneribus didicit miles habere metum.

13 At *cod. Vat.-Pal. 910*: Ac O   17–18 *om. N: an post* 12 *transferendi
quaerit Barber*   17 polles *F4V2Vo.*: pelles *F1LPDV1*   23 pauc(h)a
F1LPDV1   25–6 *post* 22 *Sandbach*   25 -que *om. N* conuicia *Broek-
huyzen*   26 perstrepat *5*: perstrepet O, *nisi quod* perstrepat *F primo*
27 sint sortes *Sandbach*   28 grauibus O, *corr. Beroaldus*   31 et *post*
thalamo *habent FLPDV*
XI 5 uentorum (*Postgate*)...motum *Owen*: Venturam...mortem *NF1LDV1*:
noctem *F3, P in ras., V2Vo.*

ista ego praeterita iactaui uerba iuuenta:
    tu nunc exemplo disce timere meo.
Colchis flagrantis adamantina sub iuga tauros
    egit et armigera proelia seuit humo,   10
custodisque feros clausit serpentis hiatus,
    iret ut Aesonias aurea lana domos.
ausa ferox ab equo quondam oppugnare sagittis
    Maeotis Danaum Penthesilea ratis;
aurea cui postquam nudauit cassida frontem,   15
    uicit uictorem candida forma uirum.
Omphale in tantum formae processit honorem,
    Lydia Gygaeo tincta puella lacu,
ut, qui pacato statuisset in orbe columnas,
    tam dura traheret mollia pensa manu.   20
Persarum statuit Babylona Semiramis urbem,
    ut solidum cocto tolleret aggere opus,
et duo in aduersum mitti per moenia currus
    nec possent tacto stringere ab axe latus;
duxit et Euphraten medium, quam condidit, arcis,   25
    iussit et imperio subdere Bactra caput.
nam quid ego heroas, quid raptem in crimina diuos?
    Iuppiter infamat seque suamque domum.
quid, modo quae nostris opprobria nexerit armis,
    et famulos inter femina trita suos?   30
coniugii obsceni pretium Romana poposcit
    moenia et addictos in sua regna Patres.
noxia Alexandria, dolis aptissima tellus,
    et totiens nostro Memphi cruenta malo,
tris ubi Pompeio detraxit harena triumphos!   35
    tollet nulla dies hanc tibi, Roma, notam.

21 *noua el. in FLPDV*   23 mitti *Tyrrell*: missi *O*: misit *Itali*   24 Ne *PDV*   25 quam *F1L, P primo, DV1*: qua *NF4, P corr., V2Vo*.   arces (artes *F1*) *O, corr. Baehrens*   26 surgere *O, corr. Burman sen., Schrader* 27 crimine *O, corr. V2*   29 nexerit *Bailey*: uexerit *O*: uexerat *ς* 31 Coniugis *O, corr. Passerat*   35 Tres *NF4P2Δ*: Res *L*: Re *P1*: Hec *F1*

issent Phlegraeo melius tibi funera campo,
  uel tua si socero colla daturus eras.
scilicet incesti meretrix regina Canopi,
  una Philippeo sanguine adusta nota,   40
ausa Ioui nostro latrantem opponere Anubim,
  et Tiberim Nili cogere ferre minas,
Romanamque tubam crepitanti pellere sistro,
  baridos et contis rostra Liburna sequi,
foedaque Tarpeio conopia tendere saxo,   45
  iura dare et statuas inter et arma Mari!
quid nunc Tarquinii fractas iuuat esse securis,
  nomine quem simili uita superba notat,
si mulier patienda fuit? cane, Roma, triumphum
  et longum Augusto salua precare diem!   50
fugisti tamen in timidi uaga flumina Nili:
  accepere tuae Romula uincla manus.
bracchia spectaui sacris admorsa colubris,
  et trahere occultum membra soporis iter.
'Non haec, Roma, fuit tanto tibi ciue uerenda!'   55
  dixit et assiduo lingua sepulta mero.
septem urbs alta iugis, toto quae praesidet orbi,
  femineas timuit territa Marte minas?   58
haec di condiderant, haec di quoque moenia seruant: 65
  uix timeat saluo Caesare Roma Iouem.   66
nunc ubi Scipiadae classes, ubi signa Camilli,   67
  aut modo Pompeia, Bospore, capta manu?   68
Hannibalis spolia et uicti monumenta Syphacis,   59
  et Pyrrhi ad nostros gloria fracta pedes?   60

---

45 conopea *Volscus, Beroaldus*: canopeia *O*: canopia *V2*   46 et (statu**s**)
5: *om. O*   49 cane *scripsi*: cape *codd.*   51 tumidi *F4V2Vo.*   uaga Δ:
uada *NFLP*   55 haec *5*: hoc *O*   fuit *O*: fui *5*   56 dixerat *Housman*
58 *om. N*   Femineas *FLP*Δ: femineo *Korsch*   timuit *F4P*Δ: *om. F1L*:
extimuit *Korsch*   65–8 *transtulit huc Housman*, 67–8 *Passerat*   65 con-
diderunt *Scaliger*   65–6 *post* 60 *Bailey*   68 capte *Heinsius*
59 monu(i)menta *O*: momenta *Damsté* (*an melius in 61?*)

Curtius expletis statuit monumenta lacunis,
  at Decius misso proelia rupit equo,
Coclitis abscissos testatur semita pontis,   63
  est cui cognomen coruus habere dedit: 64
Leucadius uersas acies memorabit Apollo: 69
  tantum operis belli sustulit una dies.   70
at tu, siue petes portus seu, nauita, linques,
  Caesaris in toto sis memor Ionio.

XII

Postume, plorantem potuisti linquere Gallam,
  miles et Augusti fortia signa sequi?
tantine ulla fuit spoliati gloria Parthi,
  ne faceres Galla multa rogante tua?
si fas est, omnes pariter pereatis auari,   5
  et quisquis fido praetulit arma toro!
tu tamen iniecta tectus, uesane, lacerna
  potabis galea fessus Araxis aquam.
illa quidem interea fama tabescet inani,
  haec tua ne uirtus fiat amara tibi,   10
neue tua Medae laetentur caede sagittae,
  ferreus armato neu cataphractus equo,
neue aliquid de te flendum referatur in urna:
  sic redeunt, illis qui cecidere locis.
ter quater in casta felix, o Postume, Galla!   15
  moribus his alia coniuge dignus eras.

---

61 Curtius *V2*: Curius *N*, *P corr.*, *V1Vo.*: Durius *F1L*, *P primo*, *D*
62 Ac *LPDV1*   63 adscisos *N*   64 Et *O, corr. Puccius*   70 tanti
operis bellum *Housman*
XII 4 facias *F1LP1DV1*   7 iniecta *Volscus, Beroaldus*: intecta *uel*
in tecta *O*   12 aerato *uel* armato *Heinsius*: aurato *O*   cataphractus
F4DV2: catophratus *NF1LPV1Vo.*   14 Sic redeunt *V2Vo.*: Si credunt
N: Si credent *F1LPDV1*

quid faciet nullo munita puella timore,
    cum sit luxuriae Roma magistra suae?
sed securus eas: Gallam non munera uincent,
    duritiaeque tuae non erit illa memor.   20
nam quocumque die saluum te fata remittent,
    pendebit collo Galla pudica tuo.
Postumus alter erit miranda coniuge Vlixes:
    non illi longae tot nocuere morae,
castra decem annorum, et Ciconum mors Ismara capta,   25
    exustaeque tuae mox, Polypheme, genae,
et Circae fraudes, lotosque herbaeque tenaces,
    Scyllaque et alternas scissa Charybdis aquas,
Lampeties Ithacis ueribus mugisse iuuencos
    (pauerat hos Phoebo filia Lampetie),   30
et thalamum Aeaeae flentis fugisse puellae,
    totque hiemis noctes totque natasse dies,
nigrantisque domos animarum intrasse silentum,
    Sirenum surdo remige adisse lacus,
et ueteres arcus leto renouasse procorum,   35
    errorisque sui sic statuisse modum.
nec frustra, quia casta domi persederat uxor.
    uincit Penelopes Aelia Galla fidem.

XIII

Quaeritis, unde auidis nox sit pretiosa puellis,
    et Venere exhaustae damna querantur opes?
certa quidem tantis causa et manifesta ruinis:
    luxuriae nimium libera facta uia est.

---

18 cui sis *Palmer*   tu(a)e   *O, corr.* ∫   25 mors ∫ mons *O*   capta
Fontein: calpe *NF1Vo.*: talpe *F4LPDV* 26 mox *Wittig* 29 Lampathie sithicis *N, similia cett.* 34
lacus *NF4∆*: latus (? *ex* laturus) *F1*: latreus *LP*   35 lecto *O, corr. F?,* ∫ reuocasse *Vo.*   38
penolopes *PVo.*: penelope *NDV1*: penelope *FL*: *corr. V2*   Aelia *Gulielmius*: l(a)e(l)lia *O*
XIII 2 uenerem *O, corr.* ∫ exhausto *N*   3 rapinis *Palmer*

Inda cauis aurum mittit formica metallis,   5
    et uenit e Rubro concha Erycina salo,
et Tyros ostrinos praebet Cadmea colores,
    cinnamon et multi pastor odoris Arabs:
haec etiam clausas expugnant arma pudicas,
    quaeque gerunt fastus, Icarioti, tuos.   10
matrona incedit census induta nepotum
    et spolia opprobrii nostra per ora trahit.
nulla est poscendi, nulla est reuerentia dandi,
    aut si qua est, pretio tollitur ipsa mora.
felix Eois lex funeris una maritis,   15
    quos Aurora suis rubra colorat equis!
namque ubi mortifero iacta est fax ultima lecto,
    uxorum fusis stat pia turba comis,
et certamen habent leti, quae uiua sequatur
    coniugium: pudor est non licuisse mori.   20
ardent uictrices et flammae pectora praebent,
    imponuntque suis ora perusta uiris.
hoc genus infidum nuptarum, hic nulla puella
    nec fida Euadne nec pia Penelope.
felix agrestum quondam pacata iuuentus,   25
    diuitiae quorum messis et arbor erant!
illis munus erant decussa Cydonia ramo,
    et dare puniceis plena canistra rubis,
nunc uiolas tondere manu, nunc mixta referre
    lilia uimineos lucida per calathos,   30
et portare suis uestitas frondibus uuas
    aut uariam plumae uersicoloris auem.
his tum blanditiis furtiua per antra puellae
    oscula siluicolis empta dedere uiris.

---

6 erythraea *ς*   9 clauias *fort. N*   puellas *Markland*   10 gerunt *Scioppius, Guyet*: terunt *O*: iterant *Heinsius*   i(y)cariote (-ore *F1LP1*) *O*, *corr. V2*   23 Hic *F4*   hic nulla *NV2Vo.*: innupta *uel. sim. cett.*   27 erat *codd. nonnulli* discussa *N*   30 uirgineos *O, corr. Fruter*   32 uersicoloris *F4PDV1*: uiricoloris *NF1LV2*: uaricoloris *V2Vo.*: uitricoloris *Ellis*   33 antra] rara *N*

hinnulei pellis totos operibat amantis,   · 35
  altaque natiuo creuerat herba toro,
pinus et incumbens lentas circumdabat umbras;
  nec fuerat nudas poena uidere deas;
corniger Arcadii uacuam pastoris in aulam
  dux aries saturas ipse reduxit ouis;   40
dique deaeque omnes, quibus est tutela per agros,
  praebebant uestri uerba benigna foci:
'Et leporem, quicumque uenis, uenaberis, hospes,
  et si forte meo tramite quaeris auem:
et me Pana tibi comitem de rupe uocato,   45
  siue petes calamo praemia, siue cane.'
at nunc desertis cessant sacraria lucis:
  aurum omnes uicta iam pietate colunt.
auro pulsa fides, auro uenalia iura,
  aurum lex sequitur, mox sine lege pudor.   50
torrida sacrilegum testantur limina Brennum,
  dum petit intonsi Pythia regna dei:
at mons laurigero concussus uertice diras
  Gallica Parnasus sparsit in arma niues.
te scelus accepto Thracis Polymestoris auro   55
  nutrit in hospitio non, Polydore, pio.
tu quoque ut auratos gereres, Eriphyla, lacertos,
  delapsis nusquam est Amphiaraus equis.
proloquar:—atque utinam patriae sim uerus haruspex!—
  frangitur ipsa suis Roma superba bonis.   60
certa loquor, sed nulla fides; neque enim Ilia quondam
  uerax Pergameis Maenas habenda malis:

---

35 hinulei *Scaliger*: Atque hunili (?)*N*, *sim. cett.* **tutos** *Sterke*: positos
Heinsius   37 l(a)etas *F1*, ς   39 Arcadii *Hertzberg*: Atque dei *O*:
Idaei *Volscus*: atque sui *Heinsius*: cornigerique dei ς   42 uestri *Barber*:
uestris *O*: nostris ς   focis *O*, *corr. Barber*   53 mox *F1LPDV1*   lauri-
gero *DV1*: aurigero *cett.*   55 Te *Itali*: Et *O*   56 pio *NF4Vo*:
tuo *cett.*   58 Dilapsis (-us) *O*, *corr.* ς   59 uanus *V2*   60 suis]
sitis *N*

35

sola Parim Phrygiae fatum componere, sola
  fallacem patriae serpere dixit equum.
ille furor patriae fuit utilis, ille parenti: 65
  experta est ueros irrita lingua deos.

XIV

Multa tuae, Sparte, miramur iura palaestrae,
  sed mage uirginei tot bona gymnasii,
quod non infamis exercet corpore ludos
  inter luctantis nuda puella uiros,
cum pila ueloces fallit per bracchia iactus,   5
  increpat et uersi clauis adunca trochi,
puluerulentaque ad extremas stat femina metas,
  et patitur duro uulnera pancratio:
nunc ligat ad caestum gaudentia bracchia loris,
  missile nunc disci pondus in orbe rotat;   10
gyrum pulsat equis, niueum latus ense reuincit,   11
  uirgineumque cauo protegit aere caput,
et modo Taygeti, crinis aspersa pruina,   15
  sectatur patrios per iuga longa canis;   16
qualis Amazonidum nudatis bellica mammis   13
  Thermodontiacis turba lauatur aquis;   14
qualis et Eurotae Pollux et Castor harenis,   17
  hic uictor pugnis, ille futurus equis,
inter quos Helene nudis capere arma papillis
  fertur nec fratres erubuisse deos.   20
lex igitur Spartana uetat secedere amantis,
  et licet in triuiis ad latus esse suae,

XIV *priori continuat N1*   3 ludos *Auratus*: laudes *O*   5 ueloci...
iactu *Scaliger*   15–16 *transtulerunt post* 12 *Canter et Scaliger, post* 10
Palmer et Otto   17 habenis *NF4V2Vo.*: athenis *F1LPDV1: corr. s,*
Volscus   19 capere arma *NVo.*: capere arma *F4*: est armata *F1*: arma
L: armata *PDV*   capillis *F1LPDV*   22 tuae? *dubitanter Barber*

36

nec timor aut ulla est clausae tutela puellae,
    nec grauis austeri poena cauenda uiri.
nullo praemisso de rebus tute loquaris   25
    ipse tuis: longae nulla repulsa morae.
nec Tyriae uestes errantia lumina fallunt,
    est neque odoratae cura molesta comae.
at nostra ingenti uadit circumdata turba,
    nec digitum angusta est inseruisse uia;   30
nec quae sint facies nec quae sint uerba rogandi
    inuenias: caecum uersat amator iter.
quod si iura fores pugnasque imitata Laconum,
    carior hoc esses tu mihi, Roma, bono.

XV

Sic ego non ullos iam norim in amore tumultus,
    nec ueniat sine te nox uigilanda mihi:
ut mihi praetexti pudor est releuatus amictus
    et data libertas noscere amoris iter,
illa rudis animos per noctes conscia primas   5
    imbuit, heu nullis capta Lycinna datis!
tertius (haud multo minus est) cum ducitur annus,
    uix memini nobis uerba coisse decem.
cuncta tuus sepeliuit amor, nec femina post te
    ulla dedit collo dulcia uincla meo.   10

testis erit Dirce tam sero crimine saeua,
    Nycteos Antiopen accubuisse Lyco.

23 Non *FLP*   27 Non *FLPDV*   28 adoratae *N*   domi *O, corr. ç,*
Canter   31 sit (facies) *PV2*   33 leonum *N*
XV 1 Hic *N rubricator, sed* s *in mg. scriba*   3 pr(a)etexti *N*: pr(a)etexta
cett.: pr(a)etext(a)e ç   releuatus *Fontein*: uelatus *O*: sublatus ç: ablatus
Heinsius: elatus *Guyet*: amotus *Barber, ex* amotus *corruptelam ortam esse*
suspicatus   amictus *LPDV1*: amicus *NFV2Vo.*: amictu ç   7 haud *F2?,*
LPDV: aut *NVo.*: hanc *F1*   cum] iam *Postgate*   10 *post hunc u. uu.*
45–6, 43–4 *Fischer*   11 *noua el. in codd. praeter Vo.*: *lacunam ante*
11 *statuit Broekhuyzen*   11 sero *Phillimore*: uero *O*: uano *Franz*

a quotiens pulchros uulsit regina capillos,
    molliaque immitis fixit in ora manus!
a quotiens famulam pensis onerauit iniquis,   15
    et caput in dura ponere iussit humo!
saepe illam immundis passa est habitare tenebris,
    uilem ieiunae saepe negauit aquam.
Iuppiter, Antiopae nusquam succurris habenti
    tot mala? corrumpit dura catena manus.   20
si deus es, tibi turpe tuam seruire puellam:
    inuocet Antiope quem nisi uincta Iouem?
sola tamen, quaecumque aderant in corpore uires,
    regalis manicas rupit utraque manu.
inde Cithaeronis timido pede currit in arces.   25
    nox erat, et sparso triste cubile gelu.
saepe uaga Asopi sonitu permota fluentis
    credebat dominae pone uenire pedes.
et durum Zethum et lacrimis Amphiona mollem
    experta est stabulis mater abacta suis.   30
ac ueluti, magnos cum ponunt aequora motus,
    Eurus ubi aduerso desinit ire Noto,
litore sub tacito sonitus rarescit harenae,
    sic cadit inflexo lapsa puella genu.
sera, tamen pietas: natis est cognitus error.   35
    digne Iouis natos qui tueare senex,
tu reddis pueris matrem; puerique trahendam
    uinxerunt Dircen sub trucis ora bouis.
Antiope, cognosce Iouem: tibi gloria Dirce
    ducitur in multis mortem habitura locis.   40
prata cruentantur Zethi, uictorque canebat
    paeana Amphion rupe, Aracynthe, tua.

---

13 ussit *O, corr. R. Titius*   14 immites *D*: i mites *V*: inmittens
(immict- *F1*, immit- *F4*) *cett.*   21 es *P*: est *cett.*   22 uincta *P*: uicta
cett.   27 uago Δ   asopi *DV1*: (a)esopi *cett.*   30 tabulis *O, corr.* ς
32 sub aduerso...notho *N*: in aduersos...not(h)os *cett.*: *corr. Lachmann*
33 sub *Liuineius*: sic *O*: si ς: iam *Havet*: subtractae...harenae *Richardson* 41 Parta (-ca *Vo.*) *O*,
corr. ς

at tu non meritam parcas uexare Lycinnam:
 nescit uestra ruens ira referre pedem.
fabula nulla tuas de nobis concitet auris: 45
 te solam et lignis funeris ustus amem.

XVI

Nox media, et dominae mihi uenit epistula nostrae:
 Tibure me missa iussit adesse mora,
candida qua geminas ostendunt culmina turris,
 et cadit in patulos nympha Aniena lacus.
quid faciam? obductis committam mene tenebris,   5
 ut timeam audaces in mea membra manus?
at si distulero haec nostro mandata timore,
 nocturno fletus saeuior hoste mihi.
peccaram semel, et totum sum pulsus in annum:
 in me mansuetas non habet illa manus.   10
nec tamen est quisquam, sacros qui laedat amantis:
 Scironis media sic licet ire uia.
quisquis amator erit, Scythicis licet ambulet oris,
 nemo adeo ut noceat barbarus esse uolet.
luna ministrat iter, demonstrant astra salebras,   15
 ipse Amor accensas percutit ante faces,
saeua canum rabies morsus auertit hiantis:
 huic generi quouis tempore tuta uia est.
sanguine tam paruo quis enim spargatur amantis
 improbus? exclusis fit comes ipsa Venus.   20
quod si certa meos sequerentur funera casus,
 talis mors pretio uel sit emenda mihi.

XVI 2 Ti(y)buri *NF₁LP₁*   4 lympha *F₄* 5   7 distulero haec *N*:
h(a)ec (*ex* hoc *P*) distulero *cett.*   9 pulsus *FLP*Δ: portus *N*   11 l(a)edit
F₁LPDV₁   12 scilicet *NV₂Vo.*: si licet *FLPDV₁*: *corr.* 5   13 Scythiae
inscr. Pomp. (= *CIL* 4. 1950)   ambulet *inscr.*, *PV₂Vo.*: ambulat
NFLDV₁   14 adeo *inscr.*, 5: deo *O*   feriat *inscr.*   16 praecutit
Guyet: concutit *Postgate*   20 exclusis *O*: extrusis *Luck*   et cuius sit
(5) *Palmer*   fit] it *Struchtmeyer*

afferet haec unguenta mihi sertisque sepulcrum
　　ornabit custos ad mea busta sedens.
di faciant, mea ne terra locet ossa frequenti,　　　　　25
　　qua facit assiduo tramite uulgus iter!—
post mortem tumuli sic infamantur amantum.
　　me tegat arborea deuia terra coma,
aut humer ignotae cumulus uallatus harenae:
　　non iuuat in media nomen habere uia.　　　　　　30

XVII

Nunc, o Bacche, tuis humiles aduoluimur aris:
　　da mihi pacato uela secunda, pater.
tu potes insanae Veneris compescere flatus,
　　curarumque tuo fit medicina mero.
per te iunguntur, per te soluuntur amantes:　　　　　5
　　tu uitium ex animo dilue, Bacche, meo.
te quoque enim non esse rudem testatur in astris
　　lyncibus ad caelum uecta Ariadna tuis.
hoc mihi, quod ueteres custodit in ossibus ignis,
　　funera sanabunt aut tua uina malum.　　　　　　10
semper enim uacuos nox sobria torquet amantis;
　　spesque timorque animos uersat utroque toro.
quod si, Bacche, tuis per feruida tempora donis
　　accersitus erit somnus in ossa mea,
ipse seram uitis pangamque ex ordine collis,　　　　15
　　quos carpent nullae me uigilante ferae,
dum modo purpureo tumeant mihi dolia musto,
　　et noua pressantis inquinet uua pedes.

---

23 huc *O, corr. Guyet*　　25 ne *D*: nec *cett.*　　29 humer *V2Vo.*:
humeri *N*: humor (ign. humor *DV1*) *FL*, ?*P1, DV1*: humet *P2*　　cumulus
FV1: cumulis *N, P corr., D*: tumulis *L*, ?*P primo*: tumulus *V2Vo*.
XVII 2 pacato *O*: pacatus *Guyet*　　3 flatus *nescioquis*: fastus *O*: fluctus
Passerat　　12 animos *cod.Burmanni*: animo *O*: animum *V2*　　toro *Palmer*:
modo *O*　　16 carpent *scripsi*: carpant *codd.*　　17 tumeant *Phillimore*:
numen *et sim. O*: spument *ϛ*

40

quod superest uitae per te et tua cornua uiuam,
    uirtutisque tuae, Bacche, poeta ferar.   20
dicam ego maternos Aetnaeo fulmine partus,
    Indica Nysaeis arma fugata choris,
uesanumque noua nequiquam in uite Lycurgum,
    Pentheos in triplices funera rapta greges,
curuaque Tyrrhenos delphinum corpora nautas   25
    in uada pampinea desiluisse rate,
et tibi per mediam bene olentia flumina Naxon,
    unde tuum potant Naxia turba merum.
candida laxatis onerato colla corymbis
    cinget Bassaricas Lydia mitra comas,   30
leuis odorato ceruix manabit oliuo,
    et feries nudos ueste fluente pedes.
mollia Dircaeae pulsabunt tympana Thebae,
    capripedes calamo Panes hiante canent,
uertice turrigero iuxta dea magna Cybebe   35
    tundet ad Idaeos cymbala rauca choros.
ante fores templi crater antistitis auro
    libabit fundens in tua sacra merum.
haec ego non humili referam memoranda coturno,
    qualis Pindarico spiritus ore tonat: 40
tu modo seruitio uacuum me siste superbo,
    atque hoc sollicitum uince sopore caput.

---

21 flumine *FL1PDV1*   24 rapta *Scaliger*: grata *O*   27 Naxon] Diam
Palmer   30 Cinget *V2*: Cingit *O*   35 Cybebe *Itali*: cy(i)be(l)le *O*
36 Fundet *O, corr. Canter*   37 cratere antistes et auro *Heinsius*
38 libabit *Foster*: Libatum *O*

XVIII

Clausus ab umbroso qua ludit pontus Auerno,
    fumida Baiarum stagna tepentis aquae,
qua iacet et Troiae tubicen Misenus harena,
    et sonat Herculeo structa labore uia;
hic ubi, mortalis dexter cum quaereret urbes,   5
    cymbala Thebano concrepuere deo:—
at nunc inuisae magno cum crimine Baiae,
    quis deus in uestra constitit hostis aqua?
his pressus Stygias uultum demisit in undas,
    errat et in uestro spiritus ille lacu.   10
quid genus aut uirtus aut optima profuit illi
    mater, et amplexum Caesaris esse focos?
aut modo tam pleno fluitantia uela theatro,
    et per maternas omnia gesta manus?
occidit, et misero steterat uicesimus annus: 15
    tot bona tam paruo clausit in orbe dies.
i nunc, tolle animos et tecum finge triumphos,
    stantiaque in plausum tota theatra iuuent;
Attalicas supera uestis, atque omnia magnis
    gemmea sint ludis: ignibus ista dabis.   20
sed tamen huc omnes, huc primus et ultimus ordo:
    est mala, sed cunctis ista terenda uia est.
exoranda canis tria sunt latrantia colla,
    scandenda est torui publica cumba senis.
ille licet ferro cautus se condat et aere,   25
    mors tamen inclusum protrahit inde caput.

XVIII 1 alludit *Lambinus*   2 Humida *O, corr. Scaliger*   5 mortales
NVo.: mortalis *cett.*   8 *post hunc u. lacunam statuit Guyet*   9 hic
Guyet   19–20 signis*.'*. . .Lydis *Barber* (Lydis *iam Phillimore*)   21 huc
(omnes) *F4P2*: hoc *O*   sed manet (*Keil*) hoc omnes, huc *Palmer*   24 torui
pro u.l. F2, V2Vo.: torti *L, ?P, DV1*: torci *F1*: troci *N*: curui *P corr.*

Nirea non facies, non uis exemit Achillem,
  Croesum aut, Pactoli quas parit umor, opes.
hic olim ignaros luctus populauit Achiuos,
  Atridae magno cum stetit alter amor.   30
at tibi, nauta, pias hominum qui traicis umbras,
  huc animae portant corpus inane tuae:
qua Siculae uictor telluris Claudius et qua
  Caesar, ab humana cessit in astra uia.

XIX

Obicitur totiens a te mihi nostra libido:
  crede mihi, uobis imperat ista magis.
uos, ubi contempti rupistis frena pudoris,
  nescitis captae mentis habere modum.
flamma per incensas citius sedetur aristas,   5
  fluminaque ad fontis sint reditura caput,
et placidum Syrtes portum et bona litora nautis
  praebeat hospitio saeua Malea suo,
quam possit uestros quisquam reprehendere cursus
  et rabidae stimulos frangere nequitiae.   10
testis, Cretaei fastus quae passa iuuenci
  induit abiegnae cornua falsa bouis;
testis Thessalico flagrans Salmonis Enipeo,
  quae uoluit liquido tota subire deo.
crimen et illa fuit, patria succensa senecta   15
  arboris in frondis condita Myrrha nouae.
nam quid Medeae referam, quo tempore matris
  iram natorum caede piauit amor?

27 Nerea O   29–30 *hic alienos esse putant multi*   29 sic *Heinsius*
32 Huc O: Hoc ς, *Lachmann*   portant *scripsi*: portent O   tu(a)e O:
suae *Heinsius*   33 Qua...qua O: quo...quo *Barber*   34 humano *R.M. Henry*
XIX 4 capt(a)e NΔ: liber(a)e *FLP*   10 rabidae ς: rapid(a)e O   12
aiegno N   boui O, corr. ς   15–16 *post* 20 *Postgate*   17 Medeam
Guyet

quidue Clytaemestrae, propter quam tota Mycenis
    infamis stupro stat Pelopea domus?   20
teque, o Minoa uenumdata Scylla figura
    tondens purpurea regna paterna coma?
hanc igitur dotem uirgo desponderat hosti!
    Nise, tuas portas fraude reclusit amor.
at uos, innuptae, felicius urite taedas: 25
    pendet Cretaea tracta puella rate.
non tamen immerito Minos sedet arbiter Orci:
    uictor erat quamuis, aequus in hoste fuit.

XX A

Credis eum iam posse tuae meminisse figurae,
    uidisti a lecto quem dare uela tuo?
durus, qui lucro potuit mutare puellam!
    tantine, ut lacrimes, Africa tota fuit?
at tu, stulta, deos, tu fingis inania uerba: 5
    forsitan ille alio pectus amore terat.
est tibi forma potens, sunt castae Palladis artes,
    splendidaque a docto fama refulget auo,
fortunata domus, modo sit tibi fidus amicus.
    fidus ero: in nostros curre, puella, toros!   10

XX B

Nox mihi prima uenit! primae data tempora noctis!   13
    longius in primo, Luna, morare toro.   14
tu quoque, qui aestiuos spatiosius exigis ignis,   11
    Phoebe, moraturae contrahe lucis iter.   12

19 Clytaemnestram *Guyet*   21 teque *Guyet*: Tuque *O*   22 Tondens
O: tondes *Keil*   purpuream...comam *Markland*   25–6 *post* 28 *Hous-*
man   25 *aliter dist.* Leo, Barber
XX 4 Tantisne *N, sim. cett.*: *corr. Heinsius*   in lacrimis *O, corr. Heinsius*
7 Ast *N*   10 ego *Heinsius*   11 spatiosius *NV2*: -osus *cett.*
11–30 *separauit Scaliger, qui* 11–12 *post* 14 *transtulit*   13 data ç: date *O*: da...nocti *Palmer*

foedera sunt ponenda prius signandaque iura 15
  et scribenda mihi lex in amore nouo.
haec Amor ipse suo constringit pignora signo:
  testis sidereae torta corona deae.
quam multae ante meis cedent sermonibus horae,
  dulcia quam nobis concitet arma Venus! 20
namque ubi non certo uincitur foedere lectus,
  non habet ultores nox uigilanda deos,
et quibus imposuit, soluit mox uincla libido:
  contineant nobis omina prima fidem.—
ergo, qui pactas in foedera ruperit aras, 25
  pollueritque nouo sacra marita toro,
illi sint quicumque solent in amore dolores,
  et caput argutae praebeat historiae,
nec flenti dominae patefiant nocte fenestrae:
  semper amet, fructu semper amoris egens. 30

XXI

Magnum iter ad doctas proficisci cogor Athenas,
  ut me longa graui soluat amore uia.
crescit enim assidue spectando cura puellae:
  ipse alimenta sibi maxima praebet amor.
omnia sunt temptata mihi, quacumque fugari 5
  possit: at ex omni me premit ipse deus.
uix tamen aut semel admittit, cum saepe negarit:
  seu uenit, extremo dormit amicta toro.
unum erit auxilium: mutatis Cynthia terris
  quantum oculis, animo tam procul ibit amor. 10

---

19 cedant *F₁LPDV₁*   19–20 *post* 14 *Lachmann*   22 uigila *N*:
uigilata *Palmer*   23 nox *O, nisi quod* modo *P: corr.* ς   25 tactas ς
XXI 3 spectandi *N*: spectanti *nescioquis*   6 Possit *O*: posset *Richards*
exsomnis *Barber*: exsomnem *iam Heinsius*   7 admittit *F4Δ*: amittit *N*,
sim. cett.   8 amica *O, corr. Scaliger*

nunc agite, o socii, propellite in aequora nauem,
   remorumque pares ducite sorte uices,
iungiteque extremo felicia lintea malo:
   iam liquidum nautis aura secundat iter.
Romanae turres et uos ualeatis, amici,   15
   qualiscumque mihi tuque, puella, uale!
ergo ego nunc rudis Hadriaci uehar aequoris hospes,
   cogar et undisonos nunc prece adire deos.
deinde per Ionium uectus cum fessa Lechaeo
   sedarit placida uela phaselus aqua,   20
quod superest, sufferre, pedes, properate laborem,
   Isthmos qua terris arcet utrumque mare.
inde ubi Piraei capient me litora portus,
   scandam ego Theseae bracchia longa uiae.
illic uel stadiis animum emendare Platonis   25
   incipiam aut hortis, docte Epicure, tuis;
persequar aut studium linguae, Demosthenis arma,
   librorumque tuos, docte Menandre, sales;
aut certe tabulae capient mea lumina pictae,
   siue ebore exactae, seu magis aere, manus.   30
aut spatia annorum aut longa interualla profundi
   lenibunt tacito uulnera nostra situ:
seu moriar, fato, non turpi fractus amore;
   atque erit illa mihi mortis honesta dies.

---

11 equora *F*: (a)equore *cett.*   19 li(y)cheo *et similia O*: Lechaei *Guyeⁱ*
25 stadiis *uel* spatiis *Fontein, Broekhuyzen*: studiis *O*   26 hortis *N*: ortis *cett.*
27 Prosequar *ς*   28 libaboque *Suringar*   docte *O*: culte *Heinsius*:
alii alia   32 situ *Heinsius*: sinu *O*

XXII

Frigida tam multos placuit tibi Cyzicus annos,
  Tulle, Propontiaca quae fluit isthmos aqua,
Dindymis et sacra fabricata in uite Cybebe,
   raptorisque tulit quae uia Ditis equos?
si te forte iuuant Helles Athamantidos urbes,   5
  at desiderio, Tulle, mouere meo.
tu licet aspicias caelum omne Atlanta gerentem,
  sectaque Persea Phorcidos ora manu,
Geryonis stabula et luctantum in puluere signa
  Herculis Antaeique, Hesperidumque choros;   10
tuque tuo Colchum propellas remige Phasim,
  Peliacaeque trabis totum iter ipse legas,
qua rudis Argoa natat inter saxa columba
  in faciem prorae pinus adacta nouae;
et si qua Ortygie uisenda est, ora Caystri,   15
  et quae septenas temperat unda uias;
omnia Romanae cedent miracula terrae:
  natura hic posuit, quidquid ubique fuit.
armis apta magis tellus quam commoda noxae:
  Famam, Roma, tuae non pudet historiae.   20
nam quantum ferro tantum pietate potentes
  stamus: uictrices temperat ira manus.
hic Anio Tiburne fluis, Clitumnus ab Vmbro
  tramite, et aeternum Marcius umor opus,
Albanus lacus et socia Nemorensis ab unda,   25
  potaque Pollucis nympha salubris equo.

XXII 1 annos *F3?*, *L2P*: annus *NF1L1VVo.*: amnis *D*   2 qua Δ
3 Dindy(i)mus *O, corr. Palmer* in uite *Havet*: inuenta *NF4LPVo.*: iu-
uenta *F1DV*: e uite *Haupt*   ci(y)be(i)l(l)e *O*   4 qua *O, corr. Itali*
5 seu *Luck* iuuant *DV*: iuuat *cett.*   6 at *Phillimore*: Et *O*: Nec *ς*, *Luck*
15 Et *NF4Vo.*: At *F1LDV*: Aut *P*   si qua] sis qua *Haupt*   Ortygie
Butler et Barber: orig(a)e *O*: Ortygia et *Haupt*: Ortygiae *Lachmann*   16
qua *O, corr. Palmer* 15–16 *post* 6 (*in* 6 *recepto* nec) *Housman* 23 flues *O, corr.* ς clitumnus *F4*:
uarie corruperunt cett. 24 martius *O, corr.* ς 25 socii *NLPVo.*: sotii *F*: sotiis *DV*: *corr. Puccius*
26 ly(i)mpha *P2,* ς

47

at non squamoso labuntur uentre cerastae,
    Itala portentis nec furit unda nouis;
non hic Andromedae resonant pro matre catenae,
    nec tremis Ausonias, Phoebe fugate, dapes,   30
nec cuiquam absentes arserunt in caput ignes
    exitium nato matre mouente suo;
Penthea non saeuae uenantur in arbore Bacchae,
    nec soluit Danaas subdita cerua ratis;
cornua nec ualuit curuare in paelice Iuno   35
    aut faciem turpi dedecorare boue;

*   *   *

arboreasque cruces Sinis, et non hospita Grais
    saxa, et curtatas in sua fata trabes.
haec tibi, Tulle, parens, haec est pulcherrima sedes,
    hic tibi pro digna gente petendus honos,   40
hic tibi ad eloquium ciues, hic ampla nepotum
    spes et uenturae coniugis aptus amor.

XXIII

Ergo tam doctae nobis periere tabellae,
    scripta quibus pariter tot periere bona!
has quondam nostris manibus detriuerat usus,
    qui non signatas iussit habere fidem.
illae iam sine me norant placare puellas,   5
    et quaedam sine me uerba diserta loqui.
non illas fixum caras effecerat aurum:
    uulgari buxo sordida cera fuit.
qualescumque mihi semper mansere fideles,
    semper et effectus promeruere bonos.   10

27 nunc *N*   28 furit (*et* fluit) ϛ: fuit *O*   una *O, corr.* ϛ   36 boue *F3DV*:
boui *cett. post hunc u. lacunam statuit Liuineius*   37 senis *O* (cinis *superscr.*
N2): *corr.* ϛ   38 curtatas *Puccius*: curuatas *O*   40 H(a)ec *F primo, LP1*

forsitan haec illis fuerint mandata tabellis:
  'Irascor quoniam es, lente, moratus heri.
an tibi nescio quae uisa est formosior? an tu
  non bona de nobis crimina ficta iacis?'
aut dixit: 'Venies hodie, cessabimus una: 15
  hospitium tota nocte parauit Amor,'
et quaecumque uolens reperit non stulta puella
  garrula, cum blandis dicitur hora dolis.
me miserum, his aliquis rationem scribit auarus
  et ponit diras inter ephemeridas!   20
quas si quis mihi rettulerit, donabitur auro:
  quis pro diuitiis ligna retenta uelit?
i puer, et citus haec aliqua propone columna,
  et dominum Esquiliis scribe habitare tuum.

XXIV

Falsa est ista tuae, mulier, fiducia formae,
  olim oculis nimium facta superba meis.
noster amor talis tribuit tibi, Cynthia, laudes:
  uersibus insignem te pudet esse meis.
mixtam te uaria laudaui saepe figura,   5
  ut, quod non esses, esse putaret amor;
et color est totiens roseo collatus Eoo,
  cum tibi quaesitus candor in ore foret.
quod mihi non patrii poterant auertere amici,
  eluere aut uasto Thessala saga mari,   10
haec ego non ferro, non igne coactus, et ipsa
  naufragus Aegaea uera fatebar aqua:

XXIII 11 fuerint *N*: fuerant *cett.*   15 dixit *P*: dixi *cett.*   cessauimus
O, corr. ς   16 parabit *Heinsius*   17–18 *dist. Housman*   17 dolens
O, corr. Broekhuyzen   18 ducitur *O, corr.* ς   19 auari *O, corr.* ς
20 diras *NF4Vo.*: duras *cett.*   22 prae *Barber*   signa *O, corr. Beroaldus*
XXIV 4 meis? *dist. N*   6 esse *N, P corr., V2*: s(a)epe *cett.*   9–12
uarie dist. edd.   10 Eluere *F4, P corr.,* Δ: Fluere *NF1L*   11 H(a)ec
O: hoc *Foster*   ipsa] ista *Barber*   12 uerba *O, corr. Passerat*   fatebar
ς: fatebor *O*

correptus saeuo Veneris torrebar aeno;
  uinctus eram uersas in mea terga manus.
ecce coronatae portum tetigere carinae,   15
  traiectae Syrtes, ancora iacta mihi est.
nunc demum uasto fessi resipiscimus aestu,
  uulneraque ad sanum nunc coiere mea.
Mens Bona, si qua dea es, tua me in sacraria dono!
  exciderant surdo tot mea uota Ioui.   20

XXV

Risus eram positis inter conuiuia mensis,
  et de me poterat quilibet esse loquax.
quinque tibi potui seruire fideliter annos:
  ungue meam morso saepe querere fidem.
nil moueor lacrimis: ista sum captus ab arte;   5
  semper ab insidiis, Cynthia, flere soles.
flebo ego discedens, sed fletum iniuria uincit:
  tu bene conueniens non sinis ire iugum.
limina iam nostris ualeant lacrimantia uerbis,
  nec tamen irata ianua fracta manu.   10
at te celatis aetas grauis urgeat annis,
  et ueniat formae ruga sinistra tuae!
uellere tum cupias albos a stirpe capillos,
  a! speculo rugas increpitante tibi,
exclusa inque uicem fastus patiare superbos,   15
  et quae fecisti facta queraris anus!
has tibi fatalis cecinit mea pagina diras:
  euentum formae disce timere tuae!

14 uinctus *LPDV*: uictùs *NFVo*.   19 dea es *Beroaldus*: deo est *O*
XXV *priori continuant FLPDV*   8 ire *NV2Vo*.: esse *cett*.   13 cum
F1LPDV cupias *LPD*: cupies *VVo*.: capias *NF*   14 a!] iam *Bailey*
18 form(a)e *NF4V2Vo*.: domin(a)e *cett*.

NOTES

I

In this elegy Propertius proclaims his poetic intentions and asserts his achievement. In so doing he echoes passages in which other poets had spoken on such subjects: Horace (*Od.* III, xxx, 13–14, 7–8; and cf. lines 3 and 34 here), Virgil (*Georg.* III, 8 ff. and 17 ff.; and cf. lines 9–12 here), Lucretius (I, 117–18 and 925–30; and cf. lines 3 and 17–20 here), Theocritus (xvi, 48 ff.; and cf. lines 25 ff. here), and above all Callimachus (Prologue to the *Aitia*, quoted in the notes below; and cf. lines 1, 5–8, 14, 21 and 38 here).

The elegy falls into two parts, the first (1–20) an assertion of achievement, the second (21–38) a prophecy of enduring fame.

* **1. Callimachi...Philitae:** Callimachus of Cyrene and Philitas of Cos, Greek poets active in the third century B.C., of whom Quintilian (*I.O.* x, 1, 58) says (*elegiae*) *princeps habetur Callimachus, secundas confessione plurimorum Philitas occupauit.* Both wrote elegiac narrative poems and elegiac epigrams, among other works. There is no surviving evidence that either wrote elegies resembling in content the amatory elegies of Propertius; he invokes them apparently as masters of metrical and stylistic technique, and perhaps as concerned (though in a different manner from himself) with the subject of love.

Callimachus was in controversy with his contemporaries about the criterion of quality in poetry. The following two passages illustrate his opinions, and help to explain much of the sentiment and imagery both of this elegy and of Elegy iii below. From the Prologue to the *Aitia* (fr. 1, 17–28): 'Be off, pernicious brood of Jealousy, and learn to judge poetry by the poet's art, not by the mile. Do not expect high-sounding verse to be produced by me: thundering is not my business but Jupiter's. For when first I ever put a writing-block upon my knees, Lycian Apollo said to me: "...Poet, fatten the beast you offer to the gods, but keep your style lean, if you please. And another thing: do not ride in the ruts the waggons make, or drive in the tracks of all the rest, along the broad high road, but find and follow new ways, though narrow, of your own."' From the conclusion of the *Hymn to Apollo* (105–12): 'Envy came whispering in Apollo's ear: "This is a poor sort of poet, I think, who cannot sing as much and as loud as the sea." But Apollo pushed Envy away with his foot and said: "The Assyrian river runs broad and deep, but also it sweeps along all sorts of dirt and floating débris. And the water that the Bees (a name for certain priestesses) bring to Deo (a name for Demeter = Ceres) is no common kind, but such as issues clean and pure from a holy spring, a slender trickle, essence of perfection."'

sacra Philitae: the value of the phrase seems to be 'Philitas whose shade we worship', the attribute standing for the person as in IV, i, 46 *Caesaris arma* = 'warrior Caesar'; and cf. Virg. *Georg.* I, 59 *palmas...equarum* = 'prize-winning mares'. Literally, the *sacra Philitae* are (on the above supposition) rites or offerings paid to the dead poet, for which cf. Serv. on *Aen.* x, 519 *sacra mortuorum*. For the 'variation' from *Manes* to *sacra* cf. Mart. x, lviii, 13–14 *per ueneranda mihi Musarum sacra, per omnes iuro deos....* (Alternatively one might understand *sacra Philitae* as worship (of the Muses) performed *by* Philitas (as priest = poet, cf. line 3 here and Hor. *Od.* III, i, 3 *Musarum sacerdos*). Then the invocation is 'o spirit of Callimachus, o mysteries (= poetry) of Philitas'; in Mart. VII, lxiii, 5 *sacra Maronis* is parallel to *Ciceronis opus* and so must stand for Virgil's poetry or poetic art.)

2. nemus: typically the haunt of poets, cf. Hor. *Od.* I, i, 30, *Epist.* II, ii, 77, Tac. *Dial.* 12, etc.; perhaps here, more particularly, setting of the fountain where Callimachus and Philitas are imagined as drawing inspiration (cf. line 6 and later III, iii, 13 and 52), or conceivably of their tombs (though we have no information that they were buried in a grove).

3–4. primus ego...choros: 'see, first (of my race) I come, a priest (with water) from a spring that is pure and clear, to join Greek measures with Italian rites (*literally* to carry Italian holy things in Greek dances)'. The claim is parallel to that of Horace in *Od.* III, xxx, 13–14 (*dicar*) *princeps Aeolium carmen ad Italos deduxisse modos*, but there is a difference of imagery. The poet is a priest (of the Muses or of Apollo), and his making poetry is an act of worship—Italian worship, as it is Latin poetry. To this process he is applying some kind of formal artistry derived from the Greeks; or, if the matter is viewed in a different perspective, he is giving an Italian content to a literary form established by the Greeks, in this case the Hellenistic elegists Callimachus and Philitas. Concerning his relation to the work of these two, see the note on line 1 above. In saying *primus* he may mean to imply that his achievement is greater than, or that it is different from, that of Catullus and Gallus and Tibullus; but it is as likely that he is simply rejoicing in his own originality and achievement, without any particular intention to compare himself with others.

ingredior: this here suggests both (*a*) 'entering on' a new enterprise, subject, etc.; cf. Virg. *Georg.* II, 175–6 *tibi res antiquae laudis et artis ingredior, sanctos ausus recludere fontes*...; and also (*b*) the solemn gait of a priest in a procession, the character of the motion being illustrated by Quint. *I.O.* IX, 4, 139 *cum debeant sublimia ingredi,...acria currere, delicata fluere.*

sacerdos: for the poet as priest cf. IV, vi, 1–10 and Hor. *Od.* III, i, 3 *Musarum sacerdos.* The idea may come from Callimachus, in some of whose Hymns (2 and 5) the poet speaks as officiant in a religious ceremony; but as early as Hesiod (*Theog.* 100) the poet is 'servant of the Muses'.

puro de fonte: the purity of the water symbolizes the refined perfection of the poetry; the idea is ultimately from Callimachus, cf. *Hymn to Apollo* 110 ff. Δηοῖ δ' οὐκ ἀπὸ παντὸς ὕδωρ φορέουσι μέλισσαι, ἀλλ' ἥτις καθαρή τε καὶ ἀχράαντος ἀνέρπει πίδακος ἐξ ἱερῆς ὀλίγη λιβάς, ἄκρον ἄωτον (translated above, on line 1). As in the passage from Callimachus just quoted, the water in the metaphor here is evidently supposed to be drawn for some ritual purpose (cf. for instance IV, vi, 7 *spargite me lymphis*). But the water of inspiration which the poets drink at the Muses' fountain (cf. line 6 below and III, iii, 5, etc.) is not far out of mind.

orgia ferre: cf. Sen. *H.O.* 594–5 *nos Cadmeis orgia ferre tecum solitae condita cistis,* where the *orgia* are holy objects carried by worshippers in some ritual procedure; cf. also Virg. *Georg.* II, 475–6 *Musae, quarum sacra fero.*

per: 'in' the dances, as we say. *per* may indicate *where* the holy things are carried (cf. *per uias, per domos,* etc.), or *how* they are carried (cf. *per insidias,* etc.), or the circumstances in which they are carried (cf. *per uinum,* etc.); it is not necessary to choose here.

choros: the rhythmical movements of those performing the ritual, accompanied by music; the term could include a processional march, or movements of arms and body by stationary performers.

53

5–6. dicite...aquam: 'tell me, where is the grotto in which together you spun your fragile (i.e. delicate) thread of song (*or* refined your poetry to such perfection)? How did you enter there? Where is the spring from which you drank?' The terms are again largely Callimachean. For *tenuastis* cf. on 8 below (*tenui*). *antrum* (= ἄντρον) seems to have been introduced into the diction of Latin poetry by the poets who followed Hellenistic precedent, though ἄντρον happens to be seldom exemplified in the fraction of Hellenistic poetry which has come down to us; the Latins use *antrum* sometimes to mean 'glen' (cf. I, i, 11 and Housman on Manil. V, 311), more usually to mean 'cave'; and they associate such a haunt with Apollo and the Muses, as at III, iii, 14 and 27 below, Hor. *Od.* III, iv, 40 *Pierio...antro*, etc. In *quoue pede* the surface meaning (with *ingressi*) is simply 'how (did you enter)?'; but there is also allusion (*a*) to the idea of a happy outcome in phrases such as *secundo pede*, etc. (e.g. Ov. *Fast.* I, 514 *ripaque felici tacta sit ista pede*), and (*b*) to the choice of the elegiac metre by Callimachus and Philitas, *pes* = metrical foot becoming a poetic shorthand for metre (as in Domitius Marsus' epigram on the death of Tibullus: *qui...caneret forti regia bella pede*). Regarding *quamue bibistis aquam* cf. III, iii, 2, 5, 32, 52 below and note on 3–4 above.

7–8. a ualeat...eat: 'begone, say I to any man who detains Phoebus (i.e. the god of poetic inspiration) with tales of war (i.e. a voluminous and high-sounding sort of poetry); tooled finely to perfection (*literally* finished with fine pumice) must my verse proceed'. For the Callimachean sentiment cf. the Prologue to the *Aitia*, quoted on line 1 above. (But while Callimachus in rejecting the epic was differing from his contemporaries on a point of literary taste, Propertius is at odds with his in a matter of national and moral sentiment: war, stock subject of epic, was Rome's speciality.)

tenui pumice: *tenuis* is the Latin adjective corresponding to the Greek λεπτός or λεπταλέος. It is here (in a metaphor, with which cf. *tenui cura limare aliquid*) said of a fine-grained abrasive which gives a smooth finish to an artefact; elsewhere (e.g. Hor. *Epist.* II, i, 225 *tenui deducta poemata filo*) it is said of a finely spun thread as opposed to a coarse one; in the passage from Callimachus' *Aitia* quoted on line 1 above the corresponding Greek word has to be translated 'lean'. It includes principally two ideas: (*a*) the perfection of finish given to a product by the skill and care of the artist or artisan, and (*b*) the removal of super-fluous mass (cf. II, xxxiv, 32 *non inflati...Callimachi* and the opposite in Catull. xcv, 10 *tumido...Antimacho*).

9. quo: ablative, 'whereby', referring to *exactus...uersus* of line 8.

me...sublimis: cf. Virg. *Georg.* III, 9.

9–10. a me nata...Musa: here *Musa* is not (for the moment) a goddess, but a personification of Propertius' poetry. *nata* is from Callimachus' Prologue to the *Aitia* (see above), fr. 1, 19–20 μηδ' ἀπ' ἐμεῦ διφᾶτε μέγα ψοφέουσαν ἀοιδὴν τίκτεσθαι.

11–12. et mecum...rotas: the *triumphator* is now the poet (in line 10 it was his *Musa*); and the Cupids (because his is love-poetry) ride with him in his chariot in the procession like the children of a real *triumphator*; and other poets (his imitators) march behind like a *triumphator*'s soldiers.

secuta: with this supply the sense of *incedit* or the like, from the context; or supply *est*.

13. quid frustra...habenis: the image has shifted, from a procession to a race; the admiring followers of the preceding line are now competitors trying to pass the man who leads the field.

missis...habenis: cf. Virg. *Aen.* V, 662 *immissis...habenis.*

in me: with *certatis*, after the pattern of *pugnare in....*

14. non datur...lata uia: it seems that the rivals are baffled because there is no room to pass, the development of the metaphor being led by an idea (really quite different) of Calli-machus, that of the narrow way followed by the fastidious and original poet, as opposed to the populous and popular highway: cf. Prologue to the *Aitia* 25–8 [πρὸς δέ σε] καὶ τόδ' ἄνωγα, τὰ μὴ πατέουσιν ἄμαξαι, τὰ στείβειν, ἑτέρων δ' ἴχνια μὴ καθ' ὁμά [δίφρον ἐλ]ᾶν, μηδ' οἷμον ἀνὰ πλατύν, ἀλλὰ κελεύθους [σπεῦδ' ἰδίας], εἰ καὶ στεινοτέρην ἐλάσεις (see translation on 1 above).

15. multi: arising from the implication of the previous line, that Propertius' kind of poetry is *not* for the many to attempt.

tuas laudes annalibus addent: 'shall add new praises of you (*or* new glorious feats of yours) to the record of history'. In the word *annalibus* is a reminder, perhaps accidental, but significant, of the *Annales* of Ennius, regarding which see III, iii, 1 ff. below and the note on III, iii, 6 in particular.

16. Bactra: the city or region of Bactra (neut. plur.), standing here as elsewhere (e.g. IV, iii, 7 and 63) as typical objective in a war against the Parthian empire. The prospect of such a war, to wipe out the humiliation of the disaster at Carrhae in 53 B.C., was much talked of in the decade following the end of the civil wars. In 20 B.C. Augustus reached a peaceful settlement with the Parthians; as there is no hint of this here, one can date this elegy with probability before that year.

17. quod pace legas: cf. on 7–8 above.

de monte Sororum: from Helicon, abode of the Muses.

18. detulit intacta...uia: cf. Lucr. I, 117–18 *Ennius...qui primus amoeno detulit ex Helicone perenni fronde coronam*, and 925–6 *auia Pieridum peragro loca nullius ante trita solo*; cf. also Callimachus fr. I, 27–8 (see on lines I and 14 above).

19. Pegasides: the Muses, because of their association with the spring Hippocrene (on Helicon), which first gushed up where Pegasus struck the ground with his hoof.

20. non faciet capiti...meo: 'will not suit' or 'do for' my head—a common use of *facio* with dative.

dura corona: 'a rugged wreath', symbolizing here the austere sentiments of epic poetry (with perhaps also a glance at the technical roughness of pre-Virgilian Latin epic verse; cf. Ov. *Trist.* II, 424 *Ennius ingenio maximus, arte rudis*).

21. Here begins the second part of the elegy, in which the poet predicts that his fame will increase in time to come.

inuida turba: cf. Callimachus fr. I, 17 Βασκανίη and *Hymn to Apollo* 105 Φθόνος (see translations in note on line I above for context), also *A.P.* VII, 525, 4 ὁ δ' ἤειδεν κρείσσονα βασκανίης (Callimachus being subject).

23. omnia post obitum fingit maiora uetustas: here, if the text is right, *omnia* is (as often) a colloquial or rhetorical exaggeration; cf. for instance Virg. *Aen.* I, 32 *errabant acti fatis maria omnia circum*. [*omnia* is given here by the usually less reliable branch of the tradition; *N* has *Famae*, which taken with *uetustas* would yield the sense 'Fame growing old magnifies (things)'. It is possible that the line is garbled in both branches.]

24. ab: 'after'.

* **25 ff.** The proposition of the preceding couplet (23–4) that *reputations grow with the passing of time* is not especially well illustrated by the example of the Trojan war, which in the terms of line 25 better illustrates the rather different proposition that *great events would be forgotten unless preserved by poetry*, and was in fact so applied by Theocritus (xvi, 48 ff.) in the passage which Propertius is here echoing: τίς δ' ἂν ἀριστῆας Λυκίων ποτέ, τίς

κομόωντας Πριαμίδας ἤ θῆλυν ἀπὸ χροιᾶς Κύκνον ἔγνω, εἰ μὴ φυλόπιδας προτέρων ὕμνησαν ἀοιδοί; But Propertius is thinking as much of Homer (with whom he compares himself in 33-5) as of Troy; the underlying idea is that the fame of the Homeric poems has grown, and the fame of Troy with it. The idea of reputation growing appears in the terms of line 30.

25. equo...abiegno: the Wooden Horse.

pulsas: 'battered'. The Horse is spoken of as if it were (as indeed some rationalizers of legend supposed) an engine of war, such as a battering-ram.

* **nosceret:** 'could ever have come to know about...'; the reference of the imperfect subjunctive in this construction is not exclusively to the present time; cf. for instance II, xiii, 49-50 *non ille Antilochi uidisset corpus humari, diceret aut 'o mors, cur mihi sera uenis?'* (the subject being Nestor); and perhaps III, vii, 43 below.

26. Haemonio...uiro: 'the Thessalian hero', i.e. Achilles.

27. Iouis cum prole Scamandro: Scamander = Xanthus is called offspring of Jupiter at *Il.* XXI, 2 ὅν ἀθάνατος τέκετο Ζεύς. He and Simois his neighbour river are together opposed to Achilles at *Il.* XXI, 305-7. For the short final vowel of *prole* left short before initial *sc-* in the proper name cf. below III, xi, 67 *nunc ubi Scipiadae*, III, xix, 21 *uenumdata Scylla*; Tibullus and Ovid allow themselves the same licence before *smaragdus* and *Zacynthus*. [*Iouis cum prole Scamandro* is an emendation, probable despite its extent, since it fulfils very stringent requirements of sense, syntax and metre; it was made, I am told, by G. Wolff when still a student at Leipzig. *N* is void at this point; and the other branch of the tradition has *Iouis cunabula parui*, a nonsense in this context.]

28. Hectora...: the asyndeton is for variety.

rotas: the wheels of Achilles' chariot (or by a metonymy the chariot itself), dragging the body of Hector thrice daily around the tomb of Patroclus; a process repeated on successive days (*Il.* XXIV, 12 ff.). The story being well known, few words are needed to recall it.

maculasse: this probably recalls *Il.* XXII, 401-4; in which case it means 'befouled' (with dust, etc.) and has *rotas* for subject and *Hectora* for object.

29. Deiphobumque...etc.: minor Trojan heroes in the Iliad, Deiphobus and Helenus being sons of Priam, and Polydamas the counsellor of caution whom Hector overrode.

[**Pulydamanta et in armis**... is conjecture; the tradition has confused the name.]

30. qualemcumque: 'sorry creature', cf. Sen. *Apocol.* 9 *hic qualiscumque est, quid de nobis existimabit?*: taking it with *in armis* we get 'that sorry warrior'.

31-2. Ilion...Troia: cf. Virg. *Aen.* v, 756-7 *hoc Ilium et haec loca Troiam esse iubet*, and also *Aen.* III, 3 where the Servian commentary says that *Ilium* is the city and *Troia* the country (though commonly of course it is the name of the city too). The two names are brought in here simply to give weight to the language (cf. *Oetaei...dei* in 32), and if there is a distinction between them it is of value only because it prevents the irritation of a tautology.

32. Oetaei...dei: Hercules, who ended his mortal life on the pyre on Mount Oeta. He attacked and took Troy because Laomedon refused him the reward promised him for killing the sea-monster. Later, it was his bow in the hands of Philoctetes which killed Paris and fulfilled the fated condition of Troy's capture by the Greeks.

34-5. posteritate...crescere...laudabit: apparently an aural echo of Hor. *Od.* III, xxx, 7-8 *postera crescam laude*....

34. posteritate: 'with the passing of time'.

35. meque inter seros laudabit Roma nepotes: i.e. 'I shall still be praised at Rome in the talk of generations now far off.' With *seros...nepotes* cf. Virg. *Georg.* II, 57-8 *arbos...seris factura nepotibus umbram.*

36. auguror: 'prophesy'.

37-8. ne...contempto: the negatived participle (here used as an adjective) carries the emphasis in the sentence: 'that it shall be no obscure grave in which the stone shall say my bones are laid, so much is assured, if the Lycian god approves my prayer'. The perfect *prouisum est* shows that he means he has already achieved enough to assure his immortality; he is not (in this elegy) speaking of new poetic enterprises in prospect. The condition added in *probante deo* softens the arrogance of the prophecy of his own immortality: it may be pious, or formal, or superstitious. (Some prefer to take *probante deo* as = 'since the Lycian god, etc.', i.e. as cause, not condition.)

Lycio...deo: cf. Callimachus fr. 1, 22 (translated in the note on line 1 above). Callimachus is recalled here at the end of the elegy, as at its beginning. Later (IV, i, 64) Propertius will call himself 'the Callimachus of Rome'.

II

On the power of poetry to immortalize its subjects and its author. After an introductory couplet[1] (1-2), the elegy falls into three sections of eight lines apiece: examples from legend of the power of song (3-10); the poet's poverty compensated by his talent and its powers (11-18); the immortality that poetry confers (19-26). Lines 19 ff. echo Hor. *Od.* III, xxx, 1 ff. The concluding couplet (25-6) strikes a note similar to that of the concluding couplet of the preceding elegy; the two pieces are closely related.

1. interea: this is most easily taken as recalling the mind from the thought of something in the future (here the prospect of posthumous fame in lines 35-8 of the preceding elegy) to something near at hand, as for instance at Virg. *Aen.* XI, 22-3 *interea socios inhumataque corpora terrae mandemus....* If this is so, we can render it here 'But now...'. For the connective in the opening sentence of an elegy cf. II, x, 1 (*sed*) and III, xvii, 1 (*nunc*). [*interea* seems also to be used sometimes by Virgil to transfer attention to a new scene or stage of action, with a value nearer to that of 'and now...' than of 'meanwhile'; e.g. *Aen.* VI, 703 *interea uidet Aeneas in ualle reducta....* And Catullus seems sometimes to use it with the value 'this being so...', e.g. at ci, 7 *nunc tamen interea haec....* Either of these values would be admissible here too, the connexion in thought with the preceding elegy varying slightly according to which is chosen. That there is a connexion in thought with the preceding elegy is clear. Some editors run the two elegies together, though they are presented as separate in the MS tradition. Other editors detach this opening couplet from Elegy ii and make it the final couplet of Elegy i; an incidental result of this transfer would be to leave Elegy i consisting exactly of 20 + 20 lines, and Elegy ii exactly of 8 + 8 + 8. The question is open. The text here printed follows the MSS.]

orbem: 'accustomed round', i.e. here a limited range of topics (those of love-elegy) repeatedly traversed; the word is commonly used of the orbits of heavenly bodies and is said of a caller's round of social calls at Juv. v, 20-1 *ne tota salutatrix iam turba peregerit orbem.*

[**2. ut** is (probably) a conjecture; the tradition has *gaudeat in*

[1] See also, however, note on line 1 below.

59

solito tacta puella sono. But *gaudeat in* (a regular construction) would make a statement about the girl's *taste*, not in place here, and would leave *tacta* unsupported. At III, xx, 4 below the tradition has *in* where sense requires *ut.*]

3–8. Examples from legend of the power of song (or poetry). Orpheus held wild nature spellbound; Amphion charmed the stones till they went of their own accord to form the wall of Thebes; the Cyclops Polyphemus wooed the sea-nymph Galatea with song. (In the story of Polyphemus given by Theoc. xi and Ov. *Met.* XIII, 749 ff. his wooing was unsuccessful. Propertius may have known another version, in literature or art.)

3. [The MS tradition here gives *detinuisse,* which is confirmed as appropriate in meaning by (e.g.) Cic. *Paradoxa* v, 37 *tabula te stupidum detinet* and Mart. XIV, clxvi, 2 *detinuit...feras* (of Orpheus' lyre also: an apparent echo which supports the MS reading in Propertius here without necessarily authenticating it). But I have accepted a conjecture *delenisse* (or *delinisse*: the word is variously spelt), since this verb in one of its special uses gives a strong and valuable sense which fits exactly here, namely 'bewitched': cf. Plaut. *Cist.* 517 *tu me delenis* ('you are putting a spell on me'); *Amph.* 844 *delenitus sum profecto ita ut me qui sim nesciam*; Quint. *I.O.* v, 8, 1 *ii qui traduntur...Sirenum cantu deleniti uoluptatem saluti praetulisse.* The expulsion of *delinisse* from the tradition by the more obvious *detinuisse* would be palaeographically easy to explain. The conjecture also yields an excellent rhythm, and removes the reiteration of the sound -*tinuisse* within the couplet.]

6. membra: used of various kinds of component parts, e.g. the rooms of a house or timbers of a ship.

7. fera...Aetna: cf. Virg. *Ec.* v, 28 *montesque feri.*

8. rorantis: referring to the spray thrown up by Galatea's chariot as it skims the sea.

9. et Baccho et Apolline: Apollo as providing inspiration, Bacchus as encouraging it; cf. IV, vi, 75 *Bacche soles Phoebo fertilis esse tuo.*

11. quod: followed by *at* in line 15, *quod* here has almost the value of 'granted that' or 'although'; cf. Lucr. II, 532–5 *nam quod rara uides magis esse animalia quaedam...at regione locoque alio terrisque remotis multa licet genere esse in eo*; a similar effect is found sometimes with a subjunctive verb, e.g. Ter. *Eun.* 785 *sane quod tibi nunc uir uideatur esse hic, nebulo magnus est*; Ov.

Met. VII, 705 ff. *liceat mihi uera referre, pace deae: quod sit roseo spectabilis ore, quod teneat lucis, teneat confinia noctis, nectareis quod alatur aquis—ego Procrin amabam*; Ov. *Her.* xviii, 41–2 *tam gelidus quod sis, num te tamen...incaluisse negas?*

11–14. Luxurious features characteristic of rich men's houses: pillars of marble from Taenarum in Laconia, ceilings coffered with ivory between gilded beams, orchards with trees as fine as those of the Phaeacian king Alcinous in book VII of the *Odyssey*, elaborate artificial grottoes containing pools and fountains fed by the Aqua Marcia, the great aqueduct which brought water to Rome from sixty miles or so away to the E.N.E.

12. camera auratas inter eburna trabes: the word order helps to convey the alternation of materials in the coffering of the roof; cf. another such effect at III, xvii, 25. For the separation of *inter* from *trabes* cf. III, iv, 18 below, perhaps also III, xiv, 5.

13. Phaeacas: an adjective-form *Phaeacus* is nowhere else exemplified, but cf. *Thraca palus* in Val. Fl. II, 201. [The MS tradition here gives *Phaeacias*, which is the normal form of the adjective but would here involve an abnormal scansion *Phaeăcias*.]

[**16. nec** is conjecture; *N* is blank here, and the other branch of the tradition has *et*, which would emphasize (rather awkwardly) the volume of the poet's output. *nec* emphasizes the persistent favour of the Muse, and seems very much more to the point. The omission of the word in *N* suggests an omission or something hard to read in the common ancestor of our MSS.]

16. nec defessa = *et indefessa* = *et assidua*; cf. Tac. *Ann.* XVI, 22 *assiduum...et indefessum*.

Calliopea: the Muse named by Propertius as his (or elegy's) patroness elsewhere also; cf. below III, iii, 38 and 51, and IV, vi, 12. She appears in converse with Callimachus also, in Call. fr. 7, 22. Later Calliope became associated especially with epic poetry, but in Propertius' day the departments of the several Muses were not yet firmly fixed by convention.

[**17. es**: the tradition has *est*.]

18. carmina erunt formae tot monumenta tuae: either (*a*) 'so many poems will be the record of your beauty', *tot* introducing an explanation of the previous statement, as often (e.g. II, xvi, 33 *tot iam abiere dies etc.*); or (*b*) 'each poem will be a record of your beauty', *quot* being supplied with *carmina*.

19–21. Three of the Wonders of the World: the Pyramids, the temple of Jupiter at Olympia, and the great tomb built in the fourth century B.C. for King Mausolus of Halicarnassus by his widow Artemisia.

19. Pyramidum sumptus: i.e. the costly Pyramids. One thinks here of Shakespeare *Sonnet* 64 *When I have seen by Time's fell hand defaced* | *The rich proud cost of outworn buried age.*

20. caelum imitata domus: the temple, which housed the famous chryselephantine statue of Jupiter by Pheidias, is a palace that vies in splendour with the heavens themselves, or with the palace of Jupiter in heaven, the *domus omnipotentis Olympi* of *Aen.* XI, 1, etc.

Iouis Elei: because Olympia was in the territory of Elis.

21. Mausolei diues fortuna sepulcri: the form of expression is parallel to that in line 19 above. *fortuna* here = 'wealth'.

24. pondere uicta: cf. Mart. I, lxxxii, 6 *uicta est pondere...suo* (a portico).

25. ab aeuo: for *ab* of cause cf. IV, iii, 39 *putris ab aestu*; but here time causing things to be forgotten is thought of almost as a personal agent, cf. on III, v, 14 below. For *ab* of the agent with an intransitive verb (*excidet*) cf. the common construction *cadere ab aliquo* = fall in battle by someone's hand.

26. (non)...excidet: 'will (not) be forgotten'; *excido* in this sense is used absolutely (as well as with dative of the person forgetting).

ingenio stat sine morte decus: here *ingenio* may be either dative ('the glory genius wins is everlasting') or ablative ('it is genius (alone) that makes glory everlasting').

III

This elegy also is concerned with Propertius' attitude to his own poetry. But while the previous two proclaimed his achievement, this one is more concerned with his reasons for not attempting epic poetry and patriotic subjects. The elegy purports to record a dream the poet has had; and it falls into two halves, equal in length and partly corresponding in content. In the first half Propertius, on Mount Helicon, is contemplating a poem on Roman history (1–12), but is interrupted by Apollo, who warns him to know his limitations, and directs him for further advice to the Muses in a nearby grotto (13–26). Now begins the second half of the poem, with a description of the grotto and its occupants (27–36); on this follows a speech by the Muse Calliope, in which she repeats in different terms the warning already given by Apollo and tells Propertius that love-poetry must be his subject (37–52). The intervention of Apollo (for which cf. Virg. *Ec.* vi, 2 ff.) is a motive from Callimachus (cf. fr. 1, translated in note on III, i, 1 above), and so also are the dream and the imparting of information by the Muses (cf. e.g. Call. fr. 7, 19 ff.). The application of these motives is Propertius' own.

1. molli...in umbra: i.e. at ease in a shady grove.

2. Bellerophontei...umor equi: the spring Hippocrene, cf. on III, i, 19 above. Bellerophon rode Pegasus, against the Chimaera. It will be noticed that the whole of the first half of the pentameter is here filled by a single word, and that both resonant and rich in associations; cf. III, xiv, 14 *Thermodontiacis*.

3. reges, Alba, tuos: this would be a compliment to Augustus, because the Julii claimed descent from the Alban kings; cf. Tac. *Ann.* IV, 9, and the prominent references to Alba in the *Aeneid*, e.g. I, 7 and XII, 826. Servius on *Ec.* vi, 3 says that Virgil at one time attempted a poem on *gesta regum Albanorum, quae coepta omisit, asperitate nominum deterritus*.

4. tantum operis: in apposition to the idea *reges...et regum facta...hiscere*. For the phrase itself cf. III, xi, 70 below.

hiscere posse: *hisco* primarily means 'open the mouth', and is very often combined with *non possum* or *non audeo* in contexts where someone does not dare or cannot bring himself to open his mouth to say something, because fear or reverence or incapacity causes him to keep it shut. The connotation given to *hiscere posse* by this common usage with the negative is exploited in our present passage in a sentence of positive form, the meaning of which seems to be: 'in my dream I thought that I could dare, with these (poor) powers of mine, to raise my voice (*literally* open my mouth) to tell of the kings of Alba and their deeds'. *neruis* is said here (I think), as elsewhere, of 'strength' or 'powers' and so in particular of the capacity to sustain a vigorous and elevated style of utterance; and thus taken it may be either instrumental or a kind of ablative absolute indicating circumstances (like *tanto...ciue* in III, xi, 55 below). (*neruis* can, however, alternatively be taken as meaning 'with my lyre', i.e. the *strings* of the accompanying lyre.)

5. tam magnis...fontibus: 'that potent spring'; for this sense of *magnus* cf. Cic. *Fam.* IV, 3 *haec tibi ad leuandas molestias magna esse debent*; for the rendering of *tam* cf. on III, viii, 2 below.

6. Ennius: the creator of the Latin hexameter, whose *Annales* recounted the history of Rome from the beginnings to his own day. He lived *c.* 240–*c.* 170 B.C.

7–12. The events listed are specimens of the content of Ennius' *Annales*. The list displays a number of small peculiarities, which it is convenient to note here together.

(*a*) Line 8 appears to refer to an event of the second century B.C., while line 12 refers to the geese saving the Capitol from the Gauls in 390 B.C. If the two lines were interchanged, the chronological sequence of the list, now irrational, would become correct. But there is no evidence that the line-order has become dislocated in the MSS.

(*b*) The *Curii fratres* of line 7 must be the three champions who fought the three *Horatii* in the war between Rome and Alba; see e.g. Liv. I, 24. But their name elsewhere is always *Curiatii* (not easy to use in dactylic verse).

(*c*) In line 7 *pila* is neuter plural, and must mean weapons (of victors or vanquished) dedicated as a memorial. But in D.H. III, 22 the Ὁρατία πίλα is feminine singular, a column (*pila*) in the forum commemorating the event in question. In Liv. I, 26 the place of the trophy is called *Horatia pila* (? neut. pl.).

(*d*) The role of the *Lares* (line 11) in repulsing Hannibal is not recorded elsewhere.

(*e*) The reference intended in line 8 must be to the triumphal return of L. Aemilius Paullus after his conquest of Perseus, king of Macedon; the enormous booty and the fact that the conqueror entered Rome by sailing up the Tiber from the sea are dwelt on in the accounts of Livy (XLV, 35) and Plutarch (*Aemilius Paullus*). But this happened in 167 B.C., so cannot have been described in Ennius' *Annales*, since Ennius was dead by then. There was indeed another L. Aemilius Paullus who won the sea victory over King Antiochus of Syria at Myonnesus in 190 B.C., but if Propertius has this in mind, he has evidently attached to it some distinctive features of the other event.

It is a fair inference from the above that in enumerations such

as we have in this passage (7–12) Propertius is concerned with
poetical or rhetorical effect and not necessarily attentive to
accuracy of detail or 'logical' sequence. We have also to be
prepared for references to stories which we know in versions
different from those in which we know them.

12. Iouem: i.e. the temple of Jupiter on the Capitol. The
geese (cf. Liv. v, 47) gave warning of the ascent of the Gauls.

13. Castalia: adjective, agreeing with *arbore*, from the
fountain *Castalia*. This fountain was really on Parnassus, not
on Helicon; the dream blends images that are properly distinct.

ex arbore: this evidently = 'from the (Muses') grove',
arbore being a (very unusual) collective singular for plural.

14. aurata nixus ad antra lyra: 'standing at (the entrance
of) a grotto, (one arm) resting on his golden lyre'. There is a
grotto in the grove, a typical feature of this scenery; cf. I, i, 5
and line 27 here below. Apollo stands in a pose evidently
characteristic of him in works of art, and what this is can be seen
(as I have learned from Mr M. H. Braude) in the picture of the
Building of the Walls of Troy in the Casa di Sirico at Pompeii,
and on a neo-Attic *puteal* of the late first century B.C. in the
Museum at Naples (289): the god stands in a relaxed attitude,
lyre at side, with a forearm resting on it, so that he appears to
lean on it rather than actually does so. (But cf. too II, xxx, 38.)

15. flumine: the metaphor suggests the voluminous flow of
epic poetry, and further recalls Call. *Hymn to Apollo* 107 ff. τὸν
Φθόνον ὡπόλλων ποδί τ᾽ ἤλασεν ὧδέ τ᾽ ἔειπεν· Ἀσσυρίου ποταμοῖο
μέγας ῥόος, ἀλλὰ τὰ πολλὰ λύματα γῆς καὶ πολλὸν ἐφ᾽ ὕδατι
συρφετὸν ἕλκει (translated in note on III, i, 1 above).

[**17. hinc** here is a probable though not indispensable emend-
ation, recommended by sound as well as sense. The MS
tradition gives *hic*.]

18. mollia prata: 'soft sward'.

paruis...rotis: i.e. a light-built car.

19. ut tuus in scamno iactetur saepe libellus: two ideas
are combined: (*a*) the book is always at hand, and in evidence,
on the stool (which serves as an 'occasional' table), and (*b*) it is
much handled. *saepe* may indicate either the frequent thumbing
of a particular volume, or that this will happen in many cases
('on many a stool...').

21. praescriptos...gyros: poetic plural. The *gyrus* is a ring
used for training horses, here a metaphor for course or range.

praescriptos is said because Apollo (or fate) has gifted Propertius for particular kinds of poetry, 'prescribing' or 'marking out' this course for him.

[21. **praescriptos euecta...gyros:** the text here printed incorporates a conjecture; the tradition has *praescripto seuecta...gyro*. 'straying from...' (*euecta*) is more effective here than 'withdrawing' (*seuecta*), and (though this is not a decisive consideration) *seuehor* is nowhere else found.]

22. **non est...grauanda:** 'must not be overloaded'.

23. **alter remus aquas alter tibi radat harenas:** here *alter...aquas* may seem otiose. But the combination it helps to make is valuable, providing the picture of a boat proceeding coastwise. This picture is context of the advice to keep, while so proceeding, as close as possible to the shore.

24. **maxima turba:** this, after *tutus eris*, must mean 'it is roughest' (*literally* 'there is most commotion', with *turba* = *tumultus* as often). But the meaning more immediately suggested by *maxima*, 'it is most crowded' (*literally* 'the crowd is largest'), is still present in the background, recalling the Callimachean exclusiveness; cf. Call. fr. 1, 25 ff. (see note on III, i, 14 above and translation in note on III, i, 1) and Call. in *A.P.* XII, 43 οὐδὲ κελεύθῳ χαίρω τίς πολλοὺς ὧδε καὶ ὧδε φέρει...σικχαίνω πάντα τὰ δημόσια.

25–6. **dixerat...:** this couplet concludes the first half of the elegy; cf. line 51 *talia...* concluding the second half.

26. **quo:** '(leading) to which'.

noua: because Propertius' poetry goes a new and original way; cf. Call. fr. 1, 25 ff. (and references under 24 above) for the background.

27–32. Description of the Muses' grotto; situated in or near the grove (13) and containing a spring (32). For this combination cf. III, i, 2, 5, 6; and for the grove and spring cf. lines 1 and 2 of the present elegy. There appear to be (in the dream) two springs on Helicon, and Propertius is being directed away from one and towards the other.

27. **affixis...lapillis:** the walls of the grotto are decorated with a mosaic of fragments of marble or other semi-precious stone.

28. **cauis...pumicibus:** 'from its rocky vault'. (The plural may suggest a rock ceiling with many cavities.)

pendebant, etc.: as *fictilis* in line 30 shows, real things are meant, cult-objects hung from the cavern roof or walls.

tympana: tambourines, to accompany sacred dances or other ritual movements.

29. orgia Musarum: holy objects used in the worship of the Muses; cf. on III, i, 4 above.

Sileni patris: for the association of Silenus with poetic inspiration cf. Virg. *Ec.* vi.

30. Tegeaee: i.e. Arcadian.

31. mea turba: here *turba* represents whatever plural is required by the context, e.g. 'birds dear to me', or 'my fellow servants (of Venus)'. Venus is mistress both of the doves, as sacred to her, and of the poet, as poet of love.

32. lacu: the pool or basin that goes with a fountain.

Gorgoneo: because the horse Pegasus, whose hoof struck the spring Hippocrene on Helicon (cf. on 2 above), had himself sprung from the blood of the Gorgon Medusa. (We seem to be back at Hippocrene, as in line 2, although in 25–6 the poet was being directed away from it to a different spring. The imagery in fact is not worked out exactly or consistently.)

33. diuersae: though attached grammatically to *Puellae* as an adjective, *diuersae* here has really an adverbial value, 'severally'. [*iura* = here 'provinces' is an emendation; the tradition has *rura*.] The nine *Puellae* are the Muses.

35. in thyrsos: i.e. 'to twine about the Bacchic wands'. The *thyrsus* belongs to Bacchus and his attendants, for whose association with poetry cf. line 29 above.

36. rosam: the collective singular, common in speaking of flowers.

37. contigit: 'laid her hand on me'.

38. Calliopea: cf. on III, ii, 16 above.

39. cycnis: with *uectabere* this means the car as well as the team which draws it; cf. the common use of *equi* in the same way. The swan-drawn chariot is an attribute of Venus; cf. Hor. *Od.* III, xxviii, 13–15 *quae Cnidon...iunctis uisit oloribus.*

40. fortis: regularly of martial spirit, and here (I think) with *equi*; cf. Virg. *Aen.* XI, 705–6 *forti...equo.* A *fortis equus* will be a war-horse, or perhaps (giving more value to the epithet) a fiery charger.

sonus takes its value from the context, so here = 'neigh' or 'snort'.

41. nil tibi sit: 'be it no care of yours to...'; evidently the phrase is a variant of *ne tibi sit*, for which cf. Tib. III, ix (= iv, iii), 3 *nec tibi sit duros acuisse in proelia dentes* (a boar is addressed).

praeconia...flare: 'sound (*or* blow) the summons'.

classica here evidently = 'martial', and this value for the adjective *classicus* can easily be extracted from the old sense of *classis* = 'army'. Moreover *classicum* (neut. subst.) is the regular word for a trumpet-call in various military contexts.

rauco...cornu: 'on the blaring horn'; *raucus* refers to the vibrant quality of the sound.

[**flare** is an emendation; the tradition has *flere*.]

* **42. Aonium...nemus:** the grove of the Muses on Mount Helicon in Boeotia, the adjective being from *Aonia* = *Boeotia*.

cingere Marte: 'beset with war'. [*cingere* is probably a conjecture; the tradition has *tingere* = ?? 'dye with (blood of) war'.]

43. aut quibus...: the indirect question depends on the sense of *dicere* or the like, supplied from the preceding couplet.

Mariano...signo: this need mean no more than 'under Marius' standards', i.e. under his leadership; but in fact it was Marius who established the eagle as sole standard of the legion.

43–4. The reference is to the victories of Marius over the Teutones and Cimbri at Aquae Sextiae and the Raudine Plains, in 102 and 101 B.C.

45–6. aut...uectet: the sense of 'how' has to be supplied to introduce the indirect question.

45. Sueuo...sanguine: the Suevi were a German tribe. They crossed the Rhine in 29 B.C. and were defeated by C. Carrinas (Dio C. LI, 21).

47. alienum ad limen: these lovers are pursuing women who belong to other men.

48. canes: i.e. 'you will make poetry about' (the sort of wars that lovers wage). There may be a play also on *signa canunt* = 'the trumpets sound', as sign for battle to begin.

ebria signa: 'tipsy warfare', *signa* being used by a metonymy in the same way as *castra* often is.

nocturnae...fugae: 'of (or as we should say, and) midnight rout', the genitive defining further the nature of the 'tipsy warfare'. With *fugae* here cf. II, i, 28 *Siculae classica bella fugae*; the exact value of *fuga* in these passages is hard to be sure of; perhaps, a running fight?

49. excantare: i.e. compel to come out by reciting a poem like a magic spell.

50. ferire: 'outwit'; cf. IV, v, 44 (*Thais*) *cum ferit astutos...Getas* (in a play); this use of *ferio* is no doubt a metaphor from fencing.

52. Philitea...aqua: for Philitas cf. on III, i, 1 above; for the *aqua* cf. III, i, 3, 6, contrasting line 5 of this elegy.

IV

This elegy is to be read in conjunction with Elegy v, as will appear from comparison of their opening and concluding couplets. The poet begins on a 'high' theme, an impending campaign, in a 'high' manner; but in lines 15 ff. he declares that his own role will be that of a spectator, a languishing lover still. This attitude is here presented without apology; but in the following elegy it is moralized with an argument that is at least partly in earnest, and the poet there forecasts that he will turn in time to subjects more 'serious' than love, speculations about the nature of the world and the causes of physical phenomena, and what awaits us after death.

1. Arma...ad Indos: the expected campaign against Parthia, cf. lines 4 and 6 here and on III, i, 16 above. The *Indi* here stand for the East in general, as do the *Seres* (Chinese) in IV, iii, 8 and often in Horace's Odes. For *ad = adversus* cf. II, xxiv, 25 *Lernaeas pugnat ad hydras*.

deus Caesar: cf. IV, xi, 60 where Augustus is also called *deus*. In this Propertius goes further than Virgil and Horace, who only speak of Augustus as assured of deification after death, or use terms that imply his divinity without actually asserting it.

2. gemmiferi...maris: the Indian Ocean, including its offshoots the Red Sea and the Persian Gulf.

* **3. magna uiris merces:** 'here is high reward for our brave men'. [*uiris* here is an emendation for *uiri* (vocative) which is given by the MS tradition but is difficult because of the following *tua* in line 4, which must refer back to Caesar. The change is small and easy but not certainly necessary, since Propertius is very fond of and free with apostrophe; see for instance III, xi, 36–7 below, and III, vii *passim*, and B.B.'s note on II, ix, 15–16. For alternative emendations see App. Crit.]

parat: i.e. is about to yield (triumphs).

4. tua: i.e. Caesar's (if the text is right).

5. sera, sed...ueniet: i.e. *sera ueniet, sed ueniet*...to the dominion of Italy, here symbolized by the rods of the Roman lictors.

6. assuescent Latio Partha tropaea Ioui: i.e. the spoils of Parthia will find in Latium (or with Roman Jupiter) their lasting home. *Jupiter* here can mean either the god (*J. Capitolinus*) in whose temple the spoils are dedicated; or the climate of the country, and so the country itself. *assuescent* (cf. 'become acclimatized') suggests that the latter meaning is at least somewhere in mind. *Latio = Latino =* (in poets) Latin or Roman according to context.

7. expertae bello: 'proved in war' (*expertae* being passive; whereas *expertae belli* would mean 'having experience of war').

prorae: it seems most natural to take this as vocative, to match *equi* in the following line (where see note), especially as *dare uela* is often used absolutely with the meaning 'set sail'; the exhortation *date lintea* is then addressed to the ships. But *prorae* could be genitive with *lintea* or dative after *date*, the exhortation being addressed to the members of the expedition generally.

8. et solitum armigeri ducite munus equi: the army marching to war is headed by the cavalry or a part of them; cf. Tac. *Ann.* I, 51 *pars equitum et auxiliariae cohortes ducebant*, and III, iii, 40 above *nec te fortis equi ducet ad arma sonus*. This is a regular thing, and so a *solitum munus* of the cavalry. It appears then that in the present passage *ducite* is intransitive (= 'lead the way'), as in the sentence of Tacitus just quoted, that *solitum...munus* is in apposition to this idea ('lead the way, your usual duty'), and that *equi* is vocative. The strange word order is not stranger than that in, for instance, line 18 below. (The alternative would be to take *munus* as accusative directly governed by *ducite*. But no such expression is known, and it is hard to see what it could mean.)

armigeri...equi: the horses are so called because ridden by armed men, not as armoured themselves: the armoured horse was an eastern invention.

9. Crassos clademque piate: though the last vocatives were (see on 7 and 8 above) the ships and horses of the expedition, all these exhortations are felt as addressed to 'the expedition'.

Hence when the poet now uses terms appropriate only to the men of the expedition, in this line and line 10, he does not need to warn us that it is not to ships and horses that he is speaking.

Crassos: Crassus' son perished with him in the disaster at Carrhae in 53 B.C.

Crassos clademque piate: 'pay the ghosts of the Crassi their due and purge our defeat'. *piare* includes the ideas of fulfilling a religious obligation and of purging a fault.

10. Romanae consulite historiae: 'see that you serve Rome's history well', i.e. by adding honour to it; cf. Liv. *Praef. iuuabit tamen rerum gestarum memoriae principis terrarum populi et ipsum consuluisse,* where Livy hopes to serve Rome's history by writing it.

* **11. sacrae:** the adjective *sacer* is elsewhere used always of things, not of deities. Perhaps it can stand here because Vesta is thought of as the sacred hearth or fire (cf. *lumina*), and not purely as a person. [Some, however, would read *sanctae*.]

13–14. The scene imagined is of a triumph. For the asyndeton between the two sentences cf. III, xii, 34 below, etc.

16. incipiam: this word can (here) be disregarded in translation. *incipio* and *cogor* are used occasionally by Propertius as a kind of metrical or syntactical padding.

titulis oppida capta legam: 'and read the names of the captured cities in their superscriptions'. Pictures of the cities would be carried in the triumphal procession, with their names, etc., written over or under them.

17–18. The accusative in line 17 and the accusative and infinitive in line 18 are both governed by the sense of *spectare incipiam* in the preceding couplet, despite the intervention of *oppida capta legam.*

17. tela fugacis equi: a rather loose possessive genitive: 'the arrows that are shot from horses in flight'; a technique characteristic of the Parthians. These *tela*, and the *arcus* of the 'trousered warriors', are spoils of war displayed in the triumphal procession.

18. et subter captos arma sedere duces: 'and the captive chieftains sitting beneath the (captured) arms'; apparently on a vehicle in the procession. For the separation of *subter* from *arma* cf. III, ii, 12 above and IV, viii, 31 *altera Tarpeios est inter Teia lucos.*

71

19. tuam serua prolem, Venus: Augustus, adopted son of J. Caesar, the Julii claiming descent from Venus through Iulus = Ascanius. (But the expression could also include the Julian *line*, and indeed the Roman race, as *Aeneadae*.)

19–20. hoc...caput: for *caput* with demonstrative or adjective indicating simply a person cf. below III, xvii, 42 *hoc... caput* = 'me', IV, xi, 55 *dulce...caput* = 'my dear one'. Another meaning of *caput* that may be relevant here is 'stock' (said literally of a vine-stock). The reference is certainly to Augustus, perhaps also the line he represents. The sentence as a whole seems to mean either (*a*) 'may he be saved for ever, in whom you see the sole survivor of Aeneas' line'; or (*b*) 'may it live on for ever, this stock sprung from Aeneas which you see still living now'. With *ab Aenea* cf. Cic. *Brut.* 62 *si ego me a M' Tullio esse dicerem*; the phrase forms an adjective meaning 'descended from Aeneas'.

21. haec: i.e. in prospect from the expedition which is subject of the poem, and associated (cf. line 13) with the triumph imagined in lines 13–18. (The thought of the triumph is no doubt present in lines 19–20 still: the poet's prayer there echoes the imagined prayers of the cheering crowd.)

22. Sacra...Via: along which the triumph passed before ascending the Capitol.

V

See introductory note to Elegy iv, with which this elegy is to be read in conjunction. Lines 1–18 are a retort, by implication, to those who hold that men should live, and poets praise, the life of action; this means really, says the poet, an acquisitive materialism, which breeds strife and misery and leads to no valuable result. In lines 19–46 Propertius affirms his present dedication to poetry (and gaiety and love), and looks forward, in a passage reminiscent of Virg. *Georg.* II, 475ff., to devoting his later years to the study of natural philosophy; in fact, he asserts the values of the aesthete and intellectual. Lines 1–18 proceed in groups of six lines, lines 19–46 in groups or multiples of four. The final couplet 47–8 recalls the final couplet of the preceding elegy.

This elegy concludes the series of five elegies on the poet's literary purpose and achievement which head the present book.

Some editors have wished to treat Elegies IV and V, though they are separated in the MS tradition, as a single piece, in which the poet's thought moves through a series of phases—as for instance in the first elegy of Book II. For a similar idea respecting Elegies I and II above, see note on III, ii, I.

I. Pacis Amor deus est, pacem ueneramur amantes: contrast III, iv, I; and compare III, iv, 22 with lines 47–8 below.

2. sat mihi cum domina proelia dura mea: sc. *sunt*. [*sat* is an emendation; the MSS give *stant*.]

3. nec tamen... : 'but then neither...'. The *tamen* answers the reproach (of self-indulgence and laziness) which the statement in the preceding line would be likely to attract from censorious Romans. The poet says that though he may be no man of action (2), he is, however, also (3–6) free from avarice and extravagance.

3–6. Gold, costly tableware, large holdings of fertile land, collector's pieces—these are typical possessions of a rich man.

3. carpitur auro: 'is consumed by greed for gold'; cf. Virg. *Georg.* III, 215 *carpit enim uires* (of the bull) *paulatim uritque uidendo femina.*

4. e gemma diuite: either (*a*) 'from costly jewelled cups'; or (*b*) 'from cups of costly (?) crystal' (or some other semi-precious mineral). For the expression cf. Virg. *Georg.* II, 506 *ut gemmā bibat.*

6. nec miser aera paro clade, Corinthe, tua: 'nor is it my folly to acquire (i.e. as a collector) bronzes from the ruin of Corinth'. The reference is to antique vessels made of a bronze alloy, alleged (e.g. by Pliny, *N.H.* XXXIV, 6) to have occurred accidentally through the melting of metals in the conflagration that followed the capture of Corinth by the Romans in 146 B.C. *miser* may be said, as here, of one afflicted with an exaggerated or misguided craving; cf. *miser ambitionis, misera ambitio*, etc.

* **7. o prima infelix fingenti terra Prometheo:** 'o primal clay ill fashioned by Prometheus', who according to the legend thus created man. *infelix* is attached grammatically to *terra*, but really goes with the whole sentence; Prometheus' work did not turn out well, but according to the next line (8) the fault was not in the *material*.

8. ille parum caute pectoris egit opus: 'in his work on the heart he was not careful enough'; the heart was conceived as the seat of intelligence, and *pectoris* here corresponds to *mentem* and

73

animi in lines 9 and 10. [Some prefer the conjecture *parum cauti pectoris egit opus* = 'did too careless a job' (*literally* the job of too careless a mind).]

9. corpora disponens: 'busy designing our bodies'.

mentem non uidit: 'he overlooked (i.e. forgot) the mind'.

in arte: 'when he was doing his work'.

10. recta animi primum debuit esse uia: 'the mind should have been set on the right way first of all'.

11. nunc: 'as it is...'.

*   **maris in tantum uento iactamur:** 'see how we are driven far out to sea by the storm that tosses us'; the metaphor refers to restless human ambition.

11–12. et hostem quaerimus: 'and go in search of an enemy'; the reference is to the Eastern campaign projected so soon after the end of the civil wars.

12. atque armis nectimus arma noua: 'and add new wars to wars (in an endless chain)'; cf. Lucr. V, 1202 *uotis nectere uota*.

13–17. haud ullas portabis...ab Iro: the thought expressed in these lines ('riches are of no use when you are dead') is related to what has gone before by the unexpressed idea that men's motive in making war is gain.

13. portabis: an imaginary addressee.

14. ab inferna...rate: for *ab* with something inanimate, viewed as agent, cf. Ov. *Ibis* 586 *ictus ab orbe* (a quoit), and III, xviii, 1 below. The *ratis* is Charon's boat. [The reading is that of the emended MSS; the tradition gives *ad infernas... rates*.]

16. cum Mario...Iugurtha: the vanquished with his victor.

17. Dulichio...Iro: the beggar Irus of *Odyssey* XVIII. 'Dulichian' is applicable by metonymy to anything in the Ithacan story, Dulichium being one of the islands in the Ithacan group.

18. optima mors Parcae quae uenit acta die: 'that death is best which comes in nature's course'; i.e. not brought on prematurely by shipwreck or battle or other hazard to which men expose themselves in the pursuit of riches. This sentiment, at this point, is required by the context. For *mors...uenit acta* cf. III, vii, 30 below *ista per humanas mors uenit acta manus*. For the expression *Parcae die* cf. Virg. *Aen.* XII, 150 *Parcarumque dies*; and for its meaning here ('natural death' or 'death at the end of one's natural span') cf. Virg. *Aen.* IV, 696–7 *nam quia nec fato merita nec morte peribat, sed misera ante diem,* and Tac. *Ann.* XIV, 62 *in Sardiniam pellitur, ubi non inops exilium tolerauit et fato obiit* ('died a natural death'); cf. also below III, vii, 31 and III, xxi, 33.

19–46. The second part of the poem. The poet sets his own way of life in contrast with the folly of greed and war.

19. coluisse Helicona: one can say *colere Musas* (worship), *colere locum* (haunt or inhabit), *colere uitam aliquam* (follow a particular way of life).

21. Lyaeo = *Baccho* = 'with wine'.

22. in...rosa: i.e. wreathed with roses, symbol of convivial elegance.

23. Venerem...interceperit: 'shall have ended love for me'.

grauis...aetas: 'the weight of (advancing) age', sobering the spirits and damping physical energy.

24. sparserit: 'shall have flecked' (i.e. besprinkled, *sc.* with white hairs).

25. Propertius looks forward here to what Virgil looked forward to in *Georg.* II, 475 ff.

26. quis deus: not 'which of the gods it is that...', but 'what Power it is that...'.

hanc mundi temperet arte domum: 'manages this household that is the world'.

27. qua uenit exoriens, qua deficit: apparently (see below) 'how the sun comes at its rising, and how it dies'; *exoriens* being used substantivally as in *El. in Maecenatem* 56 *ad extremos exorientis equos,* or as *oriens* in Ov. *Fast.* 1, 653 *septimus hinc oriens cum se demiserit undis.* For speculations on the cause of the sun's daily appearance and disappearance see Lucr. V, 650–79; the term *deficit* in our present passage may reflect the theory (one of alternatives) that the sun was worn out at the end of each day, a new sun coming into existence each morning. (To understand the passage thus, as referring to the sun, seems inevitable, because it is inconceivable that a list of this kind should not include the sun; moreover, we expect the sun to head the list, and we note that in every couplet of the passage 29–38 two principal phenomena are mentioned—winds and clouds, end-of-the-world and rainbows, earthquakes and eclipses, Bootes and the Pleiades, ocean's bounds and seasons' bounds; hence in this couplet one expects sun and moon, not moon alone. But for these considerations it would of course be natural to take *exoriens* here as a participle agreeing with *luna* in the next line, and make *luna* subject of *uenit* and *deficit* and so of the whole couplet; and many authorities do prefer so to take it. A further question concerns *deficit*, for *deficio* and *defectus* are regularly said of *eclipses* of sun or moon; here this meaning is excluded if the sun is subject, because the solar eclipse is brought in as a new topic in line 34 below; and it is virtually excluded if the moon is subject, because a reference to an exceptional phenomenon is not likely to be sandwiched between references to the moon's daily rising and to its monthly waxing; it seems to me certain therefore that *deficit* here refers to setting as opposed to rising, as indeed the parallelism *qua...qua...*, pointed by the change to *unde...*, in itself very strongly suggests.)

27–8. unde coactis...redit: here *unde = qua de causa*. The idea is that the moon becomes full again each month as the outline indicated by the horns of the crescent moon is filled in.

29. unde salo superant uenti: here intransitive *supero* (which also commonly means 'survive' or 'abound') appears to mean 'prevail' or 'have the mastery', as perhaps also in (e.g.) Virg. *Aen.* I, 537 *superante salo*; II, 311 *Volcano superante*; V, 22 *superat...Fortuna*; XII, 676 *fata...superant*. If so, *salo* is ablative of place, 'on (i.e. over) the open sea'. For the idea cf. Hor. *Od.* I, iii, 15 and III, iii, 5, where *arbiter Hadriae* is said of *Notus* and *dux Hadriae* of *Auster*. The sense of the whole is no doubt 'what causes the winds *that* lord it over the sea', rather than 'what causes the winds *to* lord it over the sea', a verb descriptive of a typical activity of the winds replacing a less colourful verb such as 'are' or 'come', by a device of style common in Latin poetry. *unde* here, as in line 30, may have its primary meaning 'whence'.

quid flamine captet (Eurus): i.e. what the purpose of his blowing is?

superant...captet: throughout all the passage 26–46, as in this line, the mood in the 'dependent questions' changes frequently and arbitrarily from subjunctive to indicative and vice versa. For the occasional use of the indicative in this construction by other Augustans cf. (for example) Virg. *Aen.* VI, 614–15 *ne quaere doceri...quae poena uiros fortunaue mersit*.

31. arces: 'stronghold'; the world is thought of as a vast edifice (cf. the *moenia mundi* of Lucretius), and the metaphor *arces* suggests the strength and solidity of a fortress; the metaphor is assisted by the choice of *subruo* for verb, this being appropriate to the overthrow of a fortification, etc., by battering or undermining. The plural in *arces* is 'poetic'; but it helps to suggest many towers, etc.

32. bibit arcus: the rainbow was supposed to draw up water, which then came down again as rain; cf. Virg. *Georg.* I, 380–1 *bibit ingens arcus.*

33. Perrhaebi...Pindi: the mountain chain Pindus in Greece, called 'Perrhaebian' here from the Perrhaebi, a people living on its western slopes.

tremuere: the perfect is of the kind used in general statements (e.g. Virg. *Georg.* IV, 213 *amisso (rege) rupere fidem* in an account of the habits of bees).

34. luxerit: from *lugeo* (but also understandable as from *luceo*, negatived by *atratis...equis* in a kind of oxymoron).

atratis...equis: the sun's horses or chariot are conceived as draped (at the eclipse) in mourning black.

35. serus uersare boues et plaustra Bootes: the constellation Bootes is supposed to be driver of the Waggon (or Plough). *serus* is said because Bootes in Homer (*Od.* v, 272) has the epithet 'late-setting'; here *serus uersare* means not that he begins late, but that he goes on late. *uersare* may mean simply 'steer' or 'drive', or that he drives the Waggon round and round the Pole. [The MS tradition is confused here; see App. Crit. The reading printed, probably correct, is given by *DV*, and either is a very clever emendation or shows that those MSS preserve evidence of the tradition not available in any others.] With *serus* sc. *est.*

36. spisso...igne: 'in a shining cluster'.

38. plenus...eat: 'and the year runs through four stages to complete its course'.

39. sub terris sint: sc. *num*, as also in 31 above.

iura deum et tormenta gigantum: i.e. gods (or their agents) sitting in judgement and giants or Titans (cf. Virg. *Aen.* VI, 580, 582, 595) suffering torment. [*gigantum*, given by one branch of the tradition, is not in *N*. Some prefer to read the conjecture *nocentum*.]

40. si furit: 'and whether...' (a new question, in asyndeton after that of the preceding line).

77

angue: collective singular, for plural.

41. aut Alcmaeoniae, etc.: a part of the verb 'to be' has to be understood, resuming the construction of line 39.

* **Alcmaeoniae...Phinei:** Alcmaeon killed his mother and was pursued by furies; Phineus (cf. Ap. Rhod. II, 176 ff.) blinded his children and was tormented by the Harpies, who prevented him from taking food. On the view here considered, their punishments are imagined as perpetuated in the underworld after death.

42. rota...scopuli...sitis inter aquas: the wheel is Ixion's; the thirst is the thirst of Tantalus, up to the neck in water which withdraws whenever he tries to drink. We expect the third item to be the stone of Sisyphus, and this no doubt is somewhere in Propertius' mind. But *scopuli* are not the kind of stone that is rolled; and the word must have been suggested by the other version of Tantalus' punishment, the rock hanging over his head and always seeming about to fall.

43. custodit...antrum: 'stands guard at the mouth of his cave'; cf. Virg. *Aen.* VI, 418 *aduerso recubans immanis in antro.* Strictly speaking, what Cerberus guards is the entry to the underworld, and the cave serves him as a kennel.

tribus...faucibus: the three-headed dog is pictured barking or about to bite.

44. Tityo iugera pauca nouem: (whether it is true that) nine acres are not enough (too few) for the bulk of Tityus, the outstretched giant. For the emphasis this gives to *pauca* cf. I, xix, 24 *flectitur assiduis certa (even* a constant) *puella minis.*

45. an ficta in miseras descendit fabula gentis: 'or if this is only a fable that has fixed itself in the minds of troubled humans'. For *descendit* cf. Sall. *Jug.* 11 *quod uerbum in pectus Jugurthae altius...descendit.* In *gentis* is expressed the idea 'mankind'.

47–8. Cf. the end of the preceding elegy.

VI

A monologue in which the poet is addressing a servant recently come from his (the poet's) mistress' presence. There has been a quarrel, which he now regrets, and he anxiously questions the servant, Lygdamus, about the state of the woman's feelings. In IV, vii and viii Lygdamus belongs to Propertius; and this is compatible with the fact that here the woman seems to have the disposal of him; see note on 41-2 below. The elegy can be divided into sections of 8 lines + 26 + 8; the long central portion containing apparently the report of the servant as repeated after him, item by item, by his anxious enquirer. The report consists partly (9-18) of the scene in the woman's apartment, and partly (19-34) of a speech by the woman herself, in which her indignation against Propertius shows that she loves him. The echoed reporting of this speech of sixteen lines verbatim is unrealistic in the setting provided; but we are hardly aware of this as we read the poem.

1. quae sentis: not 'your opinion' (with *de nostra puella*), but 'the honest truth' (with *uera*); i.e. not saying something different from what is in your mind; cf. Cic. *Ac.* II, 65 *iurarem...me ea sentire quae dicerem*; cf. also prayer-formulae such as *si...euentum bonum ita uti nos sentimus dederis*....

2. sic tibi...: 'so may you be freed from bondage to your (or, ? our) mistress'; the corresponding English idiom is 'as you hope to be...'.

3. num: 'I hope you are not...' (i.e. not here so much *expecting* as *hoping for* the answer 'no').

5-6. omnis enim debet...habere fidem: i.e. a messenger should always be truthful, and especially ought one to be able to trust a slave, who has his skin to fear for.

*   **habere fidem** may mean 'believe' or 'be believed' according to context; here it is the latter.

7. si qua tenes: 'everything that you can remember'.

8. suspensis: 'eager and anxious'; cf. *suspensus animus, uultus*, etc.

auribus...bibam: cf. Hor. *Od.* II, xiii, 31-2 *pugnas...bibit aure uulgus.* The phrase is evidently colloquial, for cf. Cic. *Att.* II, 14, 1 *sitientes aures*.

9. sicin eam...: here (and so in all that follows) the questions are not true questions, but echo the statements of the messenger in the manner characteristic of an eagerly interested listener: 'Is that so? You found her with her hair all bedraggled, and crying? Floods of tears, you say? etc.' For the force of *sicine* in this context cf. Ter. *Phorm.* 315 *itane patris ais aduentum ueritum hinc abiisse?* Sen. *Contr.* IX, 6, 3 *sicine credibile esse parricidium in sorore creditis?* (Related but slightly different is the use of *itane uero?* as preface to an *indignant* question; and slightly different

79

again are the cases in which the *sic-* in *sicine* has its full adverbial value, e.g. Sil. It. IX, 25 *sicine, sic, inquit, grates pretiumque rependis....*) With *eam* followed by *illius* in the next line cf. below (for instance) III, xxiii, 3 and 5 (*has...illae*).

11. strato...lecto: from Ov. *Fast.* II, 337 and Mart. X, xiii, 3 *stratum lectum* appears to be a regular phrase for bed or couch; so there will be no special point in *strato* here.

* **13. ac maestam teneris uestem pendere lacertis:** 'and her dress hung sadly over those soft arms?' The point in *pendere* seems to be that her dress is such as to cover her arms; but it is hard to be sure; *maestam* suggests mourning.

14. scrinia: evidently here containing *unguenta* as in Plin. *N.H.* VII, 108 and XIII, 1; elsewhere *scrinia* usually appear as *book*-boxes.

15-16. A very sober and virtuous domestic scene.

16. carpebant: of drawing the wool from the distaff in spinning.

18. iurgia nostra: either (*a*) 'our quarrel' or (*b*) 'the harsh things I said to her'.

19. Haec: i.e. 'is *this* the reward I was promised...?'

* **20. est poenae:** evidently here = 'it is punishable'; cf. III, xiii, 38 below; but *poenae est* is regularly said with the kind or amount of the punishment for subject. [Some read *poena et*.]

seruo...teste: 'even when the witness is only a slave'; for the emphasis to be inferred from the context cf. on III, v, 44 above.

21-3. ille potest...gaudet me...: these sentences, here printed as indignant questions, can alternatively be taken as indignant affirmations.

21. nullo facto: 'though I've done nothing' (presumably, nothing to deserve it).

22. [*nolo* is a very clever correction; the MSS give *nullo* or *nulla*.]

habere domi: 'take to live with him'. [Most MSS give *domo*.]

24. si placet, insultet, Lygdame, morte mea: 'if he likes, Lygdamus, he can dance for joy when I am dead'. *insulto* is said both of physical leaping and of mental exultation, and most commonly has a dative after it ('prance on...', 'exult over...', etc.); here it stands absolute (as in Virg. *Aen.* II, 329-30 *uictorque Sinon...insultans*; X, 20 *cernis ut insultent Rutuli*) and *morte mea* is ablative of cause or occasion; but the idea of dancing *on her grave* is also present, suggested by the use in passages such as

II, viii, 18 ff. *interitu gaudeat illa meo...insultetque rogis, calcet et ossa mea* (where *rogis* is probably dative).

25. illa: the supposed rival of line 22.

26. rhombi: this here is identified by *rota* as a known instrument of magic, consisting of a wheel with strings threaded through two holes near its centre, spun by twisting these strings and then alternately drawing on and releasing the ends (in fact, the familiar toy).

staminea...rota therefore = 'the wheel spun by its strings'. The rival is supposed to be drawing Propertius to her by magic made with this instrument. (*rhombus* is not really the right name for it, and belongs properly to a contrivance resembling the 'bull-roarer'. See A. S. F. Gow's note on Theoc. ii, 30.)

27. rana rubeta is a toad; *turgentis ranae portenta rubetae* means a monstrous, bloated, toad.

28. exuctis anguibus: 'from shrivelled (remains of dead) snakes'. [*exuctis* is a conjecture; the tradition has *exectis* or *exsectis* which might mean 'by gutting snakes'.]

trahunt: the toad and snake's bones, made into a philtre, draw the man magically to the woman.

29. per busta iacentia: 'among fallen (i.e. ruined) tombs', a natural haunt of owls.

30. cinctaque funesto lanea uitta toro: ? 'or a woollen fillet that has decked (girt) a bier'. Such a *uitta* would be useful to the witch, like the *plumae* of line 29, because of the evil potency supposed to derive from its associations. For *cingo* with accusative of the thing attached (instead of as usual the thing encircled) cf. Sil. It. VIII, 615 *laetos cingere ferrum*, and the alternative constructions available with *circumdare*. [*toro*, which gives a good value to *funesto*, is an emendation: the MSS give *uiro* here, as at II, ix, 16, where it is quite certainly a corruption for *toro*. Those who keep the MS reading here understand *funesto...uiro* either (*a*) as a corpse, for a *uitta* on which cf. Ov. *Ibis* 103–5 *tu quoque quid dubitas ferales sumere uittas? iam stat, ut ipse uides, funeris ara tibi. pompa parata tua est...*; or (*b*) as an effigy of her victim, used by a witch in making magic, as in Virg. *Ec.* viii, 73 ff.] If *funesto...toro* is right, it will = *lecto funebri*.

31. si non uana canunt mea somnia: 'if my dreams are not false prophets'. *canere* is said of the utterance of seers.

testor: 'I declare' (intransitive, as often and here in parenthesis).

32. ante meos...pedes: either (a) 'as he grovels at my feet'; cf. III, viii, 12 below and IV, viii, 72 *cum uix tangendos praebuit illa pedes*; or (b) 'plain for me to see'; cf. II, xiv, 17 *ante pedes... lucebat semita nobis*.

33. putris et in uacuo texetur aranea lecto: 'and on their bed, unused, will be woven dusty cobwebs'. *aranea* (fem. sing. nom.) is said sometimes for 'cobweb', more commonly for 'spider'.

34. noctibus illorum dormiet ipsa Venus: 'on the love-nights of those two Venus herself will be fast asleep'. *nox* in the elegists has often the special sense of a night of love. *ipsa* emphasizes not so much the name *Venus* as the idea of *total* frigidity which is expressed in the sentence.

35. ueris animis: 'with real feeling', 'from the heart'.

36. hac eadem rursus...curre uia: 'hurry straight back the way you came'. *eadem* here is scanned as a disyllable by synizesis.

38. iram, non fraudes esse in amore meo: 'that my love can be angry but not untrue'. For the construction cf. Cic. *N.D.* I, 121 *negat* (Epicurus) *esse in deo gratiam*.

39. me quoque...igni: 'that I too am writhing over a fire like her own'.

impositum: as, for instance, on a grill.

* **torquerier:** the old-fashioned (and colloquial) form of the infinitive is no doubt chosen here because of its rolling 'r's.

40. iurabo...esse: 'I will swear that I have known no woman for twelve days now'. The present *esse* with accusative of duration is regular, of what has been for some time and still is a fact. For the nominative and infinitive construction in *iurabo integer esse* cf. Catull. iv, 1–2 *phaselus ille...ait fuisse nauium celerrimus*; this is a Greek construction, rare in Latin.

42. per me: 'as far as it depends on me'. The point must be that Propertius is Lygdamus' master, but not his own master— the woman rules him, and may not allow him to free Lygdamus, whom she uses as her own. (The words could also mean 'through my doing'.)

VII

* A lament for a young man named Paetus, lost at sea on a business voyage (1 and 7) to Alexandria (5) from an unspecified port of origin. His ship was swept from its moorings at night by a

northerly gale (13), apparently in the Euripus (19–24), and disappeared somewhere in the stretch of sea that lies between Rhodes and Crete (unless *Carpathium mare* in line 12 is used with some poetic freedom, as may be the case). The elegy is declamatory in style, and makes much use of the stock motives (*loci*) and figures of thought and speech which rhetorical precept favoured in pathetic contexts. The free use of apostrophe and frequent changing of the person addressed (cf. 7, 11, 14, 17, 25, 29) is apt to bewilder, unless the rhetorical and ejaculatory nature of the piece is kept in mind. The total effect is powerful, and the general outline clear enough. Within the frame of a four-line introduction (1–4) and a two-line conclusion (71–2) the fate of Paetus is handled in two passages of 24 lines[1] apiece (5–28 and 47–70) which are separated by a discourse (a *locus communis*) of 18 lines on the folly of mankind in braving the perils of the sea for the sake of gain. Of the two passages directly concerned with Paetus, the first deals with the facts of the disaster, and the second gives an imaginary account of the dying man's last moments; with both are associated various kinds of pathetic comment and ejaculation. Cicero's *de Inuentione* I, 106–9 on *conquestio* and its sixteen *loci* is worth reading in connexion with these passages and with the elegy as a whole.

1. **Ergo**: for this way of beginning an elegy cf. III, xxiii, 1.

4. **semina curarum de capite orta tuo**: the metaphor appears to be from new growths sprouting from the stock (*caput*) of a vine, which are planted (as *semina*) to become vine-stocks themselves; the two words are found in juxtaposition in Virg. *Georg.* II, 354–5 *seminibus positis superest diducere terram saepius ad capita*.

5. **Pharios...portus**: Alexandria; the epithet being from Pharos, the island in the bay of Alexandria with the celebrated lighthouse.

7. **primo...excidit aeuo**: 'lost his life still young'; for the construction cf. Sen. *Ep.* 71, 11 *uita excidere*; Ter. *Andr.* 423 *uxore excidit*.

8. **noua**: 'strange'; the corpse is an object of curiosity to the fish at first.

9. **iusta piae dare debita terrae**: the term *iusta* can be used both of funeral rites and of offerings made at the grave at any

---

[1] See, however, note on line 43 for a view which would yield a different distribution.

time. Here *piae...terrae* is either (*a*) genitive, with *iusta,* and the phrase = 'tribute of due burial' (i.e. of earth to cover the dead body), the sense 'to him' being supplied after *dare*; or (*b*) dative, and the sentence = 'make offerings at the grave' (e.g. by pouring libations on to the earth), *piae* being taken adverbially with the whole sentence ('lovingly') or adjectivally with *terrae* in the sense 'which has duly received him'.

10. **rogos** here = *busta* = 'tombs'.

11. **tua:** for the appearance of the second person without Paetus having been previously addressed cf. III, iv, 4 above; and on the sudden shift of the apostrophe (in 7 'money' is addressed; in 13 the winds) see introductory note to the present elegy.

12. **Carpathium...mare:** between Rhodes and Crete; but the name is used loosely at times elsewhere, and so perhaps here too.

* 13. **Orithyia:** the legendary Athenian princess, Erechtheus' daughter, carried off by Boreas (= Aquilo).

14. **tanta:** i.e. enough that you should want to kill him.

16. **sanctos:** i.e. 'they were no sinners that that vessel carried'.

17–18. 'What is the use of appealing to the gods, crying out that you are too young to die, asking that your mother be spared the grief of losing you? There are no gods here to listen to your prayer.' Formally, there is a contradiction between this and the poet's apostrophe of Aquilo and Neptune in 14–15; but we do not feel this, because beneath the stylized rhetorical manner the sentiments are consistent: wind and sea are cruel—prayer is useless—there is none to help you.

19–20. Paetus' ship was moored; its cable became chafed and broke, and the gale swept it out to sea. As these particulars are known, the place must be known too, and being known will surely be mentioned; this gives the context of the following lines 21 ff.

21–4. **sunt Agamemnonias...mora:** 'it is that shore which bears witness to Agamemnon's love and sorrow, ill-famed through the death (for his fault) of Argynnus of the line of Athamas—the boy for loss of whom Atreus' son held back the fleet from sailing: and Iphigenia was killed for the delay'. Argynnus was a boy (grandson through his mother, Peisidice, of Athamas, king of Thebes), with whom Agamemnon fell in love when the Greek armament was at Aulis before setting out for

84

Troy. The story is mentioned in Athenaeus XIII, 603 D. Argynnus was drowned in the river Cephisus; we do not know what lies behind *poena* in line 22 here, nor any more of the circumstances.

curas: this combines the meanings 'grief' and 'love'.

[**Athamantiadae** is a conjecture, for (*poena*) *minantis aquae*. It is conceivable that better knowledge of the story would justify the MS tradition. But *Athamantiadae* is palaeographically and stylistically and genealogically plausible.]

23–4. The meaning seems to be that Agamemnon in mourning Argynnus missed an opportunity of sailing, and then began the long delay through contrary winds which led finally to the sacrifice of Iphigenia; but this is only conjecture. This couplet (23–4) may seem superfluous and irrelevant in its context; but such discursiveness is not foreign to Propertius; cf. II, xxx, 17–18. For *hoc*...instead of a rel. clause cf. III, xii, 30.

25. reddite: wind and sea, apostrophized earlier in 13–16. Paetus has surrendered his life to them; that they should give back his lifeless body is therefore (it is implied) not much to ask.

28. Et audaci tu timor esse potes: i.e. your fate may make even a brave man afraid.

29–46. A *locus communis* (see introductory note); note the succession of pointed phrases (*sententiae*) in 31–6 especially, and the examples introduced to reinforce the proposition in 39–46.

29. The ironical exhortation to do what the speaker really condemns or deprecates is a favourite 'figure' of rhetoric.

[**curuate et** is a conjecture; the tradition has *curuae et....*]

30. acta = 'brought on (by)'; cf. III, v, 18.

31. fatis = (here) the natural causes of death; cf. on III, v, 18.

32. auximus: i.e. we have opened new (additional) ways for fortune to assail us, increasing the number of such possibilities.

33. te: an imaginary 2nd person, not Paetus in particular; for cf. line 38.

ancora te teneat...: (?) 'is an anchor to hold you...?' = 'is it likely that an anchor could hold you...?' The subjunctive is akin to (though not identical with) the deliberative subjunctive.

35. uentorum est: 'belongs to', and so 'is at the mercy of'.

36. consenuit: 'reached old age'; i.e. did not come to a premature end through violence.

37. natura insidians pontum substrauit auaris: (?) 'when nature spread out the sea, she set a snare for human greed'. For *substrauit* cf. Lucr. IV, 410–11 *immania ponti aequora substrata* *aetheriis ingentibus oris.* But the simple verb *sternere* is often used of smoothing or calming the sea; so that there must be present here also the sense 'a calm sea is nature's snare for human greed'; cf. Lucr. v, 1004 *placidi pellacia ponti.*

38. ut tibi succedat, uix semel esse potest: i.e. it is a wonder if any voyage ever prospers. *tibi* is an imaginary ('ideal') second person.

* **39–46.** After the *sententiae* of lines 31–8 now follow *examples* from legend to illustrate the hazard of seafaring.

39. saxa...Capharea: the rocky promontory of Caphareus in south Euboea on which the Greeks returning from Troy were lured to destruction by Nauplius in vengeance for his son Palamedes whom they had put to death.

40. uasto...tracta salo: 'swallowed in the yawning depths of the cruel sea'. *trahere* is used (cf. line 52 below) of gulping down. *uastus* can mean either 'huge' or 'wild', and is said also of 'yawning' chasms, etc., at (e.g.) Virg. *Aen.* vi, 237 *spelunca... uasto...hiatu,* and Catull. lxiv, 156 *uasta charybdis.*

41. socium = *sociorum.*

42. [soliti...doli: here *soliti* is a conjecture: the MS tradition has *soli.*]

* **43. uerteret:** the subject is (I think) Ulysses still; for the tenses in this and in lines 44–6 cf. note on III, i, 25 above. Ploughing may have come to the poet's mind in connexion with Ulysses because of the story, probably familiar also in pictures, of Ulysses' ploughing (albeit perversely) when he feigned madness in his attempt to avoid going to Troy. (Many editors prefer to understand Paetus as subject of 43–6. My own preference depends partly on a feeling that the rhythm of 39–42 is incomplete until complemented by 43–6; and partly on the apparent dependence of *fleret* line 46 (see note) on *fleuit* line 41. It also seems unlikely that the subject should change at line 43, the verbs remaining in the third person, and this change not be indicated by a demonstrative or by the occurrence of Paetus' name earlier than line 47.)

44. uerba...mea: said as we might say colloquially in English 'if he had taken my advice...', though speaking of an occasion in legend or history; or 'if he had heeded these precepts that you have heard from me' (i.e. those of lines 33–8).

* **45. dulcis conuiua:** this apparently (but strangely) here = *dulciter conuiuans.*

46. nil nisi fleret opes: i.e. he would not have had to lament the loss of his companions, but only (and what by comparison would that matter?) the loss (= lack) of the riches which (as it was) he brought back from his travels (cf. *Odyssey* XIII, 135–8). The thought *non fleret socios* implied in the context (cf. line 41) makes *fleret opes* intelligible, as it otherwise would not be, in the sense required. (And were the words of Menelaus in *Odyssey* IV, 93–100 floating somewhere in the poet's mind?)

[The text printed is a product of a conjecture. The MS tradition has *nil ubi flere potest*.]

47–70. A pathetic imaginary account of Paetus' last moments (55–66) is framed between two pathetic *loci*: a contrast (47–54) between the delicacy of the victim and the harshness of his end, and a reproachful apostrophizing (67–70) of the Nereids who could have saved him but did not.

47–8. non tulit hic Paetus...: '(this) Paetus was not one who could (*or* used to) stand the howling of the gale and chafe his hands (those delicate hands) with hauling ropes'. Here *hic* points to the fate of Paetus, which is in our minds, when recalling something about him (47–50, especially 49–50) to set that fate in relief: for this use of *hic* cf. Tib. I, viii, 71 ff. *hic Marathus quondam miseros ludebat amantes...nunc omnes odit fastus....* The preterite *tulit* does not refer to a particular occasion but makes a general statement about Paetus in the past; cf. below III, xiii, 34 *dedere* ('used to give') and 40 *reduxit* ('used to lead home'), and IV, x, 18 *qui tulit...frigida castra* ('could stand' or 'was used to', in a general statement about Romulus). The reference to ropes in line 48 shows that Paetus is being contrasted with a sailor, who is inured to hardship and accustomed to accept the risk of death as a normal occupational hazard; the negative statement prepares (*non...sed...*) the description in the following couplet (49–50) of the comfort and luxury to which Paetus *was* used. [*hic* in line 47 is the reading of the emended MSS; the tradition is confused at this point. Otherwise the text printed and annotated here follows the tradition. The passage has been variously handled by editors and has been the subject of much conjecture.]

*   **49–50. sed...caput:** 'but in a cabin of (? panelled with) citrus wood or Orician terebinth his head was pillowed on down of many colours'. *thalamo*, which often = bedroom, here presumably refers to a cabin. *thyio*, agreeing with *thalamo*, is an

adjective formed from *thyia*, a kind of tree, for which cf. Plin.
N.H. XIII, 100. *Oricia...terebintho* (note the identical phrase in
Virg. *Aen.* X, 136) may have the value either (as ablative of
material) of an adjective parallel to *thyio* and qualifying *thalamo*,
or of a substantive phrase parallel to *thyio...thalamo*. *Oricia* =
from Oricos, in Epirus. *pluma* may either (*a*) stand simply for
cushions (stuffed with down), or (*b*) refer specifically to the
down, visible through translucent covers (cf. Cic. *Verr.* 2, V, 27
puluinus perlucidus Melitensi rosa fartus). *uersicolore* may mean
either (*a*) 'shot', i.e. iridescent, or (*b*) 'of various colours'.
[*ecfultum* here is an emendation for *et fultum*, the reading of the
MS tradition. For the suitability of *ecfultum* (or *effultum*) cf.
Virg. *Aen.* VII, 94 where the word is used of Latinus couched on
the fleeces of sacrificed sheep. For the form *ec-* see D. M. Jones
in *C.R.* (N.S.) XI, 3, pp. 198–9.]

The hiatus after *thalamo* is a 'Greek' effect.

51–4. There is a pathetic emphasis on *huic* in line 51 and
hunc in line 53; *this* man, so unaccustomed to pain or hardship,
suffered these awful things; cf. the first and fourth of the *loci
misericordiae* enumerated in *de Inu.* I, 107. The sentences com-
posing this passage can be read either as statements or as
(pathetic) questions; they are here printed as questions.

51. uiuo radicitus abstulit unguis: either as the wave tears
him from some handhold; or because Propertius supposed that
this stage of decomposition could be reached before death.

55. tamen: i.e. though at his last gasp, he yet managed to
utter the following prayer.

57–8. Three groups of forces are invoked: the gods of the
Aegaean who rule its waters, the winds, and the waves; they are
not meant to be sharply distinguished. The *et* between second
and third item of the series would be remarkable in classical
prose. (Some prefer to take *uenti* in apposition to *di*, and they
may be right, though the sea has gods other than winds presiding
over it; cf. Virg. *Aen.* XII, 182, etc.)

57. quos...penes: 'in whose power...'; cf. Ov. *Fast.* I, 119
me penes est unum uasti custodia mundi.

* **60. longas...manus:** apparently a pathetic allusion to his
fragility; cf. 59 *primae lanuginis*, 48 *teneras...manus*; at II, ii, 5
Cynthia's hands are *longae*, at IV, vii, 12 *fragiles*. For the type of
locus cf. on 51–4 above. Paetus' death is the more pitiable
because he is (*a*) young, and (*b*) frail (? and sensitive). The

second point may seem artificial, as put by the victim to the gods; but really it is put by the poet to the reader. (For a different treatment of this passage, based on an opinion mentioned in Plin. *N.H.* XI, 274 that long fingers prognosticated short life, see W. R. Smyth in *C.Q.* 1951, p. 78.)

61. alcyonum scopulis: i.e. the *desolate* rocks where the sea-birds nest.

63. Italiae regionibus: 'within the bounds of Italy'.

euehat: combining the values of *ueho* = 'carry', and *eicio* = 'cast up'.

64. hoc: i.e. his battered body.

66. quae = *et ea.*

* **67. Nereo genitore:** 'whose father is Nereus', and so 'daughters of Nereus', the sea nymphs (Nereids).

68. materno tracta dolore: i.e. drawn to the scene by (sympathy with) a mother's grief. [*Theti*: the MS tradition gives *Thetis*. The vocative normal in classical Latin is *Theti*, and cf. II, iii, 37 *Pari*. But it may be that *Thetis* should stand.]

69. uos decuit = 'you should have...'.

70. non poterat uestras ille grauare manus: the same pathetic allusion to his fragility as in 59–60.

71. numquam mea uela uidebis: 'never shall you see sail of mine'.

72. iners: 'a sluggard', or 'stay-at-home'.

*

VIII

The poet's mistress has flown into a rage with him. He professes to be glad of this (1–10), since such angry outbursts are among the symptoms of love in a woman which he as an expert has learned to recognize as infallible (11–20); they also, he now goes on (21–32) to affirm, add spice to the love-relation for the man. This discourse reaches its conclusion in lines 33–4. The remaining six lines (35–40) have no clear or valuable connexion with 1–34, and appear to be a short separate piece, like for instance II, 11; they are therefore separated in the text and will be annotated separately below, though joined in the MSS.

VIIIA (see also p. 89)

Editors understand variously the point and relevance of (especially) lines 13 ff. and 25–6, and the reader is asked to regard as provisional the text and interpretation here presented.

1. fuerat: Propertius often uses the pluperfect form of *sum* (especially) with a value as of perfect or imperfect; cf. also examples from Virgil, Tibullus and Ovid in B.B.'s note on I, viii, 35–6.

2. tot: as we should say: 'all those...'. Propertius is fond of *tot* and *tam* at the beginning of an elegy; cf. below III, xiv, 2, III, xix, 1, III, xxii, 1, III, xxiii, 1.

* [**4. insana:** recurrence of the same word in adjoining lines is not uncommon in Propertius: see examples in S-B.'s note on I, ii, 9. But not many of these are as striking as the present instance of a conspicuous word conspicuously repeated without any possibly valuable point or emphasis being gained thereby; and those that are perhaps as striking (III, xi, 59–61 *monumenta*; IV, iv, 39–40 *saeuisse...saeuos*) lend themselves to fairly easy emendation. Possibly *iratae* should be read in line 2 or *irata* in line 4.]

5. audax: i.e. 'go on, don't be afraid...'.

8. sinu: here presumably the upper part of his tunic, not (as commonly, when men's dress is in question) the fold of the toga across the breast.

[**11–12. rabida** is a correction for *grauida*, which is the reading of the MS tradition and may be due to *graui* in the preceding line. The idea is a stronger form of that expressed in Catull. xcii *Lesbia mi semper dicit male etc.* In line 12 *haec* is also a conjecture; the tradition has *et*, which can be translated 'also' and should perhaps be retained.]

13–16. Propertius can hardly be saying that a woman whose love is shown by her quarrelsomeness also displays one or other of these further remarkable symptoms; he must be saying that quarrelsomeness is one of several distinctive symptoms of love which he as an expert has learned to recognize. Hence *seu* seems to be required in line 13, in place of the MS tradition's *se*, to connect the symptoms now to be enumerated with the one mentioned already. It follows that with *euntem* in the same line must be supplied 'him' (the man she loves).

13. custodum gregibus circa seu stipat euntem: i.e. (if

the argument in the preceding note is correct) 'or again, if she sets crowds of watchers about her man (to spy on him) as he walks abroad'.

14. seu sequitur medias...uias: either (*a*) *uias* is object of *sequitur*, and the picture is as in Virg. *Aen.* IV, 68–9 *uritur infelix Dido totaque uagatur urbe furens*; or (*b*) object of *sequitur* is still 'him', as in the preceding line, and *medias...uias* is governed by the sense of *ire* contained in *eum sequitur*.

17. his...tormentis animi: either (*a*) dative, 'for (interpreting) such (signs of) anguish'; or (*b*) ablative, 'by (interpreting) such...'.

animi: this can be taken either with *tormentis* ('anguish of mind'), or with *haruspex* ('diviner of the heart's condition').

uerus = (here) *uerax*; cf. IV, i, 107 *uerus...per astra trames*.

18. certo: 'true'.

19. fides: 'love' (viewed as a bond between the lovers).

quam non...uertas: 'that one cannot turn...', i.e. 'that is not apt to get turned...'. [*uertas* is an emendation, for the tradition's *uersat*.]

20. lenta: 'placid'.

21 ff. Here begins a shift from the thought 'Quarrels are proof of love's intensity' to the thought 'Quarrels make love more exciting'.

21. aequales: friends of his own age, i.e. 'the other fellows'.

22. meam: 'my mistress'.

25–6. tecta superciliis...notas: (?) 'when your scowl shoots unspoken meaning and you signal with your gestures those wordless messages (i.e. curses) of yours'. The Latin here is imprecise in itself and could mean different things in different contexts. In Ov. *Am.* II, v, 15 ff. similar terms are used of lovers conversing by nods and signs across a dinner table, but such cannot be the meaning in this context; what must here be meant is the demeanour of one speechless with rage. The rendering above supposes that *remittis* is a metaphor from hurling missiles. *tecta...uerba* ('concealed words') could embrace many meanings: riddles, code, sign-language, expressive glances, etc.: its meaning here can only be fixed by the context. *tua...scripta*, because this is her way.

27–8. For the paradox of the 'lover' preferring that his love's course should not be untroubled cf. Ov. *Am.* II, xix, 19–36.

27. odi ego quos...somnos: 'not for me the slumber that

91

no sighs disturb'. Here *odi*, as in Hor. *Od.* I, xxxviii, 1 (*Persicos odi, puer, apparatus*), means much less than 'hate'. For the sighs and troubled rest of the lover in disfavour cf. II, xxii, 47 *quanta illum toto uersant suspiria lecto*. [*quos* is a conjecture; the tradition has *quae*, which does not seem to yield an appropriate sense.]

28. semper...uelim: i.e. 'may I be always the wan lover of an angry-tempered mistress'.

29–30. dulcior...suae: i.e. Paris enjoyed his love (*ignis*) the more when his love-making (*gaudia ferre*) was attended by resistance (cf. *arma*) on Helen's part, sweet (*grata*) because adding to the pleasure of the process. For *arma* said of a form of love-making cf. below III, xx, 20 *dulcia...arma*. What is here said of Paris' preference is not recorded elsewhere; the poet invents this particular to suit his own purpose, as he does (e.g.) Hippodamia's aversion from make-up at I, ii, 20. What has suggested to him the idea here developed is presumably the scene in *Il.* III, 427 ff. where Helen is angry but finally compliant, and the reproaches of Hector in *Il.* VI, 325 ff. [Some here emend *grata*, the reading of the tradition, to *Graia*, looking forward to line 31. But the example of Paris must illustrate what has gone *before* (lines 27–8), and cf. also line 32. Moreover the idea that he found the real warfare of others an agreeable *background* to his own erotic warfare has no place here; the point of 31–2 is simply the *contrast* between his kind of warfare and theirs.]

31. barbarus: 'fierce', or 'furious'.

32. maxima: either (*a*) 'he waged great wars in...' (ironically); or (*b*) 'all his warring was in...'. For this latter use of *maxima* cf. (?) II, xiii, 25–6 *tres...libelli, quos ego Persephonae maxima dona feram*; IV, i, 10 *unus erat fratrum maxima regna focus*.

33. aut pro te mihi cum riualibus: the thought *cum riualibus* here appears for the first time, suggested of course by the mention of the Trojan war—though in 29–32 Paris' fighting was with Helen, not with Menelaus.

VIII B

These six lines appear to be an independent piece; for another such six-line elegy cf. II, xi. The woman addressed has temporarily preferred another man to Propertius; and it is this subject that gives coherence to the little piece, which consists of two lines addressed to the woman and four lines addressed to the rival. Of course, neither woman nor rival is present; what we have here are the angry musings of the poet. The mention of rivals in line 33 of the preceding elegy may have suggested the juxtaposition of this one with it; but there is no continuity of thought or context.

35. doleres: 'you would suffer' (for treating me like this); i.e. he would turn elsewhere. As it is, she need fear no reprisals and no competitor.

[**37. nexisti:** our MSS have *tendisti*, but *nexisti* is attested for this passage by ancient grammarians.]

38. socer...nec sine matre domus: in comedy, it is the *socer* who intervenes in his married daughter's interest when a husband is suspected of keeping a mistress; and a courtesan has sometimes a *mater* who acts as her manageress, and sees that she does not let sentiment interfere with business. It may be (though we cannot know for certain) that this is the point of the reference to *socer* and *mater* here: both, in the roles described, are afflictions from the point of view of the 'lover' of elegy. For the *domus* of a courtesan cf. II, viii, 14; II, xxiv, 24; for a *mater* cf. II, xv, 20.

IX

Propertius excuses himself (1–4) to Maecenas, who has pressed him to write in a higher style, on national or epic subjects. He justifies his refusal first (5–20) by reference to his own limitations and the maxim that aptitudes differ; and secondly by reference to the example of self-knowledge and self-restraint set by Maecenas himself (21–34). Then (35–46) he declares that he will continue in his present way, as emulator of the Greek masters of elegy, Callimachus and Philitas, and as poet of love. However (47–56) he professes that he would nevertheless set no bounds to his ambition if Maecenas himself led the way (as we know from 21–34 that he won't). In conclusion (57–60) he asks Maecenas for favour all the same, while he follows the course he is now pursuing with success.

It is worth remarking that this elegy does not stand first in the book, which is thus not 'dedicated' to Maecenas.

1. eques: with point; Maecenas despite his ancestry and his personal power remained deliberately in the rank of an *eques*.

de sanguine regum: cf. Hor. *Od.* 1, i, 1.

2. fortunam...tuam: 'your station'; cf. on *eques* in line 1 above.

5. quod nequeas: sc. *ferre*. The second person in *nequeas* is 'ideal'; the subjunctive is either potential ('which you may not be able to...'), or generic ('such that you are not able to...').

* **6. et pressum inflexo mox dare terga genu:** an odd mixture of metaphors, to our ears.

* **7. omnia rerum:** cf. Tac. *Hist.* v, 10 *cuncta camporum*; *Ann.* III, 35 *cuncta curarum*; Hor. *Od.* II, i, 23 *cuncta terrarum*. The phrase here means no more than *omnia*.

* **8. palma nec ex aequo ducitur una iugo:** i.e. (?) in art there are varieties of eminence, each offering its several prize. Text and interpretation here are both uncertain. It may be that the basic idea is given by Lucr. 1, 118 *detulit ex Helicone perenni fronde coronam*; with which cf. Prop. IV, x, 4 *non iuuat e facili lecta corona iugo*. If this is right, the point of (*non*) *ex aequo...iugo* seems to be (*aequo* standing for *aequali*) that the crest of the Muses' mountain is a sloping ridge or a succession of peaks of varying height, from any of which a poet may win the palm for excellence in a particular department of his art. For *ducitur* = 'get', cf. perhaps Hor. *Od.* III, xxvii, 75–6 *tua sectus orbis nomina ducet*; *Od.* IV, iv, 59–60 *ab ipso ducit opes animumque ferro*. The negative in *nec* then goes with the whole sentence, and so embraces both *aequo* and *una* (not, that is, a single prize from a level ridge, but different prizes from different eminences). [The MS tradition here reads *Flamma...ulla*; *palma* and *una* are probable emendations, both due to scholars of the Renaissance.]

9–16. A list of eight artists (in the visual arts) illustrates the point made in the couplet 7–8 (and so makes clear the general sense of line 8).

9. Lysippo: Lysippus of Sicyon, fourth century B.C., celebrated for figures in bronze.

animosa: the word includes the meanings 'life-like' and 'spirited'.

10. Calamis: fifth-century sculptor noted for his rendering of horses.

se mihi iactat: 'vaunts himself (*or* shows himself off) to me', i.e. invites my admiration.

11. summam: 'first place' or 'primacy'; cf. Plaut. *Truc.* 728 *solus summam habet hic apud nos.*

Apelles: famous fourth-century painter; the work referred to here is his *Venus Anadyomene.*

12. Parrhasius: of Ephesus, late fifth century B.C., another painter. *parua arte* here presumably means that he excelled in detail or in miniatures.

uindicat...locum: 'claims a place of honour'; cf. *habere locum apud aliquem* = 'be held in regard'.

13. Mentoris: Mentor, early fourth century, silversmith.

argumenta...addita formae: his works depicted scenes or stories, as well as being beautiful in themselves; but there is also an allusion to the mould (*forma*) in which the artist cast his works. *magis* = (here, as the context shows and cf. III, xiv, 2 below) 'especially'.

14. Myos: Mys, fifth century, silversmith. The acanthus was used as decorative motif, e.g. on the cup in Virg. *Ec.* iii, 45 (Alcimedon) *molli circum est ansas amplexus acantho.*

flectit iter: the decorative pattern winds its way around the border of the object decorated.

15. Phidiacus signo se Iuppiter ornat eburno: 'the Jupiter of Pheidias arrays himself in (the glory of) an ivory statue'. The reference is to the chryselephantine statue of Zeus at Olympia, by the Athenian Pheidias.

16. Praxitelen: fourth-century Athenian sculptor, some of whose best-known works were in Pentelic (i.e. Attic) marble: hence *propria...ab urbe lapis.*

uendit: 'commends', i.e. causes to attract or be admired; cf. I, ii, 4 *teque peregrinis uendere muneribus*; Juv. vii, 135 *purpura* (a purple gown) *uendit causidicum.* [*uendit ab* is an emendation; the MS tradition gives *uindicat.*]

17–20. The diversity of human capacities is further illustrated by brief reference (reminiscent in some respects of Hor. *Od.* I, i) to some activities other than the arts. The conclusion in line 20 virtually repeats the proposition in line 7 above.

17. est quibus: instead of *sunt quibus*; after the Greek ἐστὶν οἷς.

Eleae...palma quadrigae: i.e. the chariot that wins the Olympic prize; literally 'the prize of the Elean chariot'. For the form of the expression cf. Virg. *Georg.* I, 59 *Eliadum...palmas equarum*, where prize-winning horses are meant.

concurrit: (?) 'falls to the lot of...', with the overtone 'contends in the race'; but *concurro* is not exemplified in either of these senses in the Th.L.L.

18. est quibus in celeres gloria nata pedes: (?) a conflation of two ideas: (*a*) *quibus gloria est in celeritate pedum*, and (*b*) *qui nati sunt in celeritatem pedum*.

20. naturae...semina: a man's natural potentialities, i.e. his 'bent'.

21–34. Maecenas himself has chosen to limit his ambitions, setting an example to which the poet now appeals. These lines develop the thought of line 2 above, just as lines 5–20 developed that of line 4.

21. at: introducing a second premise after the general proposition in line 20.

22. cogor: here perhaps 'I am constrained...' (because of the principle of conduct which he has adopted). But *cogor* in Propertius has sometimes so little value as to be hardly translatable.

23–4. cum tibi...foro: here *liceat* in the second clause has to be understood also in the first (by the figure called ἀπὸ κοινοῦ); and the verb *ponere* which governs *iura* in the second clause has to suggest (by the figure called zeugma) a kindred verbal sense suitable to govern *securis*, as it is not suitable itself; see further notes below.

23. tibi: sc. *liceat* (see preceding note).

Romano...in honore: 'as a magistrate of Rome'.

dominas: 'imperial'. *dominas* is here made an adjective by Propertius: cf. II, xxxi, 4 *femina turba*.

securis: the axes in the lictor's *fasces*, symbolizing executive power. The verbal sense to which this is object will be *habere* or *exercere* or the like, and this has to be superimposed in thought on the syntax provided by *ponere* in the following line; *ponere* itself will not yield a suitable sense.

24. ponere iura: give verdicts or rulings, i.e. 'dispense justice'.

25. uel tibi...ire: sc. *liceat* from the preceding couplet. [**hastas** is a conjecture. The MS tradition gives *hostes*.]

Medorum: standing no doubt for Eastern peoples generally, as elsewhere do the *Seres*, etc. The Eastern enemy really in mind at this period was the Parthian Empire, of which Media had long since become a part.

26. per arma: instead of the instrumental ablative *armis*. The reference is to spoils of war fixed on door or wall of the house of a victorious general.

27. ad effectum: sc. of your will.

28. insinuentur: 'come flowing in'.

29. parcis: absolutely, 'you hold back'.

et in tenuis humilem te colligis umbras: 'and shrink (*te colligis*) modestly (*humilem*) into the background (*in umbras*) like one of no account'. With *umbras* cf. our 'out of the limelight'. *tenuis* is said of a person of small rank or wealth; applied to *umbras* here it is a 'transferred' epithet.

30. subtrahis = (here) *subducis* = 'furl' or 'reef'.

ipse = *ultro* = 'deliberately'; whereas most men would act thus only under necessity.

plenos: i.e. when he could, if he wanted to, run with bellying sail before a favouring wind.

31. Camillos: generic plural, meaning 'heroes like Camillus'.

31–2. ista…iudicia: 'this choice of yours', or 'this wisdom of yours'. For the plural cf. line 22 *exemplis…tuis*; it may in both places have a certain value, as suggesting several instances.

32. uenies tu quoque in ora uirum: 'your name too will be on (all) men's lips'. The poet means 'will *live* on men's lips'; and his words carry this implication because they recall Ennius' epitaph on himself *uolito uiuu' per ora uirum.*

33. Caesaris et famae uestigia iuncta tenebis: i.e. 'you will stand at Caesar's side in history'; the metaphor is from statues in a gallery of heroes.

34. erunt takes its number from *tropaea* as nearest noun; which noun (*tropaea* or *fides*) is subject and which predicate cannot be told and does not matter.

uera: with *tropaea*, I think, but it could be taken with *fides*.

fides: cf. II, i, 36 *fidele caput*, of Maecenas' relation to Augustus. *fides* here includes affection as well as loyalty.

35–46. Propertius affirms that he will not attempt epic poetry, but will be content to emulate the Greek masters of elegy and be admired with enthusiasm (as he implies he is already) by the young of both sexes.

35. findŏ: the only example in Propertius (unless *nolŏ* is read in II, xxx, 20) of the trochaic scansion of a first person singular, and the earliest in classical poetry; Ovid has at least two instances: *Am.* III, ii, 26 *tollo* and *Pont.* I, vii, 56 *credo*. [This line is missing in *N*.]

36. sub...flumine: cf. Tib. II, iii, 19 *ualle sub alta*.

37. flebo: i.e. tell the tragic tale of....

37–8. in cineres arcem sedisse paternos Cadmi, nec semper proelia clade pari: (?) 'how the strong city of Cadmus (i.e. Thebes) fell in ruin over the ashes of the fathers, and the battles in which the fatal issue was reversed'. The wording is obscure in itself and we are expected to reach its meaning with the help of our knowledge of the story referred to, and to identify that story with the help of the context in which the passage is set. The context here requires a reference to an epic tale of war, and the wording shows that destruction of the fortified city or the citadel (*arces* could mean either) of Cadmus is in question. The reference therefore is to the destruction of the walls of Thebes by the Epigoni (Apollodorus III, 7, 2–4) when they came and avenged the defeat and death of the famous Seven Champions, their fathers. This being so, *nec semper proelia clade pari* must = *et proelia non semper pari clade*, the negative being treated as in II, xxviii, 52 *nec proba Pasiphae* = *et improba Pasiphae*, and *non semper* having the value 'no longer' as in I, xiii, 12 *nec noua quaerendo semper amicus eris*. By *cineres...paternos* must be meant the ashes (i.e. the graves or tombs) of the fathers of those who fought in this second war, perhaps with a general reference to the participants in the first war, perhaps with a specific suggestion that the bodies of the six of the seven invading champions who fell in that war were burned and buried on the scene of their defeat: in either case, there is an inverted allusion in the word *paternos* to the name and story of the Epigoni. (On the above assumptions a reference to the other legendary destruction of the citadel or palace of Thebes, by the fiery blast which killed Semele, is excluded here by the fact that that story is not a story of war. And the otherwise attractive conjecture *septem* for *semper* in line 38 is unnecessary and on the whole inexpedient, since it would bring in the two wars in inverted order and leave the point of the hexameter irretrievably obscure; moreover the Seven Champions were not all killed, Adrastus surviving.)

39. Scaeas: sc. *portas*. The ellipse is an unusual licence.

Apollinis arces: 'fortress built by Apollo', in allusion to the building of Troy for Laomedon by Apollo and Neptune.

41. pressit aratro: 'furrowed with the plough'. After the city is destroyed, the site is ploughed over by the victors to obliterate it finally. The Wooden Horse (line 42) is subject of *pressit* not as performing the act, but as causing it; there are many other instances of this in Propertius, e.g. I, xvii, 26 where *soluite uela* is said to the Nereids in a prayer for safe sailing.

Neptunia: cf. on 39.

42. Palladiae...artis equus: cf. Virg. *Aen.* II, 15–16 *equum diuina Palladis arte aedificant*; in *Odyssey* VIII, 493 it is said that Epeius made the Horse, with Athene's aid or counsel.

43. Callimachi: cf. on III, i, 1.

44. Coe poeta: Philitas of Cos; cf. on III, i, 1. [*Coe* is a conjecture. The MSS tradition has *dure*, perhaps through unconscious reminiscence of II, xxxiv, 44 *inque tuos ignis, dure poeta, ueni*.]

45. urant: 'set their hearts on fire', with enthusiasm, emulation, or (possibly) love.

46. et mihi sacra ferant: 'and worship me'; cf. Virg. *Georg.* II, 475–6 *Musae, quarum sacra fero*, and on III, i, 4 *orgia ferre*.

47. te duce: 'when (*or* if) you lead the way'; i.e. if (but only if) you set me an example, by attempting things you have hitherto regarded as beyond your powers. Propertius cannot be here imagining that Maecenas will change the principles and way of life described in 21–34 above; and so it is clear that what now follows is not what the poet hopes to do, but what he excuses himself (cf. 3–4 above) from doing. Evidently Maecenas had urged him to write on national themes, e.g. the early history of Rome (cf. 49–51) or the victories of Augustus (cf. 53–6). [As the text stands the verbs in 47–56 are future indicatives; I should prefer to read *crescat* in 52 and take them all as present subjunctives (potential); cf. III, x, 6 below where *ponat et* is necessary but *NFL* read *ponet et*.]

47–8. The 'grandest' subjects conceivable, battles of gods with Giants or Titans. For Coeus cf. Virg. *Georg.* I, 279, Hesiod, *Theog.* 134, 404.

48. Oromedon (name of a mountain in Cos according to the scholiast on Theoc. vii, 46) is not found elsewhere as name of a legendary monster; hence some would read here *Eurymedonta*, citing Homer, *Od.* VII, 58 where a Eurymedon is king of the Giants.

Phlegraeis...iugis: scene of the battle of gods and Giants, and located by some of the ancients in the volcanic area near Puteoli, by others in Thessaly. Usually one hears of the Phlegraean *plain*, not (as here) *heights*.

49. palatia = poetic plural, the Palatine Hill. We are back in the beginnings of history, when cattle grazed on the site of future Rome; cf. IV, i, 1 ff., IV, ix, 1 ff., Tib. II, v, 23 ff., Virg. *Aen.* VIII, 360–1, etc.

50. caeso moenia firma Remo: 'and the walls inviolable after Remus' death'. This wording suggests strongly (though not decisively) that the killing of Remus when he overleaped the wall somehow *rendered* the wall inviolable for the future, i.e. that his death was a blood-offering of religious potency. We do not meet this idea anywhere unmistakably expressed; but if it existed, it would explain also IV, i, 49–50.

51. eductos: 'reared'. (Listed after the event of line 50, this illustrates the fact that Propertius is not fussy about chronological sequence in his enumerations.)

siluestri ex ubere: i.e. the dugs of the she-wolf.

ex: i.e. with milk from....

52. sub tua iussa: i.e. to the height required by your command.

53. currus utroque ab litore ouantis: cf. Virg. *Georg.* III, 33 *bisque triumphatas utroque a litore gentes*, a statement made possible by the fact that in Octavian's triumph of 29 B.C. the Morini (a Belgic people on the North Sea) were included as well as the Egyptians and Eastern peoples (cf. Virg. *Aen.* VIII, 705–6 and 727).

54. Parthorum astutae...fugae = *Parthorum per astutiam fugientium*, in allusion to the well-known tactics of the Parthian horse-archers.

tela remissa: this might mean (*a*) 'arrows laid aside'; cf. Ov. *Her.* vii, 149 *ambage remissa*; Val. Fl. v, 276 *Marte remisso*; or (*b*) 'bows unstrung', *tela* standing for τόξα which includes bow and arrows together, and cf. Hor. *Od.* III, xxvii, 67–8 *Venus et remisso filius arcu*. From the context it is clear that some abatement of the Parthian menace at a date near that of Actium is referred to; presumably that achieved in 30 B.C. as a result of their internal dissensions and mentioned by Dio C. LI, 19.

55. claustraque Pelusi Romano subruta ferro: 'and the fortress of Pelusium overthrown by Roman steel'. Pelusium was a fortified town near the Canopic mouth of the Nile. In fact it was surrendered to Octavian, not taken by storm; but cf. on 38 above and III, iii, 8 for Propertius' vagueness over historical details. [*claustra*, used often specifically of a fortress guarding a key route, is a conjecture. The tradition has *castra*, which is not nearly so appropriate either to the status of Pelusium or to the verb *subruta ferro*.]

56. Antonique grauis in sua fata manus: 'and his own stroke fatal to Antony'.

57–8. In this couplet *coeptae* and *immissis* must refer to a course already entered on, a successful career already in progress; so Propertius is asking Maecenas to accept his refusal to attempt new subjects, and to approve and encourage him as a writer of love-elegy. *mollis* then in line 57 will mean 'indulgent'; cf. Ov. *Am.* II, iii, 5 *mollis in obsequium facilisque rogantibus esses*.

57. coeptae fautor cape lora iuuentae: i.e. encourage and guide my youth in its present course. There is a combination of metaphors: Maecenas is asked both to be a *fautor*—a supporting onlooker—and to take the reins.

* **58. immissis...rotis:** *immittere habenas, rudentes*, etc., is said of loosening rein or rope to let chariot or ship run faster; hence the combination *immissis...rotis* is easy and means 'my flying chariot'; cf. also *admissis equis*.

59–60. hoc mihi...fuisse tuas: there are two ways of taking this, and perhaps there are meant to be. (*a*) A common interpretation of the passage makes it a statement, and as such it is printed here: 'this honour you grant me, Maecenas, and it comes from you, that I too shall be said to have ranged myself on your side'. For *a te* then cf. Sen. *Ep.* 114, 22 *ab illo* (the mind) *nobis est habitus, uultus, incessus*. But *concedis* and *ipse* and *a te est* have not much point on this interpretation. (*b*) Alternatively, the couplet can be read as a question: 'do you leave this honour to me when it might be yours, and is it to your credit, Maecenas, that I shall be said to have ranged myself on your side of my own accord (i.e. without encouragement from you)?' This assumes that *ipse* in line 60 = *ultro* (as in line 30 above); that *a te* = 'a point in your favour' (as in Cic. *de Or.* I, 55 *uide ne hoc totum sit a me*, etc., and cf. Sen. *Prov.* 3, 2 *pro ipsis est*); and that *concedis* here means not merely 'allow', but 'give up to another what might be one's own'. This yields an obliquely phrased request for patronage on the poet's own terms, and makes a good conclusion to the elegy, as well as attaching a useful value to *concedis, a te est* and *ipse*. There may of course be a deliberate ambiguity; for play on words in various forms is found at the end of several of Propertius' elegies (e.g. III, x, IV, iii, IV, iv, IV, viii, IV, ix).

For the construction *in partis...fuisse tuas* cf. Cic. *Div. Caecil.* 66 *nationibus, quae in amicitiam populi Romani dicionemque essent*; Petron. *Sat.* 42 *fui hodie in funus*; and other exx. in Kühner–Stegmann II (i), pp. 593–4. For *ferar* cf. III, xvii, 20 below.

X

A birthday poem. For other birthday poems cf. Tibullus II, ii, III, xi and xii. The parts of the poem are: setting (1–4), prayers (5–18), celebrations (19–32).

1. uisissent: absolutely, 'had come to visit me'. [*uisissent* is an emendation. The tradition has *misissent*.]

2. sole rubente: i.e. in the red (or golden; cf. *rubicunda Ceres*) glow of early morning.

3. signum misere: 'they signalled the coming of my lady's birthday'. The metaphor is from the signal that starts a race, etc.; cf. Enn. *Ann.* 84 *consul cum mittere signum uult, omnes auidi spectant ad carceris oras.*

* **6. ponat:** absolutely, 'be stilled'; cf. Virg. *Aen.* VII, 27 *cum uenti posuere.*

minax: i.e. 'let the waves *cease from threatening* and be stilled'. [Many prefer to read *minas* here, giving *ponat* an object.]

8. et...ipse: here *et* and *ipse* both = 'even'.

Niobae lapis: i.e. 'the stone that was Niobe'.

9. alcyonum...querelis: Alcyone was turned into the seabird that has her name when she threw herself into the sea in grief for the loss of her husband Ceyx.

10. increpet...: 'lament' (with a note of complaint and indignation, cf. IV, xi, 60 *ille sua nata dignam uixisse* (= that she is dead) *sororem increpat...*).

11. felicibus edita pennis: 'born under happy auspices'. *pennis* stands for omens from the flight of birds.

12. iusta precare: 'make due prayer to'.

poscentis...deos: 'the gods who await (*literally* invite *or* require) your prayer'. The gods (*a*) have a *right* to her prayers on this occasion, and (*b*) *welcome* her prayers because they are well disposed towards her.

[**13. at** seems likelier than *ac*, which is the reading of the MS tradition, and the change is palaeographically insignificant.]

14. pollice here evidently stands by a metonymy (and as a collective singular) for 'fingers'.

[**17–18.** This couplet has been lost in *N*, no doubt because lines 16 and 18 both end with *caput*.]

17. qua polles: referring to *forma*.

18. inque meum semper stent tua regna caput: here *tua regna in meum caput* = 'your dominion over me', and *semper stent* = 'may abide for ever'.

19. inde: 'next', if construed in the *ubi* clause in 19–20; 'later', if construed in the main sentence 21–2.

20. luxerit: 'has blazed'; the fire on the altar flares up when the incense is dropped on it.

secunda: 'auspicious', as promising good.

21. sit mensae ratio: i.e. let our thought be of the dinner-table.

22. et crocino naris murreus ungat onyx: i.e. and let the scent-jar fill our nostrils with the fragrance of oil of saffron. But in the Latin every word is colourful (and resonant).

onyx: this (alabaster) being typically the material of ointment- and perfume-jars, the word can mean 'jar' without insistence on the material: cf. II, xiii, 30, and Hor. *Od.* IV, xii, 17 *nardi paruus onyx*.

murreus: probably from *murra* the perfume rather than *murra* the mineral (since it is applied to *onyx*, and since there would be no point in emphasizing the nature of the jar as opposed to its contents). And just as *onyx* can mean simply 'jar', so *murreus* may mean simply 'of perfume', not perfume of myrrh in particular; in fact the perfume in question is specified as *crocinum*, i.e. saffron.

ungat: this verb is chosen because the perfume is an oil. Its fragrance is probably conceived as an exhalation of invisible droplets; or perhaps a spray is in mind.

23. succumbat: i.e. let the dancing go on until the pipe-player is exhausted.

rauca: perhaps referring to a quality in the low notes of a pipe; cf. Virg. *Ec.* i, 57 *raucae...palumbes*.

25. ingratos adimant...somnos: 'keep dull sleep away'.

26. publica uicinae perstrepat aura uiae: i.e. and let the air in the street outside ring (with the noise of our revelling) for all to hear. [*perstrepat* is the reading of the emended MSS; the tradition has -*et*.]

27–8. sit sors et...: i.e. 'and let us play at oracles, the dice-box our fortune-teller, (asking) which of us the boy-god beats more fiercely with his wings'. The situation resembles that in Sen. *Exc. Contr.* II, 2 *assiduae contentiones erant: 'sine te uiuere non possum': 'immo, ego sine te'. qui certantium exitus esse solet, iurauimus...*; only here the *certamen* is resolved by throwing the dice. For the postponed *et* cf. III, xi, 46 below.

quem here stands, as not uncommonly, for *utrum*.

[**grauius** is an emendation; the tradition has *grauibus*, which would make the question a general one. The context surely requires something intimate to the two lovers.]

29. trientibus: cups, or measures, of wine (a *triens* being ⅓ of a sextarius, or about ½ a pint).

30. noctis et instituet sacra ministra Venus: 'and Venus attends us to prepare the holy ceremonies of night'. The metaphor in *ministra* is of a temple attendant, acolyte or the like.

32. peragamus: 'let us bring to its proper end'; there is an emphasis on *per-*.

iter: the programme of the birthday's events (but also, as an overtone here, the intercourse between the lovers which is the last of these events; for cf. II, xxxiii, 22 *noctibus his uacui ter faciamus iter*; III, xv, 4 *et data libertas noscere amoris iter*).

XI

Eight lines (1–8) on common sentiments of love-elegy (cf. I, vi, 25 ff., I, xii, 1 ff., etc.) lead to twenty lines (9–28) of legendary examples of women's power; and this complex is followed by twenty-eight lines (29–56) on Cleopatra and the shame with which she threatened Rome, and sixteen lines (57–72) on the gratitude due to Augustus who saved Rome from her. There is no return at the end of the piece to the sentiments which begin it. Despite the poet's refusal in Elegy ix to attempt 'patriotic' poetry, this elegy (like xiii below) is a 'patriotic' poem, for which the love-theme does no more than furnish what is frankly a peg.

1. **uersat:** 'governs', i.e. turns this way and that according to her whim.

2. **et trahit addictum sub sua iura uirum:** 'and leads my manhood prisoner to be her bondservant'. *addictus* is said of a debtor assigned by a legal verdict to a creditor as bondsman until he shall have paid. *addictum ducere* is said regularly of the creditor, after such a verdict, leading off his man. With *iura*, of the mistress here, cf. *sui iuris esse* of one who is free and his *own* master.

3. **criminaque ignaui capitis mihi…fingis:** i.e. charge me with being an *ignauum caput*, a feeble creature, the genitive giving the content of the charge. *fingere crimen* instead of *facere* implies that the charge is unfair.

* [5. **uentorum…motus** is a conjectured reading; the MS tradition has *uenturam mortem*. Required is something characteristic of a *sailor*'s experience (like wounds in the case of a soldier and subjection in the case of a lover); cf. II, i, 43–4 *nauita de uentis, de tauris narrat arator, enumerat miles uulnera, pastor oues*.]

7. **ista…uerba:** i.e. I used to talk like you when I was younger and still inexperienced.

9–28. Examples from legend of extraordinary powers exercised by women (not in all cases through their sexual attractions).

9. **Colchis:** Medea, the witch.

10. **et armigera proelia seuit humo:** 'and sowed (the seeds of) battles in the soil that bore armed men (for crop)'.

12. **aurea lana:** the Golden Fleece.

14. **Maeotis…Penthesilea:** the Amazon Queen Penthesilea who fought at Troy and was killed by Achilles, who loved her when he saw her beauty after death. *Maeotis* (fem. adj.) because the Amazons were associated with the region around the sea of Azov (Lake Maeotis).

* 17. **Omphale:** queen of Lydia, whom Hercules served as slave, and with whom he fell in love. The long final vowel of the (Greek) name is scanned as short, and not elided, before the following stressed vowel; this is Greek prosody, rare in the Latin poets.

18. **Gygaeo…lacu:** the name of a real lake in Lydia (cf. Hom. *Il.* II, 865, xx, 390), which Propertius here has invested with the associations of the gold-bearing river Pactolus; the suggestion evidently is that Omphale was beautified by bathing in it.

19. **columnas**: it was a Roman custom to set up columns to commemorate victories. This idea is here applied to the Pillars of Hercules, the name given to the rocks of Gibraltar and Ceuta between which are the straits of Gibraltar; these are conceived as monuments set up by Hercules to commemorate his pacification of the world, which he had freed from monsters, robbers, etc.

20. **tam**: cf. on III, viii, 2 above; one can translate (e.g.) 'with that great, rough hand...'.

traheret: of drawing the wool from the distaff in spinning.

21. **Semiramis**: queen of Nineveh who enlarged and rebuilt Babylon.

22. **ut...**: i.e. in such manner that...; in English this consecutive clause is best rendered by a participle, 'rearing a mighty edifice with walls of brick'.

23. **et duo...mitti**: still governed by the *ut* of line 22, 'in such a manner that...'; with *mitti* must be supplied *possent* from the following clause, by the construction called ἀπὸ κοινοῦ.

in aduersum: in opposite directions one to another.

24. **nec possent...**: not 'and not be able to...' but 'and be able not to...'; the construction being *possent mitti nec tangere*. The sense of the whole couplet is 'in such manner that two chariots could be despatched in opposite directions along the (top of the) wall and neither graze the side (of the other) with its axle (in passing)'. [*mitti* in line 23 is an emendation; the MS tradition gives *missi*. Sense could alternatively be obtained by keeping *missi*, and reading *ne* for *nec* in line 24.]

25. **medium, quam condidit, arcis**: 'through the middle of the city she founded'; the genitive construction after *medius* is not uncommon.

26. **Bactra**: the city, capital of Bactria.

[**25–6.** Regarding the emendations *quam...arcis...subdere* in this couplet see App. Crit.]

* 27. **nam quid...?**: here *nam* explains beforehand a proposed omission; for this usage cf. examples in Kühner–Stegmann II (ii), pp. 117–18 (under *occupatio*). The poet might find numerous illustrations of his thesis in the amours of gods and heroes, but contents himself with a single reference to Jupiter's notoriety in this respect.

* 28. **suamque domum**: cf. on III, xix, 20 below. The idea, natural in speaking of a Roman reprobate, is rather quaint when applied to Jupiter.

29–72. From here to the end the elegy is concerned with Cleopatra and Rome. Propertius has in fact moved from love to a national theme.

29. opprobria nexerit: 'has fastened disgrace upon . . .'. The point is explained by 58, etc., below, or (better perhaps) by IV, vi, 22 (Antony's Roman soldiers serving a woman). The subjunctive seems to be due to a subjunctive in the main sentence which has to be supplied (e.g. *quid raptem in crimina*). [*nexerit* is a conjecture. The MS tradition has *uexerit*.]

30. et: 'even', with *famulos*.

trita: *tero* can be said coarsely of sexual intercourse, and also of the promiscuous use of anything.

31. coniugii obsceni: 'of that shameful union', the marriage of Cleopatra and Antony, shameful to Antony and Rome.

[*coniugii* is a conjecture. The MS tradition has *coniugis*.]

32. addictos in sua regna patres: 'and for our Roman senators to be made her slaves and subjects'.

34. totiens: i.e. in Caesar's wars, and (especially) in the war of Octavian against Cleopatra and Antony.

Memphi: the city Memphis standing typically with Alexandria for 'Egypt', though it was not (as was Alexandria) really a notable scene of conflict.

35. harena: the beach where Pompey was about to land when he was murdered.

tris...triumphos: Pompey had triumphed over the Marians in Africa, over Sertorius, and over Mithridates.

37. issent...campo: 'better if the Phlegraean plain had seen you carried to the grave'. This plain was commonly conceived as located in the volcanic area around Puteoli; sometimes, alternatively, in Thessaly. Here certainly the former is meant, for (*a*) the reference in the next line to *submission* to Caesar makes a reference in this line to *death* at Pharsalus impossible; and (*b*) the moral here drawn is the same as that drawn in a famous passage of Cicero (*T.D.* I, 86), in which the point is that Pompey would have been fortunate if he had died when he was gravely ill at Naples in 50 B.C.; we expect an allusion here to this occasion, and the 'Phlegraean plains' supply it.

tibi here = Pompey, despite *tibi* = Rome in the preceding line.

38. si...daturus eras: a remarkable periphrasis for *si dedisses*.

colla daturus: 'bow the neck' (to receive chains), i.e. to surrender; cf. II, x, 15 *India...tuo dat colla triumpho*; Sen. *Apocol.* 12 *dare Romuleis colla catenis.*

39. Canopi: the city Canopus standing for Alexandria and Egypt.

40. una Philippeo sanguine adusta nota: this is variously understood: (*a*) 'sole disgrace branded (on Rome) by Philip's race'; or (*b*) 'signal disgrace branded on the race of Philip', *sanguine* being on this latter view understood as a kind of ablative of place. The first of these alternatives seems easiest grammar and likeliest sense; for why should Propertius be concerned about the honour of Philip's line? The point seems to be that in Rome's earlier encounters with Philip of Macedon's descendants (Philip, Perses, etc.) she got nothing but honour; Cleopatra alone had inflicted disgrace, by entangling Antony, with the consequences described in lines 29 ff. above and 58 below.

41. ausa: sc. *est*, a finite verb (preterite) being required here.

Anubim: the dog-headed Egyptian god. This contrast between the gods of the two nations appears also in Virg. *Aen.* VIII, 698–9.

43. sistro: a kind of rattle, used in Egyptian worship.

44. baridos: gen. (Greek form) of *baris*, a Nile barge propelled by poling; the *conti* are barge-poles.

rostra Liburna: these 'Liburnian rams' are ram-armed Liburnian galleys; the *Liburnica nauis* being a type of fast warship characteristic of Augustus' navy.

45. conopia: mosquito-nets. Like the *sistrum* (43) and *baris* (44) they are here meant to sound outlandish and suggest outlandish ways. The word is Greek, from Κώνωψ = 'gnat'.

46. iura dare: 'sit in judgement'; cf. Dio C. L, 5 of Cleopatra's ambition ἐν τῷ Καπιτωλίῳ δικάσαι; and Sen. *Apocol.* 12 *qui dat populo iura silenti*, of the judge of the dead in the underworld.

iura dare et... = *et iura dare....* For the postponed *et* cf. III, x, 27 *sit sors et....*

statuas inter et arma Mari = *inter statuas et arma Mari*. The *arma* are evidently the same as the *tropaea Gai Mari de Iugurtha deque Cimbris atque Teutonis* of Suet. *Jul.* 11. They were on the Capitol.

49. cane...triumphum: i.e. chant '*io triumphe*' as the procession passes; cf. Ov. *Am.* I, ii, 33–4 *ad te sua bracchia* *tendens uulgus 'io' magna uoce 'triumphe' canet*; and for the construction *ibid.* 25 *populo clamante triumphum.* The poet is now recalling Augustus' triumph of 29 B.C. after the death of Cleopatra. [*cane* is conjecture. The MS tradition has *cape.*]

50. longum...diem: 'long life'; whereas at II, xviii, 20 *haud longa...die* = 'at no distant time'.

51. tamen: i.e. 'after all', despite your hopes and our fears. Cleopatra is now apostrophized; Rome was apostrophized in the previous couplet.

uaga flumina Nili: 'the winding streams of Nile', apparently in allusion to the divergent mouths and their winding courses. [*uaga* is probably conjecture; the main MS tradition has *uada*, which is attested as an adjective, though not very securely, elsewhere and would mean 'shallow'.]

52. Romula uincla: cf. IV, iv, 26 *Romula...hasta*, etc. Propertius is fond of these adjectives of short form.

53. spectaui: as a spectator he saw carried in the triumph a picture of Cleopatra's death.

bracchia spectaui: The short final syllable of *bracchia* before a double consonant at the beginning of the next word is one of eight examples of this prosody in Propertius; the others being II, xvi, 43, III, i, 27 (?), III, xi, 67, III, xix, 21, IV, i, 41, IV, iv, 48, and IV, v, 17. Tibullus and Ovid have this only before *smaragdus* and *Zacynthus*, exotic words (as also are some of those involved in the Propertian passages listed).

54. et trahere occultum membra soporis iter: either (a) 'and numbness spreading unseen engulf her limbs'; or (b) 'and her limbs absorb the numbing poison as it spread unseen'. For *traho* = absorb cf. III, vii, 40 and 52. *soporis iter* must be subject or object of *trahere* (though it seems strange as either), the idea being as in Lucr. III, 530–1 *post inde per artus ire alios tractim gelidi uestigia leti.*

55. tanto...ciue: an ablative absolute construction in which the verb 'being there' (i.e. to defend you) is understood. [*haec* in this line is a conjecture, for the tradition's *hoc*. Many editors keep *hoc*, taking it with *tanto...ciue*, and read *fui* for the tradition's *fuit*; the speaker then is Cleopatra. In the text as here printed the speaker is the poet.]

56. dixit et assiduo lingua sepulta mero: the tongue dulled with long drinking is that of the poet, subject in thought of this couplet as of its predecessor (53–4); his life of dissipation (*nequitia*) is devoted to wine (cf. II, xv, 41–2 *qualem si cuncti cuperent decurrere uitam et pressi multo membra iacere mero*) as well as to women, and no doubt both attend his celebration of the victory (cf. III, iv, 15–16 above *inque sinu carae nixus spectare puellae incipiam*...). The force of *et* here is 'even'. With the metaphor *lingua sepulta mero* cf. Virg. *Aen.* II, 265 *urbem somno uinoque sepultam*. [If *hoc*...*fui* is read in line 55 and Cleopatra made the speaker, the reference to wine will be to *her* potations as in Hor. *Od.* I, xxxvii, 14 *mentemque lymphatam Mareotico*.]

57–72. Reflexions on Rome's peril and shame and on her debt to Augustus, who has proved a saviour to her like legendary heroes of the past. [The text of the MS tradition is confused in this passage. To begin with, line 58 *femineas*...*timuit*...*minas* is missing in *N*, and the word *timuit* is omitted from it in *FL*. Further, something has evidently fallen out between lines 58 and 59, as the couplet 59–60 is not a complete sentence; and lines 65–8 appear to be intrusive between the couplets 63–4 and 69–70 which both list feats commemorated (cf. 63 *testatur*, 69 *memorabit*) by concrete surviving evidence. Accordingly, in the text here offered lines 65–8 of the tradition are printed between lines 58 and 59. This transposition removes the above difficulties; and also brings the couplets 57–8 and 65–6 into a very appropriate conjunction (cf. 58 ...*timuit*...? and 66 *uix timeat*...). The total effect then is as follows.] The couplet 57–8 (Rome shamed by fearing Cleopatra) is immediately answered by the couplet 65–6 (Rome's fear unnecessary, for a saviour was at hand in Octavian); and then the four lines 67–68–59–60 point the thought of 57–8 (Rome, conqueror of so many formidable foes!), while the six lines 61–4 and 69–70 pursue the thought of 65–6 (to the monuments that recall the devotion of past saviour-heroes of Rome now is added another such). [An alternative transposition puts 67–8 after 58 and 65–6 after 60.]

57. toto...orbi: dative *toto* instead of *toti* is unusual in a classical author; cf. in Propertius I, xx, 35 *nullae* (fem. dative).

58. territa Marte: sc. in thought *femineo* from *femineas*... *minas*; cf. III, xiv, 4 below (*inter luctantis* sc. *luctans*).

65. di...di...: Romulus the founder, Octavian the saviour; but also 'the gods' collectively, who have protected Rome throughout her history.

67. nunc ubi, etc.: the proud thought of Rome's past

victories is supposed, by a rhetorical exaggeration, to fade before the shameful thought that she has been afraid of a woman.

Scipiadae: gen. sing. For the form of the name cf. Virg. *Aen.* VI, 843, Lucr. III, 1034, etc., no doubt from Ennius.

classes: 'armaments'. Perhaps the fleet with which the elder Scipio invaded Africa (cf. Liv. XXVIII, 45, XXIX, 24–7, etc.); but in old-fashioned Latin (suiting the tone of *Scipiadae* here) *classes* could mean an army too, cf. the quotation in Aul. Gell. I, 11, 3 *cum procinctae igitur classes erant et instructa acies coeptumque in hostem progredi.*

signa Camilli: cf. Virg. *Aen.* VI, 825 *referentem signa Camillum*, perhaps (but not certainly) in allusion to the *recovery* of Roman standards captured by the Gauls; perhaps to trophies won from them. Or *signa* here may be simply a symbol of military pomp.

68. capta: sc. *signa* from line 67; these *signa* will be enemy standards taken by Pompey in the war against Mithridates. [Some may favour the conjecture *capte*, reading *aut modo Pompeia Bospore capte manu*; i.e. *aut tu, Bospore capte*, etc. = *aut Bosporus captus*, etc. The attribute (*capte*) of the vocative substantive is put (regularly) in the vocative, as in II, XV, 2 *lectule deliciis facte beate meis.* For the vocative (in apostrophe, replacing a third person statement) put without a supporting *tu* or possessive pronoun, and with ellipse of the verb, cf. Virg. *Aen.* VII, 684–5 *quos diues Anagnia pascit, quos, Amasene pater* (= *quos tu pascis, o Amasene pater* = *quos Amasenus pater pascit*).]

59. uicti monumenta Syphacis: trophies or statues commemorating Rome's victory over Syphax, the Numidian ally of Carthage at the end of the second Punic war.

60. gloria: 'pride' or 'boasting', as well as 'fame'.

61–4. A list of semi-legendary heroes who saved Rome by their devotion, and of whose heroism sundry memorials still exist. Some of the examples do not fit exactly (e.g. no memorial is cited in the case of the Decii, and Valerius Corvinus neither saved Rome nor sacrificed himself by his feat of arms) but in such an enumeration the poet's concern is with the impact of the whole. *M. Curtius* (Liv. VII, 6) leapt on horseback, armed, into a chasm which had opened in the forum, because the soothsayers declared that such a sacrifice would ensure the perpetuity of the Roman state. *P. Decius*, father and son of the same name, vowed themselves to death and rode into the thick of the enemy (Liv. VIII, 9 and X, 28), to save their armies and secure victory against the Latins and the Gauls respectively. *Horatius Cocles* (Liv. II, 10, 2) held the approach to the bridge over the Tiber while the bridge was broken down and so saved Rome from the Etruscans. *M. Valerius Corvinus* or *Corvus* (Liv. VII, 26) killed a Gaul in single combat and got his cognomen from the fact that a raven perched on his helmet and harried his opponent during the combat. The feat of Curtius was supposed to be commemorated by the *lacus Curtius* in the forum (surrounded with a stone coping and called by Varro, *L.L.* V, 148 a *monumentum* of the event); the *semita* commemorating Horatius' deed is not known, but presumably was a street that bore his name; the memorial of Corvinus' feat was his name.

61. Curtius...statuit monumenta: regarding the recurrence of *monumenta* in neighbouring couplets, see on III, viii, 4 above. [I have wondered whether *momenta* should be read here, and *statuit momenta* translated 'stopped the earthquake'; cf. for the rationalization Liv. VII, 6 *seu motu terrae seu qua ui alia forum medium ferme...conlapsum...dicitur,* and for the sense of *statuere* required Prop. IV, ix, 4 *statuit fessos...boues* (halted). But *monumentum* in Varro, *L.L.* V, 148 supports the MS reading and the usual interpretation.]

69. Leucadius...Apollo: the temple of Apollo on the promontory of Leucas, overlooking the flight from Actium if not the action. This existed before the battle, but becomes by association a memorial of it. There may be present also the thought of the temple of Apollo at Actium itself, which Octavian enlarged specifically in honour of his victory; cf. Suet. *Aug.* 18, 2.

70. tantum operis = (?) *tantam molem*; the same phrase occurs at III, iii, 4.

belli can be taken both with *tantum operis* and with *una dies.*

XII

Postumus has gone with the army to the East. Propertius reproaches him for leaving his *Galla* (1–14); affirms that *Galla* will be faithful to him in his absence (15–22); and compares her (at a length which to modern tastes may seem disproportionate) with Penelope (23–38). In the vulgate text *Galla* appears in line 38 as *Aelia Galla*, but *Aelia* is due to a conjecture which is not inevitably right. The Eastern campaign anticipated is against the Parthians (cf. Elegy iv above); in 20 B.C. a settlement with the Parthians was reached without warfare, so the present elegy may be dated not later than that year.

4. ne faceres: after *rogante*.

5. auari: cf. III, iv, 3, III, v, 11–14, III, vii, 1, etc.; according to Propertius warfaring and seafaring are undertaken primarily for profit.

7. tamen: i.e. in spite of Galla's entreaties.

iniecta tectus...lacerna: this could mean that his cloak is wrapped around him, or that it serves as a blanket, or that part of it is thrown over his head as a hood; line 8 (the helmet being used to hold water) perhaps favours the last possibility.

8. Araxis: of the river Araxes, on the Armenian–Median border. [*potabis*, given here by the MSS, makes excellent sense. Equally appropriate would be *portabis*; and Tib. II, vi, 8 has *ipse leuem galea qui sibi portet aquam*.]

10. ne: i.e. fearing lest....

11. laetentur: the verb is possible because *Medae... sagittae* = (virtually) 'the Median archers'; cf. IV, i, 45 *Bruti... secures* ('stern Brutus'), IV, vi, 81 *si...pharetris Augustus parcet Eois* ('the Eastern archers').

12. armato: the *cataphractus* was an armoured horseman on an armoured horse. [*armato* is a conjecture; *aerato* is another; the MS tradition has *aurato*, which gives an improbable point.]

13. de te: 'of you'; the not uncommon partitive use of *de*, for which see also III, vii, 64 above.

14. illis...locis: hardly different from *illic*, for cf. II, xxxii, 7 *hoc utinam spatiere loco* (= here in Rome); Sen. *Ep.* 43, 1 *non est quod te ad hunc locum* (Rome) *respiciens metiaris: ad istum respice in quo moraris*.

16. moribus his: 'behaving as you do'.

[**18. suae** is an emendation: the MS tradition has *tuae*.]

19. eas: potential or jussive, 'you can go'.

* **25. et Ciconum mors Ismara capta:** the killing of the Ciconians and the taking of their town (*Ismaros* in Hom. *Od.* IX, 40, but *Ismara* in Virg. *Aen.* X, 351 and Servius *ad loc.*) are in apposition as equally important aspects of the same event; cf. *Od.* IX, 40 πόλιν ἔπραθον, ὤλεσα δ' αὐτούς, and for the apposition

II, i, 27 *ciuilia busta Philippos*. But see further note below
regarding the uncertainty of the text here. The piratical attack
on this Thracian people is the first item in the record of
Ulysses' adventures after leaving Troy, as he recounts them to
King Alcinous in the *Odyssey*. [*Ciconum mors Ismara capta* is
conjecture; the MS tradition has *ciconum mons ismara, calpe....*
The tradition's text can be defended, as *Ismara* is indeed name
of a mountain (cf. Virg. *Georg.* II, 37) as well as of a town, and
Calpe is the ancient name of Gibraltar, beyond which Ulysses'
travels carried him in some accounts. But *mons* seems very
colourless. And apart from the order of events Propertius in this
passage agrees closely with the Odyssean version of the hero's
wanderings; only the Laestrygonians and Aeolus are omitted.
Also, in mentioning each adventure he gives some fairly clear
indication of its character. Hence the bare names *Ismara* and
Calpe seem improbable; whereas *Ismara capta* is likely because
informative. Another possibility is *Ismare capte*, with the
construction discussed on III, xi, 68 above; the unfamiliarity of
that construction would help to explain the intrusion of *Calpe*.]

*   **26. genae** = (here, as at IV, v, 16) 'eyes'; usually it means
'cheeks'.

27. fraudes: the treacherous, or baneful, arts of the en-
chantress.

tenaces = i.e. 'that hold men prisoner'; the *herbae tenaces*
suggest magic herbs such as Circe might employ, but the *lotos*
(Greek nom. masc.) is the fruit in the land of the Lotophagi,
which makes those who eat it want to stay there always, for-
getting their own homes.

28. scissa: 'rent asunder'; presumably a reference to the
parting of the water when Charybdis 'sucks in'. *aquas* is
accusative of respect. [Perhaps one should consider *alternā
sicca...aquā*, taking *aqua* as ablative of privation after *sicca*; cf.
Virg. *Aen.* I, 106–7 *unda dehiscens terram inter fluctus aperit*.]

29. mugisse iuuencos: this accusative and infinitive, like
fugisse in line 31, stands in the sentence as a nominative sub-
stantive, one of the series that stand in apposition to *tot...
morae*, subject of *nocuere* in line 24. In the story in *Od.* XII,
395, the flesh of the oxen of the Sun, impiously slaughtered by the
hero's companions, emits lowing noises when being roasted.

Lampeties: gen. of Lampetie, a nymph, daughter of the Sun
(*Od.* XII, 133) and in charge of his cattle (*Od.* XII, 131 and 375).

31. fugisse: the subject (Ulysses) of the verb is understood; he has been the subject in thought all through.

Aeaeae...puellae: evidently Calypso is meant, since Circe has been mentioned in line 27, and the shipwreck of line 32 follows Ulysses' departure from Calypso in the *Odyssey*. But *Aeaea* in Homer (*Od.* x, 135) is the island of Circe. A friend points out that *Aeaeae* evokes the Greek cry of woe αἰαῖ, relevant to *flentis* here.

32. hiemis: 'of storm', the reference being to the storm of *Odyssey* v.

33. nigrantisque domos animarum intrasse silentum: the visit to the world of the dead in *Odyssey* xi.

34. Sirenum etc.: the asyndeton as in III, i, 28, III, iv, 14, III, xxii, 9, etc.

lacus: presumably rock-pools, or a lagoon.

35. renouasse: i.e. 'brought back to use'.

[**38. Aelia** is not a certain conjecture: see App. Crit.]

XIII

As in Elegy xi, a typical sentiment of love-elegy (line 1) leads to a discourse on a general theme (here, the growing menace of luxury and materialism) of national rather than erotic interest, and the original cue is gradually allowed to be forgotten. Lines 1–4 state the subject; 5–14 describe the temptations of luxury and the promiscuity which results from it; 15–24 set in contrast with this Roman promiscuity the devotion of Indian wives; 25–50 set in contrast with contemporary materialism the simplicity and innocence of primitive pastoral society; in 51–66 the poet proclaims through examples the fatal consequences of avarice, and assumes the role of a prophet to warn Rome of her danger.

1. Quaeritis: a conventional formula to introduce the subject of a piece: cf. I, xxii, 2; II, xxxi, 1.

unde auidis nox sit pretiosa puellis: 'why women's greed makes their favours dear'. *nox* has often the special sense of a night of sexual enjoyment.

2. Venere exhaustae damna querantur opes: the money squandered on sexual pleasures is said to complain of its own loss; the thought is of the ruined man complaining of his ruin.

3. ruinis: the plural may well have a value here, 'cases of (men's undoing)'.

5. Inda...formica: cf. Herodotus III, 102, and Plin. *N.H.* XI, 111 (*Indicae formicae*) *aurum ex cauernis egerunt terrae.*

6. concha Erycina: evidently 'Venus' shell', *Erycina* standing for 'of Venus' as does *Idalio* in IV, vi, 59 *Idalio...astro.* Venus herself is called *Erycina* and *Idalia* because her temples at Eryx and Idalium were famous, and the epithets thus proper to the goddess herself are then applied to things belonging to her. By 'Venus' shell(s)' mother of pearl or pearl obviously is meant, though not found so called elsewhere.

Rubro...salo: the Red Sea, Persian gulf, or adjoining area of the Indian Ocean.

7. Tyros...Cadmea: because the famous Cadmus came from Tyre.

* **8. multi pastor odoris Arabs:** here *pastor Arabs* (collective singular) = 'the shepherds (i.e. nomads) of Arabia'; and *multi...odoris* is genitive of permanent attribute, '(people) of many perfumes', as in such expressions as *magnae pecuniae homo*, or *multi ioci homo*, etc. *odor* is said (like 'scent' or 'perfume' in English) of the stuff that emits the fragrance as well as the fragrance itself; and the singular here is collective.

9. pudicas: i.e. women who keep each to her own man; cf. II, xxiii, 12 and 22.

10. gerunt: variously used of *wearing* a garment, *acting* a role, and (as here) *possessing* a moral quality; for this last cf. Val. Max. VIII, 3, 1 *sub specie feminae uirilem animum gerebat.* [*gerunt* here is a conjecture, for the tradition's *terunt.*]

Icarioti: 'daughter of Icarius' = Penelope.

11. census: (acc. pl.) = 'fortunes'.

nepotum: 'spendthrifts'.

12. nostra per ora trahit: here *per ora* = 'before our eyes'; cf. Val. Max. II, 10, 3 *gentis suae cladium indicia per ora uulgi ferre.*

13. poscendi...dandi: the man asks the woman's favours; the woman asks money; the man gives money, the woman gives herself. The following sentence (line 14) refers to the woman giving herself.

14. ipsa mora: i.e. *even* hesitation.

* **15. lex** = suttee, as will appear.

una: i.e. 'beyond compare'.

17. mortifero: here (only) of the bier that *carries the dead body*; elsewhere of what *brings death*, weapons, disease, etc.

19. certamen habent leti: i.e. they compete for the honour of dying on the husband's pyre. This is related by Cicero, *T.D.* v, 78 of the Indians; by Herodotus v, 5 of the Thracian Trausi.

23. hoc genus: the Roman sort, or breed, of wives.

23–4. nulla...nec...nec: the *pair* of negatives continuing, not cancelling, the negative in *nulla* (whereas if *nulla* were followed by a single *non* there would be cancellation); cf. Cic. *Off.* 1, 4 *nulla uitae pars...neque forensibus neque domesticis in rebus...uacare officio potest.*

Euadne: wife of Capaneus, who threw herself on his pyre.

25. pacata: 'who lived in peace'. Though a past participle in form, the word here is a pure adjective; cf. Virg. *Aen.* IV, 619 *optata.*

felix agrestum...iuuentus: 'happy those country lads...'; *iuuentus* suggests not only young lovers, but a contrast (because of *pacata*) with its common use in the sense 'warriors'.

[**30. uimineos** is a conjecture; the MS tradition has *uirgineos*, but it is the men who bring these baskets of flowers as lovers' gifts; keeping *uirgineos* one would have to give a special point to *referre* and suppose that the girls have sent their lovers out to fill their (the girls') baskets. The two epithets both occur in *Copa* 15–16 *et quae uirgineo libata Achelois ab amne lilia uimineis attulit in calathis.*]

per: possibly with the idea of distribution, i.e. 'in basketfuls'; but more probably we are to understand that the whiteness of the lilies *shows* bright (*lucet*) *through* the loose texture of the wicker baskets; for cf. IV, iii, 20 *querulas rauca per ossa tubas.*

calathos: the *calathus* was a tubular wicker basket widening at the top.

* [**32. uersicoloris** (= iridescent, when said of birds' plumage at Lucr. II, 801–5) is a conjecture; the MS tradition has *uiricoloris*, which is no word.]

33. his...blanditiis: abl. of price with *empta* in line 34.

furtiua: this epithet reads most easily with *antra*, grammatically could go with *antra* or with *oscula*, and in meaning really qualifies the proceedings described by the sentence as a whole.

34. dedere: this preterite conveys, not a single or momentary past action, but past action without implication as to frequency or duration; that the action here meant was in fact recurrent appears from the context; so also with *reduxit* in line 40 below.

35. hinnulei pellis: a deer's skin. For the choice of this to suggest primitive simplicity cf. Val. Max. IV, 3, 11 *si quis hoc saeculo uir illuster pellibus haedinis pro stragulis utatur,...nonne miserabilis habeatur?* [*hinnulei* is an emendation; the MS tradition has *Atque hinuli*, or *humili* or the like.]

*   **totos operibat amantis:** literally, 'covered...completely'; from which (I think) one extracts 'was their only covering', or 'was covering enough'. But many conclude that *totos* is corrupt.

36. creuerat: the pluperfect can be given its proper value here: the grass *had* grown, so *was* long; cf. IV, ix, 24 *lucus ubi... fecerat...nemus.*

natiuo...toro: presumably dative, the sense being *herba natiuo toro fuit,* (the luxuriant grass) 'made a natural bed'.

37. lentas...umbras: ? 'gently-swaying'; or ? 'lazy', the epithet really belonging to the whole scene, like *furtiua* in line 33 above, and cf. Virg. *Ec.* i, 4 *tu, Tityre, lentus in umbra.*

38. nec fuerat...poena: i.e. *nec pro scelere fuit*; for the tense of *fuerat* cf. on III, viii, 1 above. *poena* here apparently (and cf. III, vi, 20 above) stands for 'a matter for punishment' and so 'an offence'.

nudas...uidere deas: Actaeon, hunting, saw Artemis (Diana) bathing, and was torn in pieces by his own hounds; Teiresias, hunting, saw Athene (Minerva) bathing and was blinded. On the other hand, Paris, as a shepherd on Ida, was invited to judge the famous contest of beauty (in the nude, cf. II, ii, 14) between the goddesses. All these stories are evoked by the poet's phrases here, the two former for contrast, the last for illustration.

39. Arcadii...pastoris: collective singular for the shepherds of Arcadia, associated in poetry with the pastoral age and with the god Pan, who is subject of thought in the following lines 41–6.

uacuam: this suggests 'unguarded'; it is an age of innocence and security.

[*Arcadii* is a conjecture; the MS tradition has *Atque dei*. An alternative conjecture is *Idaei*, pursuing the thought of Paris evoked in the preceding line 38.]

41. dique deaeque omnes: vocative, the apostrophe being used for variety's sake instead of a statement in the third person. This line echoes Virg. *Georg.* I, 21 *dique deaeque omnes, studium quibus arua tueri.*

42. uestri...foci: altars, as often. Probably wayside shrines are in the poet's mind. [The text printed in 41–2 is a product of emendation. The MS tradition has *uestris...focis*.]

praebebant...uerba benigna: in inscriptions, of which a specimen follows in lines 43–6.

43–6. These lines are a fairly close translation of an epigram (*A.P.* IX, 337) of Leonidas of Tarentum (early third century B.C.):

εὔαγρει, λαγόθηρα, καὶ εἰ πετεεινὰ διώκων ἰξευτὴς ἥκεις τοῦθ' ὑπὸ δισσὸν ὄρος · κἀμὲ τὸν ὑληωρὸν ἀπὸ κρημνοῖο βόασον Πᾶνα· συναγρεύω καὶ κυσὶ καὶ καλάμοις.

43. uenaberis: 'you shall catch'; cf. Ov. *Fast.* II, 163 *mille feras Phoebe siluis uenata redibat.* (Commonly *uenari* means 'hunt' rather than 'catch', but here the context and the Greek original show that a *promise* of *good* hunting is required.)

44. meo tramite: 'in this glen of mine'. *trames* (cf. Serv. on Virg. *Georg.* I, 108) is a mountain valley making a way between two eminences; cf. ὑπὸ δισσὸν ὄρος in the epigram above. (Also a mountain path; also a path or by-way in general.)

46. calamo: the fowler's pole; cf. Mart. XIV, ccxviii *non tantum calamis sed cantu fallitur ales, callida dum tacita crescit harundo manu* (i.e. the *calamus* or *harundo* can be extended gradually by adding jointed sections, as with a modern fishing-rod).

50. aurum lex sequitur, mox sine lege pudor: the administration (or the making) of laws is perverted by money, and conscience, no longer reinforced by law, goes the same way.

51 ff. Greed for gold was the subject of lines 47–50. The awful consequences of this are now illustrated by three examples from history and legend. These are as it were steps leading up to the warning that the worst example of all is likely to be Rome herself (line 60 *ipsa*).

51. torrida: 'scorched' or 'blasted' by the lightning; cf. Lucr. V, 1220 *fulminis...plaga torrida tellus.*

sacrilegum testantur...Brennum: 'bear witness to the sacrilege of Brennus'. A Gallic horde led by Brennus (278 B.C.) was foiled by a miracle (thunder, lightning, earthquake, snowstorm) when about to sack Apollo's temple at Delphi; cf. among other authorities Cic. *Div.* I, 81.

52. intonsi: alluding to the flowing locks with which Apollo is represented.

55. scelus...Polymestoris: i.e. *scelestus Polymestor*, cf. III, V, 4 *nostra sitis*, etc. For the story of Priam's son Polydorus

murdered by his host for the sake of his treasure cf. Virg. *Aen.*
III, 49 ff.

57. Eriphyla: the seer Amphiaraus knew he would fall if
he went with the Seven against Thebes, and hid to avoid
participating; his wife Eriphyla was bribed by Polynices to
betray his whereabouts with the gift of a costly ornament (here
bracelets, elsewhere a necklace).

58. delapsis nusquam est Amphiaraus equis: the earth
opened and swallowed him up together with his chariot and
horses.

nusquam est: 'is no more'; cf. Hor. *Sat.* II, v, 101–2 *ergo nunc
Dama sodalis nusquam est.* [*delapsis* is an emendation; the old
MSS have *dilapsis*.]

59. patriae: dative of the person judging; cf. Cic. *Paradoxa*
v, 36 *an ille mihi liber, cui mulier imperat?* The poet means 'may
I be a true prophet *in the eyes of* my countrymen', i.e. 'may they
believe me (and be warned in time)'.

61. nulla fides = (here) 'none will believe'.

61–2. Ilia...Maenas: Cassandra, given the gift of true
prophecy by Apollo and then (because she broke her bargain
with him) condemned never to be believed. *Maenas* (literally
'woman in a frenzy') is usually said of a Bacchante, here of the
inspired prophetess.

neque...habenda = 'was destined not (*lit.* was not destined)
to be accounted a true prophet of (*lit.* for) the doom of Troy'.
As verb sc. *fuit.*

63. Parim Phrygiae fatum componere: 'that Paris was
building the doom of Phrygia'. The expression is figurative,
and obscure in the prophetic manner; it might refer to Paris'
proceedings generally, or perhaps in particular to the building
of the ships which took him to Greece and brought back Helen
with him (cf. generally Ov. *Her.* xvi, 107–18 and 121–4). For
componere = 'build' cf. Virg. *Aen.* III, 387 (*urbem*), Ov. *Fast.*
I, 708 (*templa*).

64. equum: the Wooden Horse.

fallacem: this is predicative.

serpere: a metaphor, suggesting by its common associations
both slow movement and insidious approach. The scene is of
the entry of the Horse into Troy; cf. Virg. *Aen.* II, 240 *medi-
aeque. ..inlabitur urbi* (and 246 ff., Cassandra's warning).

65. fuit utilis: 'was for her country's good'; *or* 'should have been...', the perfect in *fuit* being as in *potuit* = 'could have been (but was not)'.

66. experta est ueros irrita lingua deos: 'the unheeded prophetess (cf. on 55 above) found that the gods (who inspired her) were no deceivers'. Two ideas are telescoped: the *prophetess* found her inspiration vindicated; the *people* who disregarded her found that her prophecies were true.

XIV

A short essay, with a turn appropriate to the love-theme, on the advantages of a foreign custom; with which may be compared Elegy xiii, 15–24. There is an affinity here with the *laus legis* mentioned by Quintilian (*I.O.* II, 4, 33) as an exercise used in the schools of rhetoric. Regarding the athletic exercises of girls in classical Sparta cf. Eur. *Andr.* 597–600 αἳ ξὺν νέοισιν ἐξερημοῦσαι δόμους γυμνοῖσι μηροῖς καὶ πέπλοις ἀνειμένοις δρόμους παλαίστρας τ᾽ οὐκ ἀνασχετοὺς ἐμοὶ κοινὰς ἔχουσι. The details of the picture here are supplied by Propertius' imagination.

2. mage: 'especially'; cf. *magis* in III, ix, 13 above.

tot: as we should say 'the many (merits of)'; cf. on III, viii, 2 above.

3. non infamis exercet...ludos: the adjective (acc. pl.) is predicative: this activity does not attract reproach. [*ludos* is a conjecture: the tradition has *laudes*. Possibly *laudes* should be retained and taken as = 'virtues' (of strength, courage, skill, etc.) as for instance in Virg. *Aen.* IX, 252–3 *quae...digna...pro laudibus istis praemia posse rear solui?* There would then be a deliberate point in the oxymoron *infames...laudes.*]

4. inter luctantis nuda puella uiros: in thought supply *luctans* with *puella*, from *luctantis*: cf. on III, xi, 58 above.

5. cum pila ueloces fallit per bracchia iactus: there are two ways of taking this. (*a*) The ball 'causes to deceive the eye' (*fallit*) the swift throws that pass it from one player's arms to another's (*ueloces per bracchia iactus*); i.e. it is swung from the arms of one player to those of another so fast that a beholder cannot follow the throws. For *fallo* = 'cause to escape notice' cf. Ov. *Fast.* III, 22 *et sua diuina furta fefellit ope* (Mars lay with Ilia without her knowing it); *Met.* VIII, 578 *spatium discrimina fallit* (distance obscures the fact that there is a gap between two eminences). This interpretation supposes a game in which the ball is thrown from player to player with the intention that it should be dexterously caught and passed on or back. (*b*) The ball, because it is thrown quickly (*per ueloces iactus*), baffles the arms (*fallit bracchia*) of a player who is trying to intercept it. For the hyperbaton (disjointed word-order) cf. above III, iv, 18 *et subter captos arma sedere duces*; *Copa* 4 *ad cubitum raucos excutiens calamos* (of a castanet-dancer accompanied by a pipe-player). Such word-order may have descriptive value, especially in a scene of rapid and confused action; cf. above III, ii, 12 and below III, xvii, 25 and notes. In this case the game in question will be one such as the *harpastum*, on which see E. N. Gardiner, *Athletics of the Ancient World*, p. 232, and Martial, IV, xix, 6 and VII, xxxii, 10.

6. uersi...trochi: 'the bowling hoop'.

clauis adunca: the rod with a hooked end, used to keep the hoop running and to steer it.

7. puluerulentaque ad extremas stat femina metas: 'and women stand dust-grimed at the end of the track'. The *metae*, primarily the turning posts in the circus where chariots raced, here either stand by metonymy for the 'ends' of the running track, or are posts or pillars marking these ends (or the several stations of the runners). *stat* naturally suggests runners lined up for a start; and so *extremas* apparently refers here to the starting 'end'. (This may seem strange, because the common use of *meta* for 'goal' or 'end' of an enterprise comes to mind, and *extremos* to our ears suggests *the* end of a race, rather than *an* end of the track. But the end of a race does not seem likely to be meant here.)

puluerulenta: pictorially descriptive of an athlete; as they oiled themselves before exercising, they would soon be coated with the dust and sand thrown up by their activities, for an example of which cf. Mart. IV, xix, 6 and VII, xxxii, 10 *harpasta ...puluerulenta*. (Some athletes, especially wrestlers, actually dusted themselves with a powder of some kind of dry earth. This too would be among the associations of *puluerulenta* in an athletic context.)

9. ad caestum: 'for boxing'.

* **gaudentia:** with *loris*.

10. orbe: the circle described by the hand in throwing the *discus*.

11. gyrum: the ring around which horses were ridden in training.

[**15–16.** This couplet is misplaced in the MSS, interrupting the comparisons introduced by *qualis...qualis* (lines 13 and 17) and making pointless the first *et* in line 17. Some insert 15–16 after 10, others after 12. The latter transposition is adopted here; it gives a good rhythm by reserving the long sentence 15–16 to the end of the series of sentences that compose 9–16; though it does not (like the alternative transposition) make the military activities climax of the description. The omission of 15–16, preliminary to its reinsertion in the wrong place, could be due to the homoeoteleuton *canis* (16)–*caput* (12).]

15. Taygeti: Taygetus is the mountain above Sparta.

16. patrios...canis: the Laconian hounds being a well-known breed.

13–14. qualis...lauatur etc.: the sense is not 'like Amazons bathing...', but 'like the Amazons, who bathe...'.

14. Thermodontiacis...aquis: the river Thermodon in Cappadocia, original home of the Amazons.

17. qualis et...Pollux et Castor: the comparison is less with C. and P. than with the group consisting of them *and their sister* (19–20).

18. uictor...futurus: 'soon to be victorious'. They are thought of as training.

pugnis: here from *pugnus* = 'fist'.

19. capere (fertur): for the present infinitive in indirect speech indicating a time past relative to the main verb, cf. Catull. lxiv, 124 ff. *saepe illam perhibent...fudisse...conscendere...procurrere...dixisse.*

Helene: this 'tradition' (*fertur*) about her is no doubt invented by the poet; cf. on III, viii, 29–30.

20. nec fratres erubuisse: not (here) 'ashamed *of*', but 'ashamed *before*'.

21. igitur: representing what follows as corollary of what has gone before.

lex...uetat: it is not clear whether Propertius is alleging that 'the law at Sparta forbids', or only that 'custom at Sparta does not require' (which would involve an exceptional treatment of *uetat* as = *non iubet*).

secedere: 'withdraw', i.e. hide themselves; or perhaps 'be separated'.

22. suae: referring to the third person implied with *licet*, and so 'one's'.

25. nullo praemisso: without any (*nullo* masc.) intermediary paving the way; cf. Sen. *Exc. Contr.* II, 6 *quodam modo ad luxuriam a patre praemissus sum*, and the words *de rebus tute...ipse tuis* which follow here.

loquaris: potential or jussive subjective: 'you can...'.

26. longae nulla repulsa morae: 'rebuff and long delay', the rebuff being regarded as identical with the delay, and the construction being as in Virg. *Aen.* I, 27 *spretae...iniuria formae*; for the wording cf. Plin. *Pan.* 91, 2 *similis repulsae mora*.

27. errantia lumina fallunt: i.e. deceive the eyes and lead them into error, *errantia* being proleptic.

28. cura molesta comae: over-elaborate dressing of the hair. For *cura* of hair cf. Val. Fl. VIII, 237–8 *ac sua flauis reddita cura comis*. Here *molestus* is to be understood of that which is displeasing because overdone. [*comae* is conjecture: the tradition gives *domi*. Moreover *N* gives *adoratae* where the other branch of the tradition gives *odoratae*. Some doubt must still attach to the reading here.]

29. nostra: 'the Roman women' = 'our Roman women'. For *nostra* in this sense cf. II, xxv, 44 *uidistis nostras*.

30. nec digitum...uia: evidently a colloquial expression; it must mean here 'you can't find a hole big enough to slip even a finger through'. The construction is uncertain: I suppose that *est* = 'it is possible' and that *angusta...uia* is ablative of way by which.

31. facies: either this here = *forma*, with *rogandi*, and so 'manner' or 'style'; or we are told that 'you can't discover what she really looks like'.

32. caecum uersat...iter = 'turns his going blindly this way and that', i.e. 'gropes his way in the dark'.

33. pugnasque: apparently *pugnas* here stands for *palaestram*, and (probably) *iura...pugnasque* by a hendiadys for *iura... palaestrae*. For *pugna* said of boxing cf. Virg. *Aen.* V, 365 *pugnae proponit honorem* (prizes for boxing).

XV

The occasion, real or imagined, of this elegy (a fit of jealousy in the poet's mistress) is not stated directly (as for instance is the occasion of III, x above), but is allowed to become apparent (as for instance is also the occasion of III, vi above) from the words supposed to be spoken by the poet as his part of a dialogue. This speech provides the setting for a mythological narrative thirty-two lines long, introduced as a warning example; in this respect the present elegy resembles I, 20.

1. Sic ego non ... norim, etc.: the wish-formula reinforcing an affirmation or request (here an affirmation, which follows in lines 3–10); 'so may I never...'.

non...iam: 'never again...'; there has been a scene.

2. nec ueniat sine te nox uigilanda mihi: 'and may it never (again) befall me to have to lie sleepless all night, deprived of you'. Probably the force of *iam* in line 1 continues with *nec* in this line, and we are to understand that the speaker *has* just been punished in the way he describes.

3–10. The poet's statement consists of an admission (3–6) followed by a protestation overriding the admission (7–10). The emphasis given by lines 1–2 attaches to the protestation which concludes the whole.

3. ut: 'when'.

* **ut mihi praetexti pudor est releuatus amictus**: 'when the restraint of the bordered gown was lifted from me'. The *toga praetexta*, edged with purple, was worn by children of the upper orders until they were considered adult, when boys assumed the plain white *toga uirilis*. *pudor* is the feeling that you should not do (or have done) something. There were certain restrictions on his conduct, acknowledged by a boy, which did not apply to a grown man; and the state of boyhood is symbolized by the dress appropriate to it. *releuare* is found of liberation from a restraint at Ov. *Am.* I, vi, 25 *sic unquam longa releuere catena* (where the restraint removed is in the ablative); the simple verb *leuare* is found sometimes with the same construction (e.g. Virg. *Ec.* ix, 65 *ego hoc te fasce leuabo*), and sometimes also with the thing removed as direct object (e.g. Virg. *Aen.* II, 146–7 *ipse uiro...leuari uincla iubet Priamus*; and cf. Ov. *Tr.* II, 186 *pars erit e poena magna leuata mea*); there is thus nothing improbable about the construction *pudor est releuatus*. But note that *releuatus* is a conjecture. [The tradition has *praetexti* (or *-a*) *pudor est uelatus amictus*.]

4. amoris iter: 'the way of love'. For the associations of *iter* cf. on III, x, 32 above.

5–6. illa rudis animos per noctes conscia primas imbuit, heu nullis capta Lycinna datis: 'she was, indeed, my young heart's first instructress, sharing in secret those first nights of love—Lycinna, won (o innocence!) by no gifts of mine'. *imbuo* is used in various ways of doing anything or putting anything in use for the first time, and especially of first instruction or initiation. For the special sense of *noctes* cf. III, vi, 34, III, viii, 39, etc. *heu* conveys emotion, not necessarily (though often) grief; it takes its tone from the context. In this context the emotive thought is of the innocent spontaneity of Lycinna (evidently a maidservant), compared with the calculating acquisitiveness of other women the speaker has known. *rudis* is acc. pl. with *animos*.

[**7–8.** This couplet is here printed with the punctuation customary in recent editions. Elsewhere (e.g. II, xvi, 33–4 and II, xx, 21–2) Propertius favours a construction of the type exemplified in Cic. *Fam.* xv, 14 *multi anni sunt cum ille in aere meo est*; and as anacoluthic varieties of this occur—e.g. Plaut. *Aul.* 4 *hanc domum multos annos est quom possideo*—it seems possible that some colloquial variety of the same is present here, and that line 7 should be read without brackets and assuming the common ellipsis of *quam* exemplified in Vell. Pat. II, 82, 3 *haud minus pars quarta*, etc. But this cannot be determined.]

* **11. testis erit, etc.:** Propertius several times elsewhere uses *testis* to introduce an example from mythology to illustrate a point he has just made: cf. II, xiii, 52–3 (love should continue though the loved one die) *testis cui niueum quondam percussit Adonem...aper*; II, xxvi, 46–7 (Neptune too knows love) *testis Amymone...*; III, xix, 5–11 (women's wanton passions are uncontrollable) *testis Cretaei fastus quae passa iuuenci....* Here the example of Dirce does not illustrate anything that has been said in lines 1–10, and so a problem arises.

Three solutions are offered: (1) Something has fallen out between lines 10 and 11. This is always possible. (2) Lines 43–6 should be transposed to stand between 10 and 11, either as they are, or (better) in the order 45–6–43–4 (45–6 completing the protestations of 1–10, 43–4 introducing the narrative of 11–41). The couplet 43–4 then affords an excellent cue for *testis* in line 11; and if the original occasion of the poem now remains un-recollected at its end, this is also true of III, xi, III, xiii, III, xix, etc. On the other hand, the pointing of the moral at the end in 43–6 corresponds to what is done in the similar Elegy I, xx; and the lines 43–6 fit their position at the end, as given by the MSS, extremely well. (3) We may suppose that *testis erit* is used here, somewhat otherwise than in the passages quoted above, to introduce an example favouring the speaker's general purpose (to dissuade his mistress from jealousy) rather than one illus-trating the particular statement he has just made; or, perhaps, in answer to a demand supposed but not stated to have been made (e.g. that Lycinna should be maltreated in some way), just as lines 1–10 answer a complaint supposed but not stated (that Propertius has relations with Lycinna still). On this view *testis erit Dirce* could be here translated 'Think of Dirce...', and begins a new paragraph of Propertius' speech.

The text here printed is spaced, before and after the story of Dirce, so as to prejudice as little as possible the choice between the above possibilities.

[The MSS begin a new elegy after line 11, but this does not seem possible. The authority of the MSS in this department is far from decisive; e.g. *N* joins Elegies x and xi of Book IV, the other branch of the tradition joins xx and xxi of Book I, etc.]

11–12. testis...crimine...accubuisse: the accusative-and-infinitive construction in the pentameter gives the content of the *crimen*; it is not to be construed after *testis erit*, regarding which see above.

Dirce...Antiopen: the legend of Antiope and Dirce is given in two somewhat different forms by Hyginus, *Fab.* 7 and 8. Features of both appear in the version followed by Propertius here. According to Hyginus, *Fab.* 8, Antiope, daughter of Nycteus, was seduced by Jupiter. She gave birth to Amphion and Zethus; the infants were exposed on Mount Cithaeron. Persecuted for a long time by Dirce, wife of Lycus, king of Thebes, Antiope escaped at last, and sought refuge at a farmstead or shepherd's hut on Cithaeron, where Amphion and Zethus, now grown up, were living; they had been found and reared by a herdsman. They did not know that the fugitive was their mother, and Zethus was for turning her away. Dirce arrived and tried to seize Antiope. Recognition between mother and sons came about through the rustic who had brought the

boys up. Amphion and Zethus avenged their mother's mal-
treatment by tying Dirce to a bull, to be dragged to her death;
this is the subject of the famous sculpture-group known as the
Farnese Bull.

11. tam sero crimine: in the version of the story in
Hyginus, *Fab.* 7, Antiope had been wife of Lycus who put her
away, later marrying Dirce. To suppose that Dirce was jealous
and suspicious over a *past* relationship agrees with Propertius'
own defence in lines 3–10 above. [*sero* is conjecture; the MSS
tradition has *uero.*]

12. accubuisse: in other authors *accumbo* is usually said of
reclining at table; in Propertius several times of lying with a
bedfellow; cf. 11, iii, 30, 11, xxx, 36, 11, xxxii, 36, also Tib. 1, ix, 75.

[**13. uulsit:** is an emendation; the tradition has *ussit.*]

17. tenebris: used sometimes of a sunless room, hovel,
dungeon, etc.; cf. Juv. iii, 224 *quanti nunc tenebras unum con-
ducis in annum.*

18. ieiunae...negauit aquam: a compressed way of saying
that she kept her hungry and even denied her water too.

22. inuocet Antiope quem nisi uincta Iouem?: read *quem
nisi* with *Iouem*, and *uincta* with *Antiope*.

25. arces: 'heights'.

27. uaga: i.e. 'as she fled, not knowing whither'.

30. stabulis mater abacta suis: i.e. driven *by her own son*
from the cottage that *should have welcomed her*; the possessive
implies the sense of the words in italics. For a somewhat
similar use of the possessive, cf. 1, iii, 37 *meae...noctis* = 'the
night that should have been passed with me'. *stabulum* or
stabula is said in various contexts of the quarters of animals or
primitive dwellings of men, the translation depending on the
context; it is also said of inns.

32. [Eurus ubi aduerso etc. incorporates an emendation; see
App. Crit.]

*   **33. litore sub tacito:** perhaps 'down on the shore'; or 'on
the edge of the shore', as the shore slopes downward towards the
sea. For other remarkable uses of *sub* cf. III, ix, 36 *sub exiguo
flumine*; Ov. *Trist.* I, iii, 19 *Libycis...sub oris.* [*sub* here is a
conjecture; the MS tradition has *sic*, which is wanted in the
following line but not here.]

35. sera, tamen pietas: with this punctuation *uenit* or *fuit*
has to be supplied twice, to yield the sense *sera uenit pietas, sed*

tamen uenit. [Alternatively the line could be punctuated *sera tamen pietas, natis . . .*, and *sera pietas* taken in apposition to the sentence *natis est cognitus error*.]

36. senex: the man who had found and reared the boys, and now made them and their mother known to one another.

39. cognosce: i.e. 'behold the hand of Jupiter'.

42. Amphion: by the musical art here exhibited he also built the wall of Thebes, charming the stones to move into position of their own accord.

Aracynthe: evidently to be understood as an eminence on Cithaeron; cf. Virg. *Ec.* ii, 24 *Amphion Dircaeus in Actaeo Aracyntho*. The name Aracynthus occurs elsewhere only with reference to a mountain in Aetolia.

44. uestra: 'of you women'.

46. amem etc.: 'though I were ashes, burned on my funeral pyre, I still would love you, you alone'.

XVI

This elegy (a soliloquy) falls into three parts. The poet has been summoned (1–10) by his mistress to come to Tibur immediately. As it is night (and the road is unlit and infested by highwaymen) he ponders before complying, weighing the hazard against the displeasure of the woman. Then (11–20) he reflects on a commonplace of love-poetry, that the lover is immune from ordinary perils such as robbers. Finally (21–30) he pleases himself with the prospect of his mistress mourning his death, if die he should, and with thoughts about how he could wish to be buried. The disposition of the piece is thus symmetrical, in groups of ten lines each.

2. iussit adesse: the phrase has (though not inevitably) associations which make 'ordered me to report (or, present myself) at Tibur' a fair translation.

3. candida...turris: the reference is uncertain. *candida... culmina* could refer to white buildings, or to hills with white buildings on them; *turris* (acc. pl.) could be any tall buildings, cf. III, xxi, 15 below *Romanae turres...ualeatis*; the *culmina* and the *turris* may be identical or distinct.

4. et cadit in...lacus: the celebrated waterfalls. *nympha Aniena* stands for the water of the river Anio.

5. mene: for another postponement of *ne* cf. III, vi, 12 above.

6. ut timeam audaces in mea membra manus: i.e. to go in fear of ruffianly assaults (upon my person).

7. nostro timore: evidently 'fear for myself', much as at IV, vii, 65 *maternis...catenis* means 'chains endured (by Andromeda) on her mother's account'.

8. nocturno fletus saeuior hoste mihi: 'for me her tears are a fiercer foe than any that prowls by night', i.e. I am more afraid of her tears than of highwaymen.

11–20. For this topic, the lover's immunity from ordinary perils, cf. Tib. I, ii, 25–8.

12. Scironis: Sciron was a ruffian who terrorized travellers on the road between Athens and Megara. He made them wash his feet, and shoved them over a precipice as they did so. Theseus killed him.

sic: i.e. on (or in) this condition (the lover's).

media...uia: here *media* is not to be understood literally but gives by implication a certain tone to the statement: 'walk *boldly* along the road where Sciron lurks'; cf. (I think) IV, vii, 83 *media...scribe columna* 'write on my gravestone, *plain for all to read*'.

15. ministrat iter: 'lights his way', in the role of the servant who attends his master with torch or lantern.

16. percutit: shakes (the torch) vigorously to keep it alight. (*percutio* commonly means 'strike'; here, if the text is correct, it is an intensive of *quatio*.)

17. canum rabies...auertit: cf. III, v, 4 *nec bibit...nostra sitis*, and on III, xii, 11.

19. sanguine tam paruo: for the enfeebled state of the lover cf. I, v, 21–2, II, xii, 17, IV, v, 64; for 'scanty blood' (anaemia) as a symptom of feebleness cf. Val. Max. III, 8, 5 *propter exiguum senilemque sanguinem meum*. The conception is shifting slightly; the lover is now pathetic as well as sacred (line 11).

20. exclusis fit comes ipsa Venus: the poet is not *exclusus* (forbidden access to his mistress) in the situation that gives rise to this elegy; and the lover has been described in 11–18 as enjoying immunity simply as a lover, whether *exclusus* or not. But in line 19 the lover's immunity has begun to be attributed to his pathetic condition; and 'exclusion' and 'immunity' are juxtaposed in Tibullus I, ii, 7ff. and 25–8, passages which Propertius had somewhere in his mind when writing this elegy.

21. quod si certa meos sequerentur funera casus: 'but if the end of this perilous venture for me were certain death'. For *casus* = 'perils' cf. Plin. *Ep.* VI, 20, 1 (*cognoscere*) *quos ego...non solum metus uerum etiam casus pertulerim.*

22. talis mors pretio uel sit emenda mihi: 'why, I ought gladly (*literally* even) to pay for (the privilege of) such a death'; because his mistress will see that he has died for love of her.

23. unguenta: poured on the body on the pyre; cf. II, xiii, 29-30 *osculaque in gelidis pones suprema labellis, cum dabitur Syrio munere plenus onyx* (where the *pompa* has just been described, and the ignition of the pyre follows); and IV, vii, 32 *cur nardo flammae non oluere meae?*

24. custos: a metaphor; she will always be there, tending and as if watching over the grave.

25. terra...frequenti: i.e. lay my bones in the *ground* (*terra*) in a public *place* (*loco*), where there is always a busy flow of people passing by. Roadside burial was common.

27. infamantur: i.e. are made object of jibes or censorious comment.

29. aut humer...cumulus uallatus harenae: i.e. or let my grave be a little mound of soil with a fence around it.

harenae: this could mean either sand, suggesting the sea-shore, or any dry and sandy kind of soil.

ignotae: either (*a*) 'nameless'—heaped into a mound only, with no stone and no inscription; or (*b*) 'in a remote place'. Both senses are present. [*cumulus* has slight MS authority; the tradition favours *cumulis*. But the difference palaeographically is negligible, and *cumulus* yields better sense: namely the picture of a small mound (*cumulus*), enclosed by a fence (*uallatus*) of some kind, and having thus the properties of a modest but decent grave; cf. Tac. *Ann.* XIV, 9 (of the improper burial of Agrippina) *neque, dum Nero rerum potiebatur, congesta aut clausa humus* (i.e. no mound or fence). This is exactly what is wanted in the context. By contrast, an enclosure made by a number of heaps or mounds is not easy to conceive, and loses the distinctive sense of *uallatus* ('fenced', with posts or the like). To express the idea 'may my tomb be a little mound' by saying 'may I be buried as a little mound' would not be unusual language for Propertius.]

30. in media nomen habere uia: 'to have my name (or story) published on the highway'. *nomen habere* is often a phrase for 'be famous'; here the name on a gravestone is also in mind. For the force of *media* cf. on line 12 above; here its value evidently is 'in full view' or the like.

XVII

A prayer to the wine-god to bring rest to the love-tormented poet. The prayer proper (1–12 and 41–2) encloses a promise of the poet's grateful service (13–40) if the prayer is fulfilled. This service will consist partly in vine-growing (15–18), but chiefly in poetic tributes (21–40). The poetry will partly (21–8) recite the legends associated with the god, and partly (29–38) depict the god himself being honoured with music and sacrifice. It will be noticed that in lines 29–38 the poet does not say 'I will depict you as...' or 'I will tell how you...' but states directly, 'you will...'. That he means thereby 'in my poem you will...' is shown by the context in general and by lines 39–40 in particular.

1. aduoluimur: 'prostrate myself at...'.

2. pacato: this (as the text stands) has to be taken predicatively; i.e. 'calm me and give me a fair voyage' = 'give me calm and a fair voyage'. *pacatus* (which most commonly means 'peaceable' or 'no longer hostile') here is almost exactly equivalent to *quietus*, as in Lucr. v, 1203 *pacata posse omnia mente tueri*, and refers to the calm of a mind no longer disturbed by passion. The same word in Ov. *Her.* x, 65 *pacata per aequora* is said of calm seas, and thus here also suits the metaphor introduced by *uela*. A storm that needs to be calmed is in the poet's soul.

uela secunda: 'a fair voyage'; for the expression cf. on the one hand the familiar *uenti secundi* and on the other Virg. *Aen.* I, 156 *curru...secundo*; the idea is of a progress not simply swift, but easy and untroubled. Here the context shows that the thought expressed by the metaphor is: 'bring rest to my tormented soul and let me live in peace henceforth'.

3. insanae Veneris flatus: 'the stormy blasts of raging passion'. For the image of the storm-tossed lover cf. III, xxiv, 15–17 below. [*flatus* is conjecture; an alternative conjecture is *fluctus*, for which cf. Ov. *Tr.* I, ii, 87 (o winds) *tantos compescite fluctus*. The tradition gives *fastus*. But as lines 2 and 4 show, the thought at this point is not of love as a tormenting agent needing to be rebuffed but of love as a disturbance in the soul needing to be stilled. Moreover, rage (cf. *insanae*) and disdain (*fastus*) belong to conceptions of love which, though both common, are distinct.]

7. non...rudem: not without experience (sc. of love).

7–8. in astris...Ariadna: Bacchus took Ariadne (deserted by Theseus) to heaven as his bride, and made her crown into a constellation. Hence she is said to 'bear witness in the starry sky that...'.

lyncibus: drawing Bacchus' chariot. With *uecta* we understand *lyncibus* as = 'lynx-drawn chariot', just as *equis* often = 'chariot and horses'.

10. funera: a common poetic plural, and a common metonymy for 'death'. Supply *mea* from *mihi* in line 9.

11. uacuos: left desolate.

12. spesque timorque animos uersat utroque toro: 'and hope and fear torment their hearts as they shift restlessly in bed from one side to the other'. For the compressed expression cf. on III, xvi, 25 above. For the ideas compressed cf. Liv. XXV, 3, 17 *metus pudorque animum uersabat*; Prop. II, xvii, 3–4 *quotiens desertus amaras expleui noctes fractus utroque toro*; II, xxii, 47 *quanta illum toto uersant suspiria lecto*. [*animos... utroque toro* is conjecture: the tradition has *animo* (evidently a slip) ...*utroque modo*. But neither of the available meanings of *utroque modo*—'in both ways' and 'in either case'—will do here.]

13. per feruida tempora: this must form a single phrase with *tuis...donis*: 'by your gift (working) in my heated temples (*or* brain)'; cf. Ov. *Am.* I, vi, 37 *modicum circa mea tempora uinum*.

15. pangam...collis: sc. *uitibus*; for the construction cf. that of *sero* in Ov. *A.A.* II, 668 *iste serendus ager*. Normally *pango* and *sero* have acc. of the plant planted or seed sown.

16. quos carpent nullae...ferae: for *carpo* = 'strip' or 'browse on' with *collis* for object (instead of the forage consumed) cf. Ov. *Her.* xvi, 53–6 *est locus...qui nec ouis placidae... nec patulo tardae carpitur ore bouis*; perhaps also Virg. *Georg.* III, 324–5 *rura carpamus...* = (according to Servius *ad loc.*) 'let us graze...', the shepherds causing their beasts to graze the meadows being said to do so themselves. [The MSS have *carpant*.]

me uigilante: this carries an emphasis: 'and I will myself keep good guard to see that no...'.

17. dum modo: this here virtually = 'that my...may not

fail to. . .'; the connexion of thought between the couplets 15–16
and 17–18 being 'no trouble will be too great for me personally
to take, if only I can ensure that. . .'. For the value of *dum modo*
required cf. Varro, *R.R.* III, 17, 9 *tanta ardebat cura, ut archi-*
tecto permiserit uel ut suam pecuniam consumeret, dummodo per-
duceret specus e piscinis in mare. [Some editors place a full stop
at the end of 16 and attach 17–18 to 19–20. But this makes the
poet promise Bacchus his poetry in return for a good wine
harvest, whereas in fact the poetry (and the viticulture) are
promised to ensure sleep and rest from love.]

[**tumeant** (cf. *Aetna* 271 *tumeant ut dolia musto*) is conjecture;
the tradition has *numen* or the like. An alternative conjecture
is *spument*.]

19. per te et tua cornua uiuam: cf. Plaut. *M.G.* 1051 *quae*
per tuam nunc uitam uiuit, where complete devotion and
dependence seem to be meant.

cornua: the strength that wine gives; cf. Hor. *Od.* III, xxi, 18
(addressing a wine-jar) *addis cornua pauperi.* (Also relevant is
the fact that Bacchus was sometimes represented with horns.)

21. maternos Aetnaeo fulmine partus: 'how your mother
bore you, (blasted) by the Aetnaean bolt'. When Bacchus'
mother Semele was consumed by the lightning which attended
Jupiter's manifestation of himself, the unborn Bacchus was
saved (and incubated in Jupiter's thigh). The epithet *Aetnaeo*
alludes to the idea that the thunderbolts were made for Jupiter
by Vulcan and his Cyclopes in a forge under Mount Aetna;
cf. Virg. *Aen.* VIII, 416 ff. The ablative in *Aetnaeo fulmine* may
be of cause, or of manner, or of attendant circumstance; the
value of some verb has to be supplied in thought to connect it
with *partus*. Such ellipses are characteristic of Propertius; for
an example with a prepositional phrase cf. line 13 above; for
other examples with the plain ablative cf. III, xi, 55 above
tanto. . .ciue; III, xxii, 13 below *Argoa. . .columba*; I, xix, 19
quae tu. . .mea possis sentire fauilla.

22. Nysaeis: *Nysa* was an apocryphal mountain, scene in
legend of Bacchus' childhood.

choris: the host of dancing worshippers who attended Bacchus
in his triumphal (and bloodless) progress through India.

23. uesanumque noua nequiquam in uite Lycurgum:
'and Lycurgus' vain fury against the invader vine'. Lycurgus as
king of Thrace opposed the worship of Bacchus. He was made

mad, and, thinking to hew down vines, cut off his own legs and killed his own son. *in* here is with ablative and refers to the object in respect of which one feels or behaves in a given way; cf. III, viii, 28, III, xix, 28.

24. Pentheos in triplices funera rapta greges: i.e. 'and Pentheus' death, torn three ways asunder by the three (maenad) bands'. Pentheus king of Thebes opposed, like Lycurgus, the worship of Bacchus; he was torn in pieces by three bands of Maenads led respectively by his mother Agave and her sisters Ino and Autonoe. *funera* by metonymy can mean either 'death' or 'corpse'. The idea of *in triplices...rapta greges* is that the three bands tug each in its own direction. [*rapta* is conjecture; the tradition has *grata*. But *gratus* with *in* and acc. is attested only for the phrase *in uulgus*, and appears to mean 'popular with', 'pleasing to' or the like. This is not strong enough for the present context. In II, xxxiv, 40 the *ruina* of Capaneus is *grata Ioui* because it avenges an insult.]

25. curuaque Tyrrhenos etc.: the interlacing of the two noun-epithet combinations (in apposition) helps to suggest the confused scene, and the suddenness of the metamorphosis.

26. pampinea: i.e. vine-*clad*; the epithet is only intelligible in this special sense by one who knows the story. The story is that Bacchus in human form was travelling on a ship, and the crew plotted to sell him as a slave. When he disclosed himself, the sailors went mad and leapt into the sea, becoming dolphins, and the ship was suddenly overgrown with vines. For the epithet acquiring a particular sense from its context cf. III, VI, 26 *staminea*.

27. et tibi...Naxon: 'and fragrant streams flowing through Naxos in obedience to your will (*or* in your honour)....'. There was supposed to be a spring of wine on the island of Naxos.

28. potant...turba: the plural verb with collective singular noun, as not uncommonly.

29–38. This is a tableau, which the poet will describe in verse (cf. lines 39–40 below, and introductory note above).

29. onerato: sc. *tibi*.

laxatis: 'loose'; evidently the participle here has become a pure adjective, without verbal force; cf. III, xiii, 25 *pacata* etc.

corymbis: clusters of ivy-berries; implying here garlands of ivy, as the context shows.

30. Bassaricas: the βασσάρα was a garment of fox-skin worn by Bacchic worshippers; hence *Bassaricus* (like *Nysaeus* in line 22 above) is applicable to anything associated with Bacchus.

mitra: a head-dress made by winding a strip of material around the head, with a result resembling sometimes a head-band, sometimes a turban.

33. mollia...tympana: 'the wanton tambour', so called because used by Bacchic worshippers to accompany their ecstatic dances.

Thebae: standing here for Theban Bacchants; Bacchants being thought of as typically Theban because of the story of Bacchus' birth, of Pentheus, etc.

Dircaeae: a general epithet of Thebes (where there was a fountain called Dirce), but suggesting Bacchants (see on *Thebae* above) because of the story of Queen Dirce; cf. Hyginus, *Fab.* 7 *ex cuius corpore in monte Cithaerone fons est natus, qui Dircaeus est appellatus, beneficio Liberi, quod eius Baccha fuerat.* For more about this Dirce see on III, xv, 11 above.

34. calamo...hiante: apparently 'the vocal pipe'; for cf. II, xxxi, 6 *carmen hiare* (of a singer).

35. uertice turrigero: Cybele, Mother of the gods, is depicted with a battlemented crown. She is introduced here because her worship was orgiastic like that of Bacchus.

iuxta = 'nearby' (adverb).

dea magna: with conscious or subconscious allusion to the other name of Cybele, *Magna Mater*.

Cybebe: this is the form long customary in editions when metre requires the penultimate to be long. But here, as also in III, xxii, 3 and IV, xi, 51, the tradition gives *Cybelle* (or *Cybēle*) and one of these should perhaps be kept.

36. ad: 'to accompany...'.

rauca: evidently to describe a low or reverberant note; cf. on III, x, 23.

37. antistitis auro: i.e. by means of the golden ladle of the priest.

38. libabit: subject is the *crater*, said to pour the libation because the wine for this is drawn from it. [*libabit* is an emendation, for the tradition's *libatum*. It is not indispensable but seems probable.]

39–40. qualis...: as if in the previous line we had '*non imbecillo spiritu, sed tali...*'. *coturnus* (tragic buskin) and *spiritus* are both metaphors for the same thing—an elevated style.

* **41. seruitio uacuum me siste:** cf. Virg. *Aen.* IV, 634 *huc siste sororem*; the sense must be 'present someone in a given place or condition'.

42. hoc sollicitum...caput: we should rather say 'troubled heart'. *caput* here represents, as often, a person; cf. II, ix, 26 *capite hoc* (you), III, x, 18 *meum...caput* (me), IV, xi, 9–10 *nostrum...caput* (me); Plaut. *Pseud.* 723 *siquidem hoc uiuet caput* (I); Ov. *Tr.* III, iii, 45 *caput hoc barbara terra teget* (me), etc. It will be noticed that in all these instances life, death, or condition of the person is in question. Elsewhere an adjective is attached to *caput*, e.g. II, i, 36 *fidele caput* (Maecenas), III, xi, 3 *ignauum caput* (by implication, of the poet), IV, xi, 55 *dulce caput* (the speaker's mother); cf. Virg. *Aen.* IV, 354 *capitisque iniuria cari* (said by Aeneas of Ascanius); IV, 613 *infandum caput* (said by Dido of Aeneas). In all these instances the attached adjective is one that has an emotive value.

XVIII

A lament, like Elegy vii; this time for M. Claudius Marcellus, son of Augustus' sister Octavia and husband of his daughter Julia, who died at Baiae in 23 or 22 B.C. at the age of about 18; cf. Virg. *Aen.* VI, 860–86 and Servius *ad loc.* The poem falls into three groups of ten lines apiece (each developing a rhetorical *locus* usual in this kind of discourse), followed by a four-line conclusion: 1–10 reproachful apostrophizing of Baiae; 11–20 pathetic reflexions on the contrast between Marcellus' fortunate position and sudden death; 21–30 reflexions on the inevitability of death for all men; 31–4 but Marcellus has surely been translated directly to heaven, like his ancestor the conqueror of Syracuse and like Julius Caesar. This consolation, which renders no longer applicable some of the pathetic reflexions which have preceded, may strike a modern reader as implausible; and so it is, but only in the same sense as the consolation at the end of *Lycidas*. It may also seem remarkable that Marcellus is nowhere *named* in the poem; it is not necessary that he should be, since his death is in everyone's mind, being of such recent occurrence that (cf. lines 10 and 32) the funeral has not yet taken place.

1. Clausus ab umbroso...Auerno: 'enclosed by shady Avernus'; for *ab* with an inanimate thing treated as an agent

cf. on III, v, 14. (That here is meant 'enclosed by...' and not
'shut out from...' we can be sure, because the exclusion of the
sea from Avernus, an inland lake, could hardly attract mention;
whereas the admission of the sea *to* Avernus, by the making
of the *Portus Iulius* in 37 B.C., could obviously do so, and
did in Virg. *Georg.* II, 163–4. Moreover, the epithet *umbroso* is
pointless unless part of the same scene as *ludit pontus*.)

ludit: as we say 'dances'. The word (*a*) is pictorial (and cf.
umbroso), and (*b*) contrasts the permanent innocence of the sea-
water in the inland harbour with the occasional violence of the
sea outside.

2. fumida Baiarum stagna tepentis aquae: 'Baiae's
steaming pools of warm water'; we might say 'Baiae's warm
springs and steaming pools'. The phrase is a vocative in syntax
(cf. line 7) and (cf. line 8) signifies Baiae itself, the warm springs
being that place's characteristic attribute. In lines 1, 3 and 4 are
mentioned notable places in Baiae's immediate neighbourhood.
It stood in the north-west corner of the gulf of Naples, between
the promontory of Misenum (cf. line 3 and Virg. *Aen.* VI, 234)
and the Lucrine lake (which was skirted on the seaward side by
the causeway mentioned in line 4 below, and adjoined on the
landward side by lake Avernus). [*fumida* is a generally received
emendation of the tradition's *humida*.]

3. iacet: i.e. lies buried, cf. Virg. *Aen.* VI, 234. (*et* in this
line has, I think, the value 'also'.)

4. et sonat...uia: 'and where runs the echoing causeway
which Hercules laboured to build'. This causeway, supposed to
have been made by Hercules, was pierced by Agrippa when he
made the *Portus Iulius* in 37 B.C. By cutting a connexion on the
other side between the Lucrine lake and lake Avernus he made
the latter too accessible from the sea; cf. on line 1 above. *sonat*
might refer to the breaking of the sea against the embankment;
but more likely it refers to the noise of traffic on the highway
(cf. IV, vii, 4 *murmur...uiae*), amplified perhaps by being heard
across the water.

5. mortalis: acc. plural, with *urbes*, and here meaning 'of
mortal men'.

dexter cum quaereret: 'visited with good will'. For
quaerere = 'visit' cf. I, iv, 20 *nec te quaeret*.

6. Thebano...deo: Hercules and Bacchus both had Theban
mothers, Alcmene and Semele. Hercules in legend visited Baiae

(cf. line 4); it is clearly implied here that Bacchus did so too. Both *cymbala* and *deo* point away from Hercules to Bacchus, and his triumphal but pacific progress through the world; for the cymbal was not associated with Hercules, and Hercules at the time of his travels was not yet a god. It also seems likely, after the reference to Hercules in line 4, that a new person should now be in mind. We do not hear elsewhere of Bacchus visiting Baiae specifically, but we do (Sil. It. VII, 166–72 and ff.) of his coming to Campania.

7. **at nunc...Baiae:** 'but now become infamous, o Baiae, and guilty of a monstrous crime'; the vocative picks up the vocative of line 2.

8. **quis deus...hostis:** 'what malignant spirit'.

constitit: this could mean 'has taken up his abode in' or 'has posted himself in' (as it were, in ambush); one can fairly translate 'haunts' or 'lurks' (or 'lurked').

9. **his pressus Stygias uultum demisit in undas:** (?) 'by these waters undone, he turned his face to the Stygian waters below'. *his* is most easily understood as *his undis* (i.e. the lakes, etc., around Baiae, its distinctive attribute as shown by lines 1–2 and 8), in contrast with the *Stygias undas*; and the waters of Baiae are said to have undone Marcellus simply because he died at Baiae, as for instance at IV, vi, 25 (*aciem geminos Nereus lunarat in arcus*) Nereus is said to have arrayed the fleets because they get arrayed on the surface of his sea. *pressus* suggests the metaphor 'overwhelmed' or 'drowned', but need mean no more than 'undone'. *uultum demisit* seems to be a variant of a (presumably current) phrase exemplified in Val. Max. IV, 6, 3 *nec dubito quin...Plautius et Orestilla fati consortione gestientes uultus tenebris intulerint*, where the idea must be of braving the darkness of death without flinching; here *uultum demisit* suggests a drowned body sinking (though it would not in fact sink face downward), as well as the descent of the spirit or shade into the world below. In *Stygias...undas* here the thought seems to be of the infernal rivers as symbolizing the world of the dead generally, and not of Styx as the boundary-river over which the souls are ferried. The waters about Baiae are conceived as a *way into* the world of the dead because lake Avernus is supposed to be fed directly by the infernal rivers.

10. **errat:** the dead man has not yet been buried, and his ghost still haunts the vicinity of his body or of the place where he died.

For *errare* of the spirits of the dead cf. Ov. *Fast.* II, 566, etc. (This idea is not inconsistent with the descent of the spirit to the underworld at death which was implied in the preceding line; for the spirit may hover to and fro between the two worlds until laid finally to rest by, e.g., proper burial. But in any case we must not expect a uniform eschatology in Propertius, or in any poet of his date; traditional ideas, often mutually inconsistent, are exploited as suits the poetic imagination at the moment.)

spiritus: 'soul', or 'spirit'; cf. Ov. *Tr.* III, iii, 61–2 *nam si morte carens uacua uolat altus in aura spiritus*; Val. Max. IV, 5, 6 *illud tempus, quo diuinus spiritus discernebatur a corpore*. (In another context the same words *errat...spiritus* etc. could signify vapours drifting over a lake, and such a picture may be somewhere in the poet's mind here too.)

spiritus ille: Marcellus does not need to be named. His death is in all men's minds.

uestro...lacu: perhaps Avernus, because of its association with the underworld (see on line 9); perhaps the Lucrine, as nearest to Baiae. *uestro* because the name *Baiae* is plural.

11–12. optima...mater: i.e. 'his mother's love'. *pater optimus, optima mater*, etc., are said of affectionate parents appreciated as such.

12. amplexum Caesaris esse focos: he had married Julia, Augustus' daughter, in 25 B.C. (Dio C. LIII, 28). *focos* stands here for 'household' and so 'family'.

13–14. aut modo etc.: i.e. 'and only the other day, the awnings rippling over the crowded theatre, and all the things his mother's care contrived'. The reference is to games given on a magnificent scale by Marcellus as aedile, in the year of his death; cf. Vell. Pat. II, 93 *magnificentissimo munere aedilitatis edito*; evidently Octavia bore the expenses. The reference to the awnings would recall not only the show in the theatre, but also the fact that the forum was shaded with awnings through that summer, *ut salubrius litigantes consisterent*, at the expense of Marcellus (Plin. *N.H.* XIX, 24) or of Augustus himself (Dio C. LIII, 31).

14. et per maternas omnia gesta manus: for the form of expression cf. I, vi, 24 *et lacrimis omnia nota meis*; for the meaning see previous note.

15. steterat: 'stopped' (before its end or on its way); the

pluperfect has here the value of a preterite. (Servius on *Aen.*
vi, 861 says that Marcellus died in his eighteenth year. He may
be wrong; or Propertius may be using a round figure *metri
gratia*.)

17. i nunc: the ironical exhortation with pathetic effect;
cf. iii, vii, 29 above.

19. Attalicas...uestis: Attalus of Pergamum invented a
method of weaving cloth of gold. *uestis* may refer to garments,
or coverlets, or woven stuff in general; here it probably refers to
hangings, for cf. ii, xxxii, 11–12 *Pompeia...porticus aulaeis
nobilis Attalicis*; Val. Max. ix, 1, 5 *Attalicis aulaeis contectos
parietes*.

19–20. magnis...ludis: the term *Ludi Magni* is applied
especially to the *Ludi Romani*, held in September each year, and
as here a particular occasion must be in mind, this must be the
Ludi Romani held by Marcellus as aedile in the year of his death
(cf. Vell. Pat. ii, 93 in note on lines 13–14 above).

21. huc: i.e. to death; the sense of a verb of motion has to be
supplied, as quite commonly, e.g. Tac. *Ann.* xiv, 8 *magis ac
magis anxia Agrippina quod nemo a filio*. [The MS tradition has
hoc (omnes).]

23. canis: i.e. of Cerberus.

24. torui...senis: i.e. of Charon.

publica: in which all must be carried (rich and poor alike;
cf. 21).

25. ille: either (*a*) 'yonder man' (one imagined for example's
sake, like the horse in Virg. *Georg.* iii, 120 *quamuis saepe fuga
uersos ille egerit hostes*, etc.), and *cautus* is adverbial with *condat*;
or (*b*) *ille cautus* is an idiomatic phrase, to be rendered 'your
cautious man', cf. Liv. xxxiv, 4, 14 *illa locuples*.

ferro...et aere: i.e. in a tower of brass like Danae in the
legend, or behind doors bound or bolted with iron and brass.

26. caput: cf. on iii, xvii, 42 above.

27. Nirea: a Greek accusative. Nireus was handsomest after
Achilles of all the Greeks at Troy (*Il.* ii, 673).

28. Pactoli: Pactolus was a gold-bearing river in Lydia.

29–30. hic olim ignaros...: 'such cause of mourning
ravaged too the nameless mass of the Achaeans long ago';
cf. 21 above *et ultimus ordo*. *ignaros* here = *ignotos*, as sometimes
elsewhere; cf. Servius on Virg. *Aen.* x, 706 *ignarum Laurens
habet ora Mimanta*. The reference is to the plague sent on the

Greeks by Apollo in *Il.* 1, 10 and 50 ff. [One could take *ignaros* as = 'ignorant (of the cause of their affliction)'; but it would then have no *useful* value in the present context.]

30. Atridae magno cum stetit alter amor: 'when for the second time his (*or* a fit of) love cost the son of Atreus dear'. The first time was when Agamemnon's love for Argynnus caused the delay at Aulis and subsequent sacrifice of Iphigenia (see III, vii, 21-4 above and note); the second was when his love for Chryseis (see *Il.* 1, 112 ff.) made him reject her father's entreaties, on which rejection followed the plague and the quarrel with Achilles (with heavy loss of life from both) and the payment of costly amends both to Chryseis' father and to Achilles. [In the above *Atridae* is taken as dative; it could alternatively be taken as genitive, leaving more emphasis on the cost *to others* of Agamemnon's extravagances. It would also be possible to take *alter amor* as 'a new love', regarding Clytaemnestra (cf. *Il.* 1, 112 ff.) as the first, and confining the bad effects to this (one) new love.]

31. nauta, pias...qui: here as elsewhere (IV, vii, 55 ff., IV, xi, 102 ff.) Propertius conceives the good and the bad as crossing the infernal river by separate ferries. (We need not look for consistency between the ideas involved in these lines 31-2 and those in lines 9-10 above; see note on line 10.)

32. huc animae portant corpus inane tuae: 'they are bringing hither (i.e. to Rome) an empty body, without a soul to be your passenger'. The 3rd person plural in *portant* is exactly the same as the anonymous 'they' which English uses in such a context. It appears that the poet writes when the funeral cortège is on its way from Baiae to Rome with Marcellus' body; cf. Serv. on *Aen.* VI, 861 *igitur cum ingenti pompa adlatus et in campo Martio est sepultus.* [*portant* is conjecture; the tradition has *portent*. Many editors keep *portent*, and read *suae* (a conjecture) for *tuae* at the end of the line.]

animae...tuae: the genitive is after *inane* = 'empty of...'. *tuae* is said because a dead person's spirit or shade is ordinarily the ferryman's prospective passenger, and it is said in much the same way as in I, iii, 37 *meae...noctis* is said by the speaker of a night which she considers hers by right when in fact it has been denied her; cf. Tib. I, ix, 77-8 *blanditiasne meas aliis tu uendere es ausus, tune aliis demens oscula ferre mea?* In this case, as will be explained in lines 33-4, the spirit of Marcellus will not cross the river in the world below with the spirits of all the rest of the dead (including those bound for the Elysian fields, as we find in IV, vii, 59–60, etc., and as implied by *pias* here in line 31), but has already been taken up into the sky (abode of gods) like the spirit of Julius Caesar and (we are told by Propertius here but by no other extant authority) the spirit of the greatest of the Marcelli of old.

animae: this has a double appropriateness here, because it is used in two senses in which 'soul' is used in English also, namely (*a*) a dead person's spirit, and (*b*) a person carried in a ship, as for instance 'there were about three hundred souls on board', and cf. Sen. *Contr.* VII, 1, 8 *nauigium uix unius capax animae.*

33–4. qua Siculae...in astra uia: 'by the same way as Claudius, conqueror of Sicily, by the same way as Caesar, he is gone from the ways of men to the starry sky'. Julius Caesar's soul was supposed to have departed to heaven in the form of the comet which appeared at the games held by Octavian in July of the year of Caesar's assassination (cf. Suet. *Jul.* 88; Dio C. XLV, 6–7; Plin. *N.H.* II, 93–4; Ov. *Met.* XV, 844 ff.). We do not hear elsewhere of a similar translation of the great Marcellus, and the suggestion here may be Propertius' own; according to one story (cf. Plutarch, *Marcellus, ad fin.*) Marcellus' body was never found after the action in which he met his death.

Siculae uictor telluris: M. Claudius Marcellus, winner of *spolia opima* from the Gaul Virdomarus in 222 B.C., conqueror of Syracuse in 212, killed in a skirmish near Venusia in 208.

ab humana...uia: this phrase is not found elsewhere, but cf. Hom. *Il.* III, 406 θεῶν δ' ἀπόεικε κελεύθου, and Ov. *Fast.* I, 248 *humanis numina mixta locis.* The sense is 'the ways of men'.

XIX

An essay on a general proposition—that women's passions are more extravagant than those of men; in its character as an essay it has something in common with, for example, Elegies xiii and xiv above. The proposition is stated in lines 1–4; it is reinforced in lines 5–10; it is illustrated in lines 11–22 by three legendary examples of unnatural passion and three of great crimes committed under passion's influence. In lines 23–8 the final example is discussed as a warning; but there is no back-reference at the end of the elegy to the proposition from which it took its beginning. For Ovid's treatment of the same theme, with several of the same examples, cf. *A.A.* 1, 281 ff.

1. a te: the unnamed woman may be imaginary.

1–2. nostra...uobis: referring to men and women respectively.

3. ubi contempti rupistis frena pudoris: i.e. when you no longer heed (the voice of) shame, and have broken its power to bridle your desires.

4. captae mentis: 'frenzy'; cf. Liv. xxxix, 13, 12 (*uiros*) *uelut mente capta...uaticinari*, and the phrases *mente captus, animo captus,* etc.

nescitis...habere modum: 'you are no more able to keep your frenzy within bounds'.

5–8. The first of the series of *adynata* (examples of obvious impossibilities cited to emphasize *a fortiori* the impossibility of something else) is a simile as well as an *adynaton*: the fire in the dry cornfield resembles the passions in that once started it can not be controlled. The subsequent examples merely illustrate 'impossibility'.

7. Syrtes: sandbanks off the N. African coast, dangerous to shipping.

8. Malea: the southernmost promontory of the Peloponnese.

10. rabidae stimulos...nequitiae: 'the furious lust that goads you on'; the genitive is of definition, as in *spretae... iniuria formae.* [*rabidae* is a conjecture of the Renaissance; the tradition has *rapidae*, which might be kept and understood as = 'careering (*or* sweeping) headlong', for which cf. *cursus* in line 9.]

frangere: 'vanquish'; or 'check' (cf. *frangere cursum, impetum,* etc.), if we treat the metaphor as above; but with *stimulos* as substantive the literal meaning 'break' is also relevant.

11. Cretaei fastus quae passa iuuenci: Pasiphae, who loved a bull and disguised herself in a wooden image of a cow.

13. Salmonis: Tyro, daughter of Salmoneus, fell in love with the river Enipeus, and Neptune pretended to be Enipeus in order to seduce her.

14. liquido tota subire deo: *subire* (more usually construed with an accusative) could mean either 'yield herself to' or 'be submerged in'; evidently both senses are present here. *tota* is adverbial in value.

15. crimen: 'a reproach' (to womankind); cf. I, xi, 30 *Baiae, crimen amoris, aquae*; Virg. *Aen.* x, 188 *crimen, Amor, uestrum.*

patria succensa senecta: i.e. inflamed by (passion for) her aged father.

16. Myrrha: daughter of Cinyras, king of Cyprus. She fell in love with her father, and deceived him into an act of incest. As she fled from his anger she was turned into a tree (the myrrh-tree).

17. Medeae: if the text is right, as object to *referam* one must supply *nequitiam* from the context (cf. 10), or *amorem* (= *libidinem*) from the following relative clause.

17–18. matris iram natorum caede piauit amor: syntactically *matris* goes with *amor* or *iram*; in sense it throws emphasis on *natorum*.

piauit: the word is appropriate to appeasing the anger of a deity; here perhaps it suggests a numinous quality in intense passion.

19. Mycenis: it seems odd to say that the royal house of Mycenae was disgraced 'in Mycenae' or 'in Mycenae's eyes'; but the poet's language is probably influenced by the thought of great houses at Rome, one or other of which might be shamed in the eyes of Rome by the crime of a member.

21. teque: still after *quid referam* in 17.

Scylla: daughter of Nisus, king of Megara, whom she betrayed in war to Minos, king of Crete, because of love for the latter. She detached a purple lock of hair on which her father's life depended. Minos, instead of rewarding her assistance, punished her treachery by dragging her at the stern of his ship until she drowned. (So Apollodorus III, 15, 8; Ovid's version in *Met.* VIII, 6–151 differs in some respects.) Regarding the final *-a* of *uenumdata* left short before *sc-* cf. on III, i, 27 and III, xi, 53.

uenumdata: either fem. sing. vocative with *Scylla*, or neuter pl. accusative with *regna paterna*. If the former, for the combination *uenumdata...tondens* cf. the similar combination *succensa ...condita* in 15–16 above.

Minoa...figura: ablative of price; she sold herself (or her father's life and kingdom, according as we take *uenumdata* as voc. sing. fem. or acc. pl. neuter) for Minos' good looks, i.e. the hope of getting this handsome man for husband. Here as often in Propertius (and cf. line 15 above *patria succensa senecta*) extra terms have to be supplied by imagination; the meaning is a product of the poet's words and the context in which they are set.

22. purpurea...coma: the ablative is hard to classify (? 'by means of', ? 'in') but the sentence is easy to understand; cf. preceding note, and on III, xvii, 21. (It is conceivable, however, that *regna paterna* = 'royal father', the neuter abstract indicating a person, like *hospitium* in I, xv, 20 and *coniugium* in III, xiii, 20 above; in which case *coma* will be ablative of separation, as we say 'shorn of...', a construction found with *tondeo* elsewhere.)

[**21–2.** The text is uncertain. *teque* in line 21 is a conjecture; the MS tradition has *tuque*. An alternative is to keep *tuque* and transpose 15–16 to follow 20; this yields easy syntax, and a satisfying stylistic pattern in 11–24 as a whole, and brings together two offences against fathers in 15–16 and 21–2. On the other hand the traditional order of the lines affords a rational grouping (see introductory note above); and there is no obvious reason why 15–16 should have become displaced. Another remedy, keeping *tuque*, is to read *tondes* (as statement or question) for *tondens* in line 22.]

25. [**at uos...:** some prefer here to punctuate *at (uos...taedas) pendet...* etc.]

taedas: the torches of the marriage procession, symbolizing marriage (especially from the woman's point of view). The thought is: 'may you not suffer Scylla's awful fate, but be happily married in the normal way'.

26. pendet: for the story see on 21 above.

27. non tamen immerito: here *tamen* does not make a contrast with the immediately preceding sentence (25–6), but with something implied in the context, and it goes closely with *non...immerito*: 'it is not without good cause (*after all*) that Minos has been made judge of the dead' (e.g. though that is an extraordinary distinction; or, though you may have been thinking that his severity was excessive).

28. in hoste: for this use of *in* cf. III, xvii, 23.

XX

✱ In lines 1–10 here the speaker is soliciting a woman whose man is away overseas, in the province of Africa, on business or duty. In line 13 the speaker has been promised an assignation. It seems

probable therefore that we have here an elegy in two parts, like
(for instance) I, viii; and the text is printed accordingly. There
is nothing in either part to suggest that the woman addressed in
1–10 is Cynthia. If she were, the piece would be a reminiscence
of the beginning of their affair, placed here deliberately in
proximity to poems which purport to record the end of it (xxiv
and xxv). But such an effect, if intended, would be more
definitely exploited; while unless such an effect were intended
a reminiscence here of the beginning of the affair is not con-
ceivable. Nor, considering the terms of 7–10, can a resumption
of an interrupted relationship be in question. It seems clear
therefore that the woman is not supposed to be Cynthia.

XXA

'Forget that man: he will have forgotten you by now. I will be
true to you. Come to my arms.'

1. iam: 'any more', *iam* cohering with the negative implied
in the question.

figurae: referring to beauty of the whole person, not only the
face.

4. tantine, ut lacrimes...: for the sentiment and the con-
struction cf. Tib. II, vi, 42 *non ego sum tanti ploret ut illa semel.*
The woman's protector has gone to Africa, on duty or business
of some kind. [*tantine ut lacrimes* is a correction: the tradition
has *tantisne* (or *tantis*) *in lacrimis.*]

5. deos...inania uerba: the gods the man swore by in
departing, and the empty promises he made.

fingis: this cannot here mean (as it normally would) 'imagine
(what is not real)', but must mean 'delude yourself with the
thought of'.

6. alio pectus amore terat: 'hug another darling to his
breast'; that *tero* can mean 'press' as well as 'rub' is shown by
IV, ii, 62 *tellus artifices ne terat Osca manus* (of the earth on the
buried man), and so also IV, vii, 94 *ossibus ossa teram.*

7. castae: with *Palladis* (the virgin goddess Minerva).

Palladis artes: (*a*) skills such as spinning and weaving, and
(*b*) literary arts.

8–9. These particulars—well-known name, literary ancestor,
easy circumstances—point to a person of some standing, but

what standing is impossible to guess; the *doctus auus* might be on the one hand an aristocrat with literary pretensions, or on the other hand a freedman who kept a well-known school. (Those who take the poem as addressed to Cynthia suggest that the *auus* may be Hostius, an epic poet of the second century B.C., since Apuleius, *Apol.* 10, says that Cynthia's real name was Hostia.)

9. fortunata: well-to-do.

modo sit tibi: 'all you need is…'.

XXB

* The speaker looks forward to his first night with a new mistress. Presumably this is the woman addressed in xx A, for though the MSS sometimes run together poems which are wholly unrelated (cf. note on III, xv, 11), there is no reason to suspect this here; while *fidus* in lines 9 and 10 provides a cue for the theme of 11–30. Looking forward, he reflects, apparently in soliloquy (for *nobis* in lines 20 and 24 does not require the woman to be addressed, while line 13 clearly implies that she is not), on the terms on which the new relationship is to be inaugurated. In the text printed 13–14 have been transposed to precede 11–12. It may be that they fell out because of *toros|toro* in 10 and 14, and were reinserted out of order. Line 13 makes a good opening to the elegy, of the same kind as in Elegies iv, xvi, xxi, etc. And the appeal to the sun to bring evening soon fits well with the poet's insistence in lines 15 ff. on the need for long *preliminaries*. The prolongation of the night at the other end, prayed for in line 14, is not wanted for the preliminaries, but is a thought arising naturally from *nox mihi prima uenit*, and equally naturally giving rise to *tu quoque…* [This transposition is probable rather than certain.]

13. data tempora: apparently poetic plural for *datum tempus* = 'an appointment has been given me'; cf. Corn. Nep. *Pelop.* 2 *domum Charonis deuerterunt, a quo et tempus et dies erat datus.* [*data* is a correction: the tradition gives *date*.]

11. exigis: 'extend the course of…'.

12. moraturae: with *lucis*; cf. I, iii, 22 *luna moraturis …luminibus.* It means 'disposed to linger' and so 'lingering'; from the point of view of the impatient lover, 'dawdling'.

148

15. prius: 'beforehand'; for the comparative without stated point of comparison cf. *magis* in III, ix, 13, III, xiv, 2; also *Aen.* II, 596 *non prius aspicies*, etc.

foedera: i.e. the terms of an agreement (*foedus*).

iura: i.e. the terms viewed as giving the two parties their respective rights.

16. lex: 'contract'.

17. pignora: 'promises' (by a metonymy; strictly it means the securities which back a promise).

constringit: 'makes fast'. Metaphorically the seal makes the promise binding, literally it fastens the document.

18. testis: the word is suggested by the presence of witnesses at a contract (cf. lines 15–17). But what is primarily meant here is not a witness of that kind, but a witness whose evidence is invoked to prove a point; in poetic usage, a person or thing whose story illustrates the truth of what the poet has just said (in 17); cf. for instance III, xix, 11 and 13 above. (Or does *testis* here denote not an illustration, but a guarantor, as in II, ix, 41 ff. *sidera sunt testes...te nihil in uita nobis acceptius unquam?* If so, the passage should be re-punctuated to make *quam multae* etc. depend on *testis*; and this seems indeed to give a better rhythm to the passage as a whole.)

sidereae...corona deae: the crown of Ariadne, made a constellation by Bacchus. Ariadne is called *dea* because according to one account she was made a goddess by Bacchus under the name *Libera*; cf. Ov. *Fast.* III, 459–516; and in particular 460 *Theseo crimine facta dea est.* The crown is *testis* to the value of a contract in a love-affair because it is understood as Bacchus' pledge to Ariadne, who became and remains his wife; cf. Ov. *A.A.* I, 555–7. But cf. also II, ix, 41 cited above.

torta corona: the crown (in the sky) is shaped like a horseshoe, the same shape as a *torquis* (called *unca* by Propertius at IV, x, 44); presumably therefore *torta* here = 'bent'. *torqueo* can = 'bend' as well as 'twist', for cf. Virg. *Georg.* II, 448 *taxi torquentur in arcus.*

19–20. quam multae...Venus: these discussions will be needed in order to establish the mutual understanding which has been said in lines 15–18 to be necessary. [Some editors transpose this couplet to precede line 15.]

20. dulcia...arma: a metaphor for physical love-making; cf. I, iii, 16 and (?) III, viii, 29.

21. lectus: with *uincitur* this stands by a metonymy for 'union'.

22. non habet ultores nox uigilanda deos: i.e. when a lover is left to lie sleepless, alone, it is no god's concern to avenge his suffering, unless there has been a contract and a god has been invoked to sanction it.

24. omina prima: i.e. due ceremony before our union (literally 'initial auspices' such as those taken before a formal marriage).

fidem: 'our partnership', i.e. the mutual relationship of two who love or otherwise trust one another; cf. Mart. ix, lxxi (of a lion and ram who made friends) *mirum qua coiere fide*.

25. qui pactas in foedera ruperit aras: one can say in prose *pangere foedus*, and *iurare aras*; and *rumpere foedus* or *ius iurandum*; the form of expression here shown is unique to Propertius. [Renaissance scholars conjectured *tactas...aras*; cf. Virg. *Aen.* xii, 201 where Latinus says *tango aras* in making his *foedus* with Aeneas.]

26. sacra marita: the liaison is spoken of as a marriage. For the phrasing cf. ii, xxxii, 21 *famae...pudicae*.

nouo...toro: i.e. by turning to another woman.

28. argutae...historiae: 'chattering gossip'.

caput...praebeat: i.e. 'and make himself the butt of...', apparently on the model of *praebere os ad contumeliam*, and with *caput* suggesting (as it sometimes does) 'reputation'.

29. dominae: genitive after *fenestrae*.

XXI

The poet announces that he is going abroad, to Athens, in an effort to escape from the unhappy love (of Cynthia; cf. line 9) which troubles him (1–10). He imagines the stages of his journey (11–24). He imagines the new interests that he will pursue at Athens and hopes that time and distance will heal his heart's wound (25–34). The name of Cynthia here occurs in this book for the first time.

1. cogor: 'I am constrained' (e.g. by despair or the insistence of friends); but cf. also on iii, ix, 22 above.

5–6. quacumque fugari possit: '(I have tried everything) any device by which this love might be expelled'. The subjunctive *possit* indicates that expulsion by these devices might be possible; the indicative *potest* would say that it *is* possible—which experience seems to show is not the case. [A strict logic recommends *posset*, and some emend to *posset* accordingly.]

* **6. ex omni:** this expression is not found elsewhere; presumably it means either (*a*) 'from every side' (i.e. *ex omni parte*, and cf. *ex aduerso*); or (*b*) 'completely' (cf. *ex toto*). **premit:** 'besets'; cf. Virg. *Aen.* VIII, 474 *hinc Rutulus premit*; *Aen.* X, 375 *numina nulla premunt; mortali urgemur ab hoste.* **ipse deus:** cf. II, xxx, 7–8 *instat semper Amor supra caput, instat amanti, et grauis ipse super libera colla sedet*; in these passages *ipse* appears to mean either (*a*) 'unremitting', or (*b*) 'with all the power of his own presence' (cf. *praesens*).

7. uix tamen: *tamen* here does not refer to the previous sentence, but coheres with *uix*, and the sense is: 'she can hardly be got to admit me at all...'.

aut semel...cum saepe negarit: 'or (if she does, it is) just once, after many snubs'.

8. seu uenit: 'or if she complies...'; *uenio* is a sort of slang, for a woman responding to a lover's invitation, or entreaty; cf. I, v, 32 *non impune illa rogata uenit*; II, xiv, 20 *sic hodie ueniet si qua negauit heri.* Hence it is not necessarily meant here that Cynthia comes to Propertius' house.

amicta: cf. II, xv, 17 *quod si pertendens animo uestita cubaris.* [The MS tradition has *amica*.]

9–10. The construction is *quantum Cynthia procul ibit oculis (meis), tam procul ibit amor.*

9. Cynthia: the first time Cynthia has been named in this book.

11. socii: 'my friends', or 'men'; cf. Virg. *Aen.* I, 198 *o socii...*, where Aeneas is addressing his crew, and echoing the Homeric ὦ φίλοι.... Here the crew of the ship are meant; and *o socii* may have been the regular way of addressing a ship's crew (though we do not know), since sailors in the Roman navy were called *socii*.

12. remorumque pares...uices: either (*a*) 'and draw lots, each man for his fair spell at the oar', *uices* bearing its common meaning 'turn'; or (*b*) 'and draw lots for oar-stations, two men to an oar', *uices* meaning 'allotted tasks (*or* stations)' as in Virg. *Aen.* III, 634 *sortitique uices* (of Ulysses' men preparing to blind the Cyclops), and *pares* (? nominative) meaning 'in pairs'; cf. Ap. Rhod. I, 395–6 κληῖδας μὲν πρῶτα πάλῳ διεμετρήσαντο, ἄνδρ' ἐντυναμένω δοιὼ μίαν. (Virg. *Aen.* III, 510 *sortiti remos* could also be understood either way, as far as the words go. The evidence of Apollonius for ancient practice seems to favour 'stations' rather than 'turns' in both passages.)

* **13. iungiteque extremo...malo:** i.e. hoist the sail, hauling the yard that carries it up towards the top of the mast.

felicia lintea: the plural is 'poetic', for only one sail is in question.

felicia: either 'since the winds are favourable'; or proleptically (extracting a prayer from the preceding imperative) 'and may our sailing prosper'.

14. nautis...secundat iter: 'promises sailors a fair voyage'.

liquidum...iter: the epithet *liquidum* belongs properly to the sky, and is here transferred to the voyage which takes place under such a sky; in Virg. *Aen.* V, 217 (where a bird *radit iter liquidum*) there is hardly a transference, as the bird's course is through the sky. Here one can translate the epithet by adding a sentence '...and the sky is clear'.

15. turres: not necessarily what we should call 'towers' but tall buildings; cf. III, xvi, 3, and Plin. *Ep.* II, 17, 12 where Pliny's Laurentine villa has upper storeys called *turres*.

16. qualiscumque mihi tuque, puella, uale: *mihi* can be taken both with *uale* (cf. Virg. *Aen.* XI, 97–8 *salue aeternum mihi, maxime Palla, aeternumque uale*), and with *qualiscumque* ('wretchedly though you have behaved to me'). For *qualiscumque* cf. III, i, 30 above. For the postponed enclitic (-*que*) cf. III, xvi, 5 (-*ne*) above, II, xx, 12 (-*que*) and II, xxxii, 14 (-*que*, in same position as here); also Platnauer, *L.E.V.* pp. 91–2.

17. ergo ego...: i.e. and so now for the first time I shall sail the sea, and make acquaintance with the Adriatic. Taking lines 11, 15 and 17 in conjunction, it seems that he is (in imagination) leaving Rome and intending to embark at an Adriatic port on a ship which is there awaiting him. If so, *iam...aura* in line 14 will mean that the sailing season has begun, *aura* referring to the winds or weather in general, not to the favouring breeze of a particular moment.

* **18. undisonos:** a notable compound.

19. Lechaeo: Lechaeum was the port of Corinth on the Corinthian gulf. The ablative for locative in place-names of the second declension is abnormal, but exemplified in the prose of Propertius' contemporary Vitruvius.

20. sedarit: 'has brought to rest'. (*sedare* is ordinarily used of quieting a disturbance rather than of bringing rest after exertion.)

phaselus: a light sailing boat. He will have a private boat at his disposal.

21–2. quod superest...utrumque mare: he will cross the Isthmus on foot, and take ship again at Cenchreae for Piraeus.

22. arcet utrumque...: i.e. the shores of the Isthmus hold the two seas apart.

terris: = (here) 'shores'; the plural has a value.

24. scandam ego Theseae bracchia longa uiae: 'I will mount the long stretch of road that leads to Theseus' city'. *bracchia longa*, here said of the 'stretch' of road, is suggested by the thought of the Long Walls (*bracchium* being regularly said of such fortifications) which at one time had enclosed it. *Theseae* is here simply a poetic synonym for 'Athenian'.

25. A friend points out that *animum* here and *lumina* in 29 appear to echo *animo* and *oculis* in 10 above.

* **stadiis:** i.e. the Academy (a *gymnasium*, for which *stadium* would be an easy metonymy). [The MS tradition has *studiis*, but cf. *hortis* in line 26.]

26. hortis: the Garden in which Epicurus taught, and which he bequeathed to his followers.

28. librorumque tuos...sales: the form of expression is explained by the fact that *librorum sales* = 'witty books', in the same way as *canum rabies* in III, xvi, 17 above = 'mad dogs'.

docte Menandre: for the repetition of the same epithet in lines 26 and 28 cf. on III, viii, 4 and III, xi, 61; also III, x, 16–18.

30. siue...seu: the first *siue* connects with what precedes (cf. III, viii, 13), and the second connects *ebore* and *aere*; the sequence being 'pictures, or figures of ivory or bronze'.

manus: 'works of art'; cf. Mart. IV, xxxix, 3 ff. *solus Praxitelis manum Scopaeque...solus Mentoreos habes labores*; Petron. *Sat.* 83 *Zeuxidos manus uidi, nondum uetustatis iniuria uictas.*

32. lenibunt: for the archaic or popular form cf. I, iii, 25 *largibar*.

tacito...situ: i.e. will assuage the pain of my wound and let it gradually heal over. *tacito* is said of the gradual imperceptible process. *situ* is said of the growth or deposit that forms on things left long undisturbed; this is often a disagreeable phenomenon (mould, squalor, etc.), but it is not always so, and the relevance of the process here can be seen by comparing the phrases *ducere situm* and *ducere cicatricem*. [The MS tradition has *tacito...sinu*. But it is hard then to find a *useful* meaning for *tacito* in the present context.]

33. seu moriar, fato...: sc. *moriar* in the apodosis.

34. atque erit illa...dies: i.e. and that being so I shall die with honour (whereas to die of unrequited love would be, he now feels, a disgrace).

XXII

Propertius appeals to his friend Tullus, who has been living at Cyzicus for some years, to return home and start a career and a family. This is presumably the Tullus addressed in Elegies i, vi, xiv, and xxii of Propertius' first book. In I, vi he was leaving Rome for the East, and there appeared as the man of action, with whose way of life that of the lover is contrasted. His re-appearance here may be significant, for the neighbouring Elegies xxi, xxiv and xxv suggest that a new phase is about to begin for the poet.

The elegy owes something to standard forms of composition practised as exercises in the rhetorical schools (e.g. *laudes urbium*, Quint. *I.O.* III, 7, 26; *comparatio*, Quint. *I.O.* II, 4, 21), and to the rhetorical method of arguing by enumeration of examples. This characteristic it shares with pieces such as Hor. *Od.* I, vii, 1–20 and Virg. *Georg.* II, 136–76.

The structure is as follows: appeals to Tullus (lines 1–6 and 39–42) frame the argument (lines 7–38), in which eight lines of praises of Italy (19–26) are preceded by twelve lines (7–18) enumerating certain wonders of the outside world surpassed by those of Italy, and followed by twelve lines (27–38) of legendary monsters, etc., from which Italy is free. The excellence of Italy is thus established first by comparison and then by contrast. Whether there is a numerical balance in the arrangement is not clear, as lines 17–18 can be grouped either with their successors or with their predecessors; see also on 37–8 below.

The central passage containing the praise of Italy itself (19–26) consists of two groups of four lines each, the first (19–22) on moral virtues, the second (23–6) on physical beauties —it is worth remarking that those selected for mention are all springs or lakes or rivers.

1. **Cyzicus:** name both of the island and of the city on it, situated off the southern shore of the Propontis and joined to it by the isthmus of line 2.

2. **fluit:** 'is washed by'. The isthmus was no more than a causeway (perhaps artificial); cf. Ap. Rhod. 1, 938 (of Cyzicus) ὅσσον τ' ἐπιμύρεται ἰσθμός (the sea washes over the Isthmus).

3. **fabricata in uite:** this statue of the goddess consisted of (here *in* may be as in *constare in* or as in *effingere in auro*, etc.) a vine-stock, shaped by carving; cf. Ap. Rhod. 1, 1118 ff. (of the Argonauts on Dindymus, a hill on Cyzicus) ἔσκε δέ τι στιβαρὸν στύπος ἀμπέλου ἔντροφον ὕλῃ...τὸ μὲν ἔκταμον ὄφρα πέλοιτο δαίμονος οὐρείης ἱερὸν βρέτας· ἔξεσε δ' Ἄργος εὐκόσμως...(there was a stout vine-stock, growing in the wood; this they cut down, to make a holy image of the mountain's goddess...).

Dindymis: (fem. adj.) = 'of Dindymus'. [The MS tradition has *Dindymus*, which would add the hill as a separate item and leave an awkward but not impossible asyndeton before it. The tradition also has *Cibele*; regarding the form *Cybebe* printed here cf. on III, xvii, 35 above. The tradition also has *inuenta* where *in uite* (an emendation) is printed here; for the plausibility of *in uite* cf. note above.]

4. **raptorisque...equos:** Proserpine was specially venerated at Cyzicus (cf. Plut. *Lucull.* 10, etc.); it appears from our passage here that there was a version of the legend which made Cyzicus, instead of Sicily, the scene of her rape by Dis.

5-6. **si te forte..., at...:** i.e. if (= though), as may well be, you find the cities of the Hellespont pleasing, still, you must be moved by consideration of me, who miss you so much. [*at* is an emendation; the tradition has *et*.]

7. **tu licet...:** i.e. though you should travel the wide world and visit the scenes of all the wonders of legend, etc.; the concessive construction is continued or repeated through lines 7-16, and the apodosis (main sentence) follows in 17-18.

Atlanta: the giant Atlas (identified with the mountains of the same name in North-west Africa) who, in the legend, carried the sky on his shoulders.

8. **Phorcidos:** Greek genitive from *Phorcis* = daughter of Phorkys = the Gorgon Medusa; Perseus killed her and cut off her head. The head was subsequently set by Athene (= Minerva) in her aegis; so what is here meant must be the *scene of* the Gorgon-slaying. This was near Ocean according to Apollodorus

II, 4, 2; Ov. *Met.* IV, 772–9 seems to imply that it was in the same general region as Atlas.

9. Geryonis stabula: the pastures (or farmstead) of Geryon, the giant who lived in the island Erythea, beyond the pillars of Hercules; Hercules had to bring his oxen to Eurystheus.

10. Antaeique: Antaeus was the African giant whom Hercules outwrestled. For the elision in this position in the pentameter cf. I, v, 32 *non impune illa rogata uenit* (where, however, the rhythm of the sentence is different).

Hesperidumque choros: evidently here *choros* stands for 'dancing-places', by metonymy (and cf. on 8 above), or on the analogy of χορός in *Od.* VIII, 260, etc. To fetch the apples of the Hesperides was one of Hercules' labours.

* **10–11.** All the wonders so far enumerated (except the Gorgon) relate to labours of Hercules; and all were located in North Africa or further west. With line 11 begins a list of wonders in the Euxine and Eastern Mediterranean.

Phasim: the Phasis was a river of Colchis, destination of the Argonauts.

12. Peliacae...trabis: the Argo. *trabs* stands for 'ship' by a common metonymy. *Peliacae*, because the timber for the ship was cut on Mount Pelion.

legas: as often, of following an irregular course fixed by a guiding line of some kind—e.g. a coastline, a river bank, the thread that guided Theseus out of the labyrinth. Here it is the course of the Argo, fixed by the places known to have been visited on it.

13. rudis: agreeing with *pinus*, etc., in the next line; ? 'on that maiden voyage of all'. *rudis* literally means 'inexperienced' or 'untried' or 'unformed'.

Argoa natat inter saxa columba: the *saxa* are the Symplegades, the Clashing Rocks, cf. Ap. Rhod. II, 549 ff. *Argoa... columba* is a very unusual ablative, for Propertius' free treatment of which case cf. on III, xvii, 21 above. Here the sense must be 'with the aid of (abl. of instrument or attendant circumstances) the dove of Argo', i.e. the dove sent ahead of Argo between the Clashing Rocks (Ap. Rhod. II, 328 and 561 ff.). It is a further singularity of the passage that Argo, the real subject of this whole sentence, should be brought into the syntax of the sentence thus obliquely; cf. IV, vi, 49 *uehunt prorae Centaurica saxa minantis* (acc. pl.), where the fact that the figureheads are

Centaurs is obliquely indicated by the epithet attached to the stones they are poising to throw.

14. prorae...nouae: i.e. 'the world's first ship'.

* **15. et si qua...:** I think that *qua* here is adverb (*quā*) and that the meaning is 'and if *in any respect* Ephesus is wondrous' = 'and whatever the wonders of Ephesus...' = 'all the wonders of Ephesus'; cf. III, vi, 7 *si quā tenes* = 'everything you can remember'. But the reader may prefer to construe otherwise. [Some read *et sis quā...* = 'and though you be *where*...' obtaining a construction after *licet* which is parallel to those in the preceding lines, but stylistically rather harsh.]

Ortygie: this Greek (Ionic) form of the name is found and confirmed by metre in Ov. *Met.* xv, 337 *nunc sedet Ortygie; timuit etc.*; the usual Latin form is *Ortygia*. The name *Ortygia* belonged to (1) Delos (cf. Virg. *Aen.* III, 124); (2) an island off Syracuse (cf. Virg. *Aen.* III, 694); (3) a grove at Ephesus, rival claimant with Delos to the honour of being Diana's birthplace (cf. Tac. *Ann.* III, 61, Strabo XIV, 639); (4) Ephesus itself (cf. Plin. *N.H.* v, 115). Here no doubt Ephesus itself is meant, being remarkable not only for the above-mentioned grove (διαπρεπὲς ἄλσος according to Strabo) but also for the famous temple of Diana, one of the Wonders of the World. [*Ortygie* here is a restoration: the tradition has *Orig(a)e*.]

ora Caystri: in apposition to *Ortygie*, and either (*a*) poetic plural, neuter, 'Cayster's mouth'; or (*b*) feminine singular 'Cayster's bank'. Ephesus stands at the mouth of the river Cayster.

uisenda: this gerundive is sometimes an adjective, meaning 'wonderful'; e.g. in Plin. *N.H.* xvi, 242 the trunks of certain trees are said to be *magnitudinis uisendae* (genitive singular). Here the primary sense 'worth a visit to see' is also relevant; cf. Lucr. I, 726-7 *miranda...regio uisendaque.*

16. et quae septenas temperat unda uias: the *septenae uiae* are the seven streams or mouths of the Nile. The point of *temperat* is uncertain. Possibly relevant uses of *tempero* are these: (1) Virg. *Georg.* I, 110 *scatebris arentia temperat arua*, of a stream watering the land it flows through; (2) Ov. *Met.* XIII, 366 *ratem qui temperat*, of a helmsman steering a ship's course; (3) Hor. *Od.* I, xii, 14 *qui mare ac terras uariisque mundum temperat horis*, of Jupiter regulating the cycle of natural phenomena (weather, tides, seasons, etc.). The Nile *might* be said to 'water its ways' (i.e. the strips of land through which it flows); or to 'guide its waters (seaward) in seven streams'; or to 'regulate (the annual rise and fall of) its seven streams'. Evidently we have here a compressed statement about the Nile, that it has (*a*) seven mouths, and (*b*) some other property or several other properties, corresponding to the associations of the verb *tempero*.

18. quidquid ubique fuit: a strong way of saying 'everything that can be'; so often in Cicero *omnes qui ubique sunt*, etc., Plin. *Pan.* 10, 2 *qui ubique sunt homines.* The perfect tense *fuit* is stronger (because more comprehensive) than the present would be; cf. Ov. *A.A.* 1, 56 *haec (Roma) habet...quidquid in orbe fuit.*

20. non pudet: 'glories in'; the ironical understatement (meiosis) adds a positive emphasis; cf. IV, i, 38 *sanguinis altricem non pudet esse lupam.*

21. pietate: 'righteousness'. *pietas* embraces all conduct governed by a proper sense of obligation. Because Roman tradition emphasized the obligations towards family, country and gods, *pietas* is met most often in senses corresponding to these. But there are also other naturally felt obligations, to be just, humane, etc.; and in the present context (see line 22) humanity seems to be uppermost in the poet's mind. That this sense of *pietas* was common in speech if not in literature is shown by its descendant, our 'pity'.

21–2. pietate potentes stamus: in Virg. *Aen.* XII, 827 *sit Romana potens Itala uirtute propago* the same key word *potens* is associated with a similar very pronounced alliteration on 'p's and 't's. It may be that both poets are echoing the same predecessor, or one echoing the other. Note, incidentally, the effect of the initial spondee with strong stop after it.

22. uictrices temperat ira manus: 'our anger stays its hand in victory'.

23–6. The falls at Tibur, the source of the Clitumnus, the great aqueduct called *Aqua Marcia* (and the excellence of its water; cf. Plin. *N.H.* XXXI, 41 *clarissima aquarum omnium in toto orbe frigoris salubritatisque palma...Marcia*), were all celebrated 'wonders'; the lakes *Albanus* and *Nemorensis* and the *fons Iuturnae* would have their special associations for a resident of Rome. It may be that the idea which has determined the choice of all these waters to symbolize the physical excellence of Italy is the idea of *health*; cf. the end of the enumeration in line 26.

23. Tiburne: the usual adjectives of Tibur are *Tiburs* and *Tiburtinus*. Elsewhere *Tiburnus* is name of the tutelary spirit of the place.

Clitumnus: mentioned also by Virg. *Georg.* II, 146 in his 'praises of Italy'. It rises in Umbria and flows into the Tiber. Its source was a beautiful and celebrated curiosity; cf. Plin. *Ep.* VIII, 8 for a description.

24. tramite: probably 'mountain valley'; cf. on III, xiii, 44.

Marcius umor: the water of the *Aqua Marcia*, the great aqueduct which brought water to Rome from the hills in the E.N.E.; it was made by the praetor Q. Marcius Rex in the second century B.C. and was repaired by Agrippa in Propertius' day.

25. Nemorensis: sc. *lacus*, getting its name from the *nemus* of Diana near Aricia. It is now called the lake of Nemi.

socia...ab unda: because the two lakes are neighbours and both fed by streams from the Alban mount.

26. potaque...equo: the *lacus* or *fons Iuturnae*, at the foot of the Palatine, roughly between the *Atrium Vestae* and the (post-Propertian) temple of Castor and Pollux. The legend ran (D.H. VI, 13) that Castor and Pollux watered their horses there after the battle of Lake Regillus.

nympha: presumably 'water' by metonymy, as with *Ceres* = 'bread', *Bacchus* = 'wine', etc. [Some prefer to emend to *lympha*.]

27. cerastae: horned snakes. (Those mentioned by Herodotus II, 74 are specifically said to be harmless. But in Nicander's *Theriaca* 258 ff. the *cerastes* is very poisonous indeed; this poem was imitated by Propertius' older contemporary Macer, as appears from Ov. *Trist.* IV, x, 44 and Quint. *I.O.* x, 1, 56.)

28. nouis: 'strange', 'marvellous'.

portentis: 'monsters'.

29 ff. Here begins a list of legendary horrors; these by contrast illustrate the safety and innocence of Italy, whose history affords no counterpart to them.

29. non hic Andromedae resonant pro matre catenae: 'not here the ring of chains that bound Andromeda for her mother's fault'. Andromeda's mother, Cassiopea, boasted that she (Cassiopea) was more beautiful than the Nereids. For this reason Neptune sent a sea-monster to ravage the country (Ethiopia). An oracle said that Andromeda must be exposed to be devoured by it. She was saved by Perseus.

30. nec tremis Ausonias, Phoebe fugate, dapes: i.e. 'never in Italy was there a banquet that made the sun-god shudder and turn away'. Atreus killed his brother Thyestes' children and served their flesh to him at a feast; the sun turned away in horror and left the world in darkness.

31–2. nec cuiquam...: the Fates told Meleager's mother Althea that he would live until a log then on the hearth was consumed. She took it from the fire and hid it. Later Meleager killed her brothers, and to avenge them she burned the log.

in caput: against his life; cf. *capite suo dimicare*, etc.

33. Penthea: Pentheus hid in a tree to observe the Bacchantes, and was pulled down by them and torn in pieces.

34. subdita cerua: Diana being offended with Agamemnon prevented the Greek fleet from sailing from Aulis. To appease her, Iphigenia had to be sacrificed. According to one version of the story, the goddess miraculously substituted a deer for the human victim and removed Iphigenia to be her priestess among the Tauri.

35. cornua...in paelice: Hera = Juno turned Io into a cow, being jealous because Io was loved by Zeus = Jupiter. Hera in Latin is always Juno; but the Latin name here receives a certain point from the context.

36. boue: i.e. with *the features of* a cow. The essential terms of the thought are given in *dedecorare faciem* and *boue*, and the subordinate term (needed only for structure, not for meaning) is left to be supplied; cf. (e.g.) IV, iv, 83 *mons erat...festo remissus* = the *guard on the* hill was relaxed because of the holiday.

37–8. This couplet contains no verb. Hence it seems likely that something has fallen out between lines 36 and 37, and the text here is printed accordingly. On this assumption *Sinis* in line 37 (an almost certain correction of the tradition's *senis*) is probably genitive. Anyone unwilling to assume a lacuna before line 37 has to suppose that syntactical connexion is fading out as the poet hurries to the end of his enumeration, and that (*a*) *Sinis* is nominative, and the value of an appropriate verb (e.g. *non potuit curuare*, from 35) has to be supplied from what has preceded, while (*b*) the following phrases *et non hospita Grais saxa, et...trabes* have really no syntax, but indicate telegraphically, by brief and cryptic labels, well-known stories associated with that of *Sinis*.

Sinis was a ruffian killed by Theseus. He bent down pine-trees and then released them so as to rend or catapult his victims. Another ruffian killed by Theseus was *Sciron*, who kicked his victims over a cliff into the sea, the place being called *Scironides petrae* by (e.g.) Sen. *Hippol.* 1023, with which cf. *saxa* here. Another ruffian killed by Theseus was *Procrustes*, who (according to the version of his story in Hyginus, *Fab.* 38) had two beds, one longer and one shorter (cf. *curtatas* here in line 38) than normal, and adjusted his victims to these by stretching or chopping. (The proceedings of these bad men and even their names vary somewhat in the accounts of different authors; e.g. the scholiast on Eur. *Hippol.* 977 attributes the pine-bending and the lethal bed to the same person.)

crux is said elsewhere of various instruments of execution, primarily of course the cross of crucifixion, but also, e.g., the stake of impalement; here applied to the pines of Sinis (which are unmistakably identified by *arboreas*) it is a metaphor, conveying the idea of an agonizing death and assisted by the fact that Sinis fastens his victims to these trees. The feats of Theseus being now in mind, the *saxa* are inevitably the Scironian Rocks; and the *curtatas in sua fata trabes* (= the boards made short to cause the deaths of their victims) will be the bed of Procrustes. *trabs*, said occasionally of a tree-trunk, is usually said of some kind of trimmed or carpentered wood, especially beams and planks, often ships, sometimes tables, etc. [*curtatas* in line 38 is a conjecture. The tradition has *curuatas*. If *curuatas* is kept we have to suppose that pine-bending is again referred to. But it does not seem possible (in spite of Ov. *Met.* VII, 441, where *qui poterat curuare trabes* is said of the Pine-Bender) that the *cruces* and the *trabes* here, especially when separated by a different allusion in the *saxa*, should refer to the same thing.]

40. pro digna gente: 'in accordance with the deserts of your family', i.e. as your birth and rank demand.

41. hic tibi ad eloquium ciues: in their context these few words convey a great deal, viz. (roughly): you are gifted with eloquence, and here among your own people is scope for your gift, to render service and win admiration in the civic (primarily forensic) activities which (as well as the military ones you have already engaged in) befit a Roman of your station.

41–2. ampla nepotum spes...coniugis aptus amor: the epithets, grammatically attached to *spes* and *amor*, go more

161

closely in meaning with *nepotum* and *coniugis*: prospect of *many* children and grandchildren, a *well-suited wife* to love and be loved by. (In Virg. *Aen.* II, 503 *spes ampla nepotum* is said of the fifty bed-chambers of Priam's sons in his palace. It may be that the two poets are echoing a common predecessor.)

*

XXIII

The poet has lost his writing tablets, and soliloquizes on the occasion. The poem can be divided up as follows: exclamation (1–2); the tablets' virtues (3–10); messages that they carried are imagined (11–18); exclamation (19–20); the poet offers a reward for the tablets' return (21–4). These tablets are oblong slabs of wood, hinged so as to open and shut like a book; the inside surfaces are overlaid with wax, in which messages can be scratched with a pointed metal stylus, and erased again at will to free the surfaces for re-use; the edges of the blocks on the side that is written on are raised in relation to the waxed surfaces, so that these do not touch one another when the tablets are 'shut'.

1–2. Ergo: for this way of beginning cf. III, vii, 1 above.

tam...tot: for Propertius' fondness for these words cf. on III, viii, 2 above.

doctae = (here) something between 'eloquent' (this being the quality which ancient education—*doctrina*—aimed to cultivate) and 'clever' (as one says it e.g. of an animal that has picked up some tricks).

2. quibus may be either dative (with *pariter*), or ablative (with *scripta*, meaning 'on which').

periere: 'are lost', *pereo* being the proper word for this in daily life; cf. *C.I.L.* IV, 64 (a notice) *urna aenia pereit de taberna. sei quis rettulerit, dabuntur HS LXV.*

bona: probably 'good things' in the sense of clever sayings, *res bona* being regular Latin for one of these.

3. nostris manibus detriuerat usus: a mild hypallage (reversal of the expected syntactical relationship between terms in a sentence); we should expect *manus detriuerant usu.*

4. habere fidem: 'be accepted as from me'; what is said to be believed here is that the message comes from the person it purports to come from, not simply (as might be meant by *habere fidem* in another context) that what it contains is truth.

5. illae: cf. *has* in line 3. The indifference with which Propertius uses these demonstratives is worth remarking.

puellas: there is no reason to take the plural otherwise than literally; cf. III, xx above, II, xxii (*n.b.* lines 13 ff., 35 ff.), IV, viii, etc.

iam...norant: knew by now, i.e. 'had learned'.

6. diserta = (here) 'persuasive'.

8. uulgari buxo sordida cera fuit: 'they were just soiled wax on common boxwood'. *cera* is predicate to the unexpressed subject 'they', and the verb *fuit* takes its number from the adjoining predicate, as commonly.

9. qualescumque: 'poor things that they were'; cf. III, i, 30.

10. promeruere = (here) 'earned', and so 'got'. (Elsewhere *promereo* means 'deserve' or 'oblige'.)

11. Here follow (some say) imaginary specimens of communications from women in the past; or (according to others) conjectures of the poet about a message from a particular woman which the tablets were carrying when they got lost.

12. es...moratus: 'you were so late in coming'.

lente: 'unfeeling man', or 'sluggard'; both meanings are included here.

13–14. i.e. has she a rival? or has he some imaginary grievance against her?

15. dixit: the subject, on one hypothesis (see above on line 11), is an imaginary 'she'; on another hypothesis it is a current mistress.

Venies: the future with imperative force, 'you are to come'; *cessabimus* is a statement, 'we will'. [*cessabimus* is a necessary correction: the tradition has *cessauimus*.]

16. hospitium tota nocte parauit Amor: 'Love has prepared to lodge you all night long'; for the ablative *tota nocte* of a whole night's duration cf. II, xiv, 28 *tota nocte receptus amans*. As this exemplifies the wit of a *non stulta puella* (line 17) we must suppose that some further meaning is to be read into it, e.g. that the writer's *uir* (cf. III, xiv, 23–4, etc.) is out of town.

[In view of the necessary change of *cessauimus* to *cessabimus* in line 15 it may be that *parauit* here should be emended to *parabit*. This would yield a *double entendre*, as *hospitium tota nocte parabit Amor* could mean either (*a*) Love will prepare to entertain you all night long; or (*b*) Love's payment for his (i.e. your payment for your) lodging shall be a whole night of

163

love's joys (for me). In (*a*) *tota nocte* is ablative of duration; in (*b*) it is ablative of price. For *nox* in the special sense of a night of love cf. II, xxiii, 11 *quam care semel in toto nox uertitur anno.* 'prepare' and 'buy' are both regular meanings of *paro*.]

17. uolens: i.e. to receive the lover; cf. Catull. viii, 9 *nunc iam illa non uult: tu quoque impotens noli.* This seems to give *uolens* more point than if it is taken with *reperit* ('at will'). [The tradition has *dolens*, which would have to mean either 'passionately loving' or 'vexed' (e.g. at a man's delay).]

18. cum...dicitur hora: 'when a time is being appointed', 'when an appointment is being made'; cf. *dicere diem*, etc. [The tradition has *ducitur*. But written messages *before* the assignation are in question here.]

blandis...dolis: dative, 'for secret love'; cf. Tib. I, ix, 23–4 *nec tibi celandi spes sit peccare paranti: scit deus occultos qui uetat esse dolos*; 54 *rideat assiduis uxor inulta dolis*; where the reference is to a woman deceiving her *uir* with another man. (Some prefer to understand *dolis* here of feminine blandishments as part of a love-scene; or—taking it as ablative—of the secret correspondence or the riddling language whereby the meeting is arranged.)

19. rationem: reckoning, and so 'accounts'.

20. ephemeridas: ledgers.

diras: 'odious'. [*diras* is given by *N*; the other branch of the tradition has *duras* = 'merciless'. As Servius on *Aen.* III, 235 says that *Umbri...quae nos mala dira uocant*, and as Propertius was an Umbrian, *N*'s reading is not improbable. But *duras* is plausible too.]

21. donabitur auro: one distinctive use of *donare* with acc. and abl. is with reference to rewards in recognition of services rendered. *auro* is said with emphasis: the reward will be very handsome.

22. ligna: this sometimes (and evidently here) = 'firewood', as opposed to timber (*materia*). [*ligna* is a correction: the tradition has *signa*.]

23. columna: of a portico or a shop, where notices would be posted.

i puer, et citus haec...: an echo of Hor. *Sat.* I, x, 92, or perhaps of a common predecessor.

XXIV

The poet declares that he is free at last from the servitude of his love for Cynthia. Echoes of I, i, 18–30 ff. are audible in lines 9–12. The punctuation, interpretation and text of lines 9–12 are uncertain.

2. olim: long since.

oculis: i.e. by my admiration.

4. uersibus insignem te pudet esse meis: 'I feel shame to think how my verse has glorified you'. Here *te* goes with *insignem esse*, and the whole accusative-and-infinitive complex thus created depends on *pudet*, with which *me* has to be supplied.

5. mixtam...figura: 'often I mixed all manner of beauties in my praise of you'. *uaria...figura* might mean that he enumerated several 'points' (as at II, ii, 5 ff., II, iii, 9 ff.—hair, eyes, hands, movements, etc.), or that he attributed to Cynthia qualities that he had observed in various beautiful women, real or depicted; this ambiguity remains in the rendering suggested above. *figura* is shape, posture, beauty of shape or posture, an image or picture, etc.

6. ut, quod non esses, esse putaret amor: 'making love think you were what you were not'. Here *te* must be supplied with *esse*. Whether *ut* is of purpose or result does not matter. *amor* can include the love of rivals attracted by the poet's praise of Cynthia; but uppermost is the idea that he feeds his own illusion.

7–8. et color...in ore foret: 'and ah, how often have I compared your complexion to the glow of dawn (*or* of the morning star), when all its radiance had been got by painting'. As will be seen from the further notes below, there is no contradiction between *roseo* in the hexameter and *candor* in the pentameter; the former does not *insist* on pinkness, nor the latter on absolute whiteness. But in other contexts they are found in antithesis to one another; and by using them here the poet has suggested the idea of the mixture of the two colours in the complexion.

totiens: as we should say 'how many times'. (But this comparison is not in fact made anywhere in the elegies that we have.)

Eoo: *Eous* is the morning star, but the name comes to stand virtually for dawn; for cf. Virg. *Georg.* I, 288 *cum sole nouo terras inrorat Eous*. The star suggests radiance, and dawn the characteristic colours of the morning sky.

roseo: this often means pink or red, but its range is much wider: e.g. in Lucr. v, 610 *rosea sol alte lampade lucens* the colour intended must be golden, while in Virg. *Aen.* 1, 402 (Venus) *auertens rosea ceruice refulsit* the emphasis will be on radiance rather than on colour.

candor: this is said of many things, e.g. the sun, milk, wool, snow, etc.; in Plaut. *Men.* 179–80 *solem uides satin ut occaecatust prae huius corporis candoribus* it is said of radiant beauty. Thus as applied to a complexion it conveys (*a*) fairness as opposed to swarthiness, and (*b*) radiance.

9–12. The text here printed of this much discussed and emended passage (see supplementary note below) is that of some of the old editions: it can be tentatively translated as follows: 'My sickness (i.e. the compulsion to praise Cynthia in terms which flouted reality) was one which my family's friends could not rid me of, nor Thessaly's witches purge away with all the waters of the sea—about you I could not be got to confess the truth by cutting or burning or even shipwreck in the (stormy) Aegean.' This yields a likely pattern of thought in the piece as a whole: 'I was lying when I praised your beauty, as for so long I did—I was under a compulsion of which no one and nothing could rid me—because, you see, I was a helpless victim and prisoner of Love—but now I have escaped and am safe and cured—thanks be to the goddess of Sanity who has had mercy on me.' In particular, lines 13–14 stand, on this assumption, in a satisfactory relation (explanatory) to lines 11–12. [For further comment see detailed notes below, and also supplementary note at foot of page 167. It should be noted that witches, cutting, burning and escape by sea all occur in the first elegy of Book I (lines 19 and ff.), which is evidently echoed here. But there is not exact correspondence; for instance the witches who here fail to cure the man of loving were invoked in the earlier passage to make the woman love him in return. On the other hand, the fact that in that passage the object of the cutting and burning was to make the poet free to speak his mind (I, i, 28 *sit modo libertas quae uelit ira loqui*) lends some support to the interpretation of this present passage recommended above, and in particular to the meaning proposed for lines 11–12.]

9–10. quod mihi...saga mari: with the punctuation adopted in the text this clause refers forward, attributively or in apposition, to the condition of the speaker described in the following couplet: 'a failing which friends, etc., could not rid me of—I was, etc.'. [It can alternatively be read with a strong stop after it and taken as conclusion of the passage 1–8: 'and this sickness of mine (i.e. the compulsion to praise Cynthia without regard to truth) neither friends nor witches etc. could free me from'. For the relative thus introducing a conclusion cf. III, vii, 66 *ultima quae Paeto...* = 'and that was Paetus' last...'.]

10. Thessala saga: 'Thessalian' is a general epithet for witches, because Thessaly was celebrated for them.

11. non...non...et ipsa...: i.e. (on the above assumptions) *non ferro aut igne, ne naufragio quidem....* For the sequence *non...non...et* cf. II, i, 21–2 *nec...nec...et.*

ferro...igne...: the words in themselves might refer to surgery (and cautery) or to torture; in I, i, 27 surgery evidently is meant, and so no doubt here, *coactus* then meaning 'got to' rather than 'forced to'.

11–12. haec...uera fatebar: i.e. *harum rerum ueritatem*, or *haec ut re uera sunt*; for a similar construction cf. Virg. *Aen.* II, 77–8 *cuncta...fatebor uera.* He refers to the subjects of 5–8.

non...coactus...fatebar: i.e. (on the above assumptions) *non cogi poteram ut faterer* = 'I could not be (*or* could not have been) got to admit...'.

naufragus Aegaea...aqua: the context (on the above assumptions) requires this to indicate something that might normally cure a man of his unreason, or otherwise cause him to speak the truth. The idea of 'curing' may be present if the sea is thought of as able to wash away a malady, as in line 10 above. The idea of 'eliciting truth' may be present if we can infer from II, xxvi, 1 ff. that a person in danger of drowning was supposed to confess the truth; that passage runs *uidi te in somnis fracta, mea uita, carina Ionio lassas ducere rore manus, et quaecumque in me fueras mentita fateri....* For the epithet *Aegaea* cf. the arbitrarily chosen *Ionio* in the passage just quoted and the conventional *Thessala* said of the witch in line 10 above; here *Aegaea* adds not only sonority but useful associations for *naufragus*, because of the Aegean storms; cf. Hor. *Od.* III, xxix, 63 *Aegaeos tumultus.*

[**9–12.** In the above *uera* is a generally received emendation of the tradition's *uerba* (though *haec...uerba* might mean 'that these were empty words'). *fatebar* is the reading of the emended

MSS; the past tenses of lines 9–10 and 13–14 make a past tense probable in this couplet too. But the tradition has *fatebor*. Keeping *fatebor* and supposing that shipwreck aids veracity one might perhaps read *ut ipsa* for *et ipsa* and get the sense 'now I will tell the truth, without needing to be brought to it by surgery, as truthfully as if I were...'. The Oxford text reads: *hoc ego non ferro, non igne coactus, et ipsa naufragus Aegaea— uera fatebor—aqua*; and Butler and Barber's edition (p. 320) translates this text: 'This madness I myself have banished, under no compulsion of steel or cautery, though I was shipwrecked (I will confess the truth) even on an Aegean sea of passion'. This assumes a heavy emphasis on *ego* and that the sense of *auerti* is to be supplied from *auertere* in line 9, while *hoc*, a conjecture, refers to the malady indicated in the preceding *quod* clause.]

13. correptus: *corripio* is variously used of a person seizing a prisoner, and of a conflagration enveloping and consuming something.

aeno: with the cauldron of Venus (a striking metaphor, not conventional) cf. the stove or grill of III, vi, 39.

15. coronatae: in thanks for their safe arrival; cf. Virg. *Georg.* I, 303–4 *cum iam portum tetigere carinae, puppibus et laeti nautae imposuere coronas.*

16. traiectae Syrtes: 'we are past the Syrtes', dangerous sands off the African coast.

17–18. In this couplet the metaphor changes (by way of *resipiscimus*) from weathering a storm at sea to recovering from a disease; cf. (perhaps, but the text there is uncertain) III, xvii, 2–4 above.

resipiscimus: used variously of recovering consciousness, or sanity, or (metaphorically) courage.

uasto: connoting desolation, wide expanse, savagery, perhaps also (cf. on III, vii, 40 above) an engulfing maw.

aestu: heaving swell, or boiling surge; the context here admits either sense.

19. Mens Bona: Sanity. There was in fact a temple of Mens (Bona) at Rome, vowed after the defeat at Trasimene; cf. Ov. *Fast.* VI, 241 ff. and Liv. XXII, 9–10.

si qua dea es: in this formula *si qua* does not imply doubt, but rather confidence that the condition stated *is* fulfilled; cf. Virg. *Aen.* I, 603–4 *si qua pios respectant numina, si quid* *usquam iustitia est...*; *Aen.* III, 433 *si qua est Heleno prudentia uati...*; *Aen.* VII, 3–4 *ossaque nomen Hesperia in magna, si qua est ea gloria, signat* (where *magna* in line 3 and *aeternam famam* a little earlier show that no pathetic doubt is being expressed). So here 'for goddess you surely are' is meant.

20. exciderant: pluperfect because the poet's prayers to Jupiter *had* proved ineffective when he obtained relief from *Mens Bona* instead. *excidere* with dative is properly said of something being forgotten by someone (*excidit tibi cura mei,* etc.), and so strictly does not fit with *surdo* (which should mean that he never became aware of the prayers in the first place); but the tendency of *exciderant* and *surdo* is the same, that the prayers went unheeded, and no doubt the meaning here is: 'how often I prayed to Jupiter, and my prayer remained unheeded as if he had not heard'.

XXV

The poet says an angry farewell to Cynthia. The elegy is obviously to be read in conjunction with Elegy xxiv, but they do not naturally form a single piece. [*N* presents xxiv and xxv as separate elegies; the other branch of the tradition presents them as one.]

1. Risus: substantive, 'a laughing stock'; cf. Ov. *Fast.* I, 437–8 (of Priapus caught in an embarrassing situation) *at deus...omnibus ad lunae lumina risus erat*; and cf. Prop. II, xxi, 7 *et nunc inter eos tu sermo es,* II, xxiv, 15 *sed me fallaci dominae iam pudet esse iocum.* For the situation cf. Juv. i, 145 *it noua...per cunctas fabula cenas.*

positis...mensis: this is a dispensable but not otiose amplification of *inter conuiuia*, as if one were to say 'at table at dinner-parties'. The guests recline on couches, and the *mensae* (tables, and hence also 'courses') are brought and set before them.

3. quinque...annos: here one must bear in mind (*a*) that five may be a 'round' figure; cf. on III, xviii, 15 above; (*b*) that while this elegy stands last in the book, it was not necessarily the last in the book to be composed; (*c*) that we cannot, in general, be sure how exact, or how immediate, is the relation of any elegy of Propertius to the experience it reflects or appears to reflect.

4. ungue...morso: in frustration. Here the frustration is regret; elsewhere (II, iv, 3) it is disappointment, or jealousy, or helpless anger.

querere = (here, as often) 'lament *the loss of*...'.

5. ab arte: cf. on III, xviii, I for another extension of the concept of 'agency'. Cynthia's play-acting is easily treated as an agent, because it almost = 'Cynthia with her play-acting'.

6. ab insidiis: here the *ab* is of motive, cf. Cic. *Att.* IX, 7 B, 3 *scio me ab singulari amore ac beneuolentia, quaecumque scribo tibi, scribere.* But there may also be a play on *ex insidiis*, said literally of those who emerge from an ambush, and also used metaphorically, e.g. in Cic. *Or.* 38 *non ex insidiis sed aperte ac palam elaboratur ut uerba uerbis quasi demensa ac paria respondeant*, etc.

7. iniuria: i.e. my reaction to the *iniuria* I have suffered from you, a mixture of anger and grief: ? 'my wrongs', or 'my bitterness'.

8. tu bene conueniens non sinis ire iugum: the sense is 'you make harmonious partnership impossible'. *iugum* is a pair of beasts in harness, affording a metaphor for various kinds of human partnership; *bene conueniens* is a regular phrase for harmonious relations between man and woman; *ire* belongs to the metaphor of the *iugum*, being the proper word for a pair of beasts going together in harness. The metaphor is the same as in I, V, 2 (where the poet is warning off a rival) *et sine nos curso quo sumus ire pares.*

9. nostris lacrimantia uerbis: his pathetic cries moved even the stone threshold to tears; cf. I, xvi, 13 where the door is addressed and says *grauibus cogor deflere querelis, supplicis a longis tristior excubiis.* For the ablative *uerbis* (= 'because of', or 'caused to...by') with *lacrimantia* cf. II, iv, 21 *alter saepe uno mutat praecordia uerbo.*

10. nec tamen irata ianua fracta manu: i.e. door that my anger has come so near to smashing. Here the contrast pointed by *tamen* is not with the preceding sentence but with *irata*, or with an idea present in the general context: despite his anger, or though you would have expected it in the circumstances, he nevertheless did not smash the door.

11. celatis...annis: 'as the years steal by unseen', or (taking *annis* with *grauis*) 'with the weight of the years that steal by unseen'; *celatus* here seems to be used as an adjective, like *occultus*; for the meaning of the phrase here and a possible

construction cf. Hor. *Od.* I, xii, 45 *crescit occulto uelut arbor aeuo.*
(For the words in a different sense cf. Phaedrus II, 2 *mulier
annos celans elegantia*; and indeed the thought that Cynthia will
try to conceal her years is present here too; for cf. Tib. I, viii,
43–5 *tum studium formae est, coma tum mutatur, ut annos dis-
simulet uiridi cortice tincta nucis; tollere tum cura est albos a stirpe
capillos etc.*, which is shown to have been somewhere in
Propertius' mind here by the echo in line 13.)

   aetas grauis: cf. III, v, 23 above *grauis...aetas.*

   urgeat: 'press hard upon'; *urgeo* includes among its meanings
both 'press hard' (as a pursuer), and 'lie heavy on' (as a burden);
both senses are relevant here.

   16. facta: on the face of it this might be (*a*) nom. sing.
fem. = 'when you are become' (an old woman); or (*b*) acc. plur.
neut. 'that you did what you did'; or (*c*) acc. plur. neut. 'that
what you did is done *by others to you*', the sense of the words in
italics having to be understood. The juxtaposition *fecisti facta*
leads one to expect a *point* in the expression, and thus to supply
mentally what is necessary to provide it, i.e. to construe as in
(*c*) above.

   17. fatalis: either (*a*) nom. sing., with *pagina*, meaning
'prophetic', as in *fatales libri*, etc.; or (*b*) acc. pl., with *diras*,
meaning 'deadly' or 'which will surely be fulfilled'.

   18. euentum formae: 'what your beauty will come to (*or*
bring you to) in the end'; cf. *euentum pugnae, euentum fortu-
narum alicuius.*

TEUBNER TEXT VARIANTS

Readings in the Stuttgart Teubner text of 1984 (P. Fedeli) which differ from the text printed in this edition.

2.17 si qua est   3.42 tingere   4.3 uiri   5.2 stant
6.20 poena et   12 *and* 14 *interchanged*   28 exsuctis
7.21-4 *after* 38   22 poena minantis aquae   29 curuas
47 non tulit haec   51 *and* 53 *interchanged*   8.13 se stipat
29 Graia   30 Tyndaridi   35-40 *not detached*   9.38 nec
septem   57 mollia   10.28 grauibus   11.5 †uenturam melius
. . . mortem†   30 et (famulos inter . . . suos!)   49 cape
55 non hoc . . . fui (*Cleopatra*)   67-8 *after* 58
12.12 aurato   25 Ciconum mons, Ismara, Calpe   13.35 †totos†
39 Idaei   14.15-6 *after* 10   15.3 sublatus   16.29 cumulis
17.2 pacatus   3 fastus   12 utroque modo   16 carpant
24 grata   37-8 cratere antistes et auro libatum   18.9 hic
32 hoc . . . portent . . . suae   19.21-2 tuque . . . tondes
El. 20 *as one piece, with* 11-12 *not transposed but* 15-16
after 20   21.32 sinu   22.15 sis qua   24.11-12 hoc ego . .
. (vera fatebor)   24 *and* 25 *made a single piece*

In some of these passages (7.22, 8.13, 8.29, 9.38, 11.55, 12.25, 18.32, 20 A & B, 24.11-12) the choice of reading substantially affects the sense. Indications of the problem, though not of an infallibly correct solution, will usually be found in the notes or supplementary notes below.

SUPPLEMENTARY NOTES

I

1 (*pp*.51-2). Philitas: the name, so spelled in the MSS. tradition of Propertius and in modern texts of Theocritus 7.40, appears as *Philetas* in many older editions and works of reference, and so may be better known in that form. *Philitas* is better authenticated and should now be preferred.

25 (*pp*.56-7). The existing note is unsatisfactory. The movement of the poet's tnoughts seems rather to have been on the following lines. A legend may grow in impressiveness, as time passes, through the accretion to it of fabulous elements which but for this fable-making effect of time would never be heard of; this is what has happened with the story of the fall of Troy. A work of art, on the other hand, remains itself unchanged as time passes, but its reputation (and so its author's reputation too) may grow in time as it comes to be more widely and more warmly appreciated; this is what Propertius anticipates for his poems and himself. The two conceptions of time's magnifying effect are somewhat different from one another. A link between them is provided by the reference to Homer and the Homeric poems in lines 33-4. Homer tells the story of the fall of Troy (and may indeed have contributed to the enrichment of it with fabulous incidents). The poems in which he tells the story have grown since he made them, not in content but in reputation.

25 (*p*.57). nosceret: better than 'come to know about' would be 'come to hear of' or 'have come to hear of'; the knowledge being not of fact in this case, but of report.

III

42 (*p*.68). Aonium cingere Marte nemus: while *cingere* gives good sense and is palaeographically plausible enough, the tradition's *tingere* can be accepted (given the strong association of ideas exemplified in Hor. *Od*. 2.14.13 *cruento Marte*), as involving an ellipse scarcely bolder than that in *proelia seuit* at 11.10 below, or *pampinea...rate* at 17.26. T.A. Suits, CP (1970) 204-5 points out a remarkable set of repetitions of related words in this poem, thus: *molli* (1) and *mollia* (18), *neruis* (4) and *neruis* (35), *fontibus* (5) and *fonte* (51), *ora* (5) and *ora* (52), *pater* (6) and *patris* (29), *cecinit* (7) and *canes* (48), *sede* (11) and *sedem* (25), *fugantis* (11) and *fugae* (48), *tutum* (12) and *tutus* (24), *carminis* (16) and *carmina* (35), *turba* (24) and *turba* (31); *uectet* (46) and *uectabere* (39), *signo* (43) and *signa* (48). Each word occurs, as Suits puts it, once in an 'epic' and once in an 'elegiac' context. And *tingere* here in 42 would make another such pair with *tingunt* in 32.

IV

3 (*p.*69). [magna uiris merces: Heinsius' alternative conjecture
uiae merces is attractive, for sound, and plausible in itself, *uia* having
military associations (cf. Ov. *Am.* 1.9.9. *militis officium longa est uia*)
and being said of journeying by sea as well as by land.]

11 (*p.*71). sacrae: the existing note is inaccurate, for *sacer* is
sometimes, though very rarely, applied to deities, e.g. to Janus by Ovid
at *Fasti* 1.95.

V

7 (*p.*73). Prŏmēthēō: three syllables, -ĕō being contracted into
-ēō by synizesis.

11 (*p.*74). maris in tantum uento iactamur: a literal reference
to sea-faring (in pursuit of gain) is more natural than the metaphorical
significance suggested in the existing note; but the latter need not be
excluded.

41 (*p.*78). Phīnēī: two syllables; cf. on 7 above.

VI

6 (*p.*79). habere fidem: not so much 'be believed' as 'possess
credibility', i.e. 'deserve to be believed'.

13 (*p.*80). uestem pendere: the note should have pointed out that
the acc. and inf. has to depend on the idea of *uidisti*, supplied from 11
across the intervening indicative construction in 12. This is not impossible;
cf. 3.43 and 4.17-18 above. [Suringar transposed 12 with 14, as now
recorded in the app. crit. on p.20.]

20 (*p.*80). est poenae seruo rumpere teste fidem: the existing
note needs revision. *est poenae* here = 'is cause of punishment', i.e. 'is
a punishable offence', *poenae* being a predicative dative indicating 'that
which a thing occasions'. like *pallori* in 2.5.30 *hic tibi pallori ... uersus
erit*. The alternative use of the predicative dative as indicator of 'that
which a thing serves as' is excluded by the context here. [Some emend to
est poena et seruo..., comparing 13.38 below for *poena* (nominative) =
'offence', a meaning for the word which though unusual is attested there
by the metre].

39 (*p*.82). **torquerier**: the existing note needs correction. The alternative form (-*ier*) of the infinitive passive, common in Plautus, Terence and Lucretius, is thereafter only occasionally to be met in literary texts. Here (as also in Hor. *Sat*. 2.8.67 *tene, ut accipiar laute torquerier*...) it is plainly used with colloquial effect, but this does not prove that in Propertius' day it was common in everyday conversation. It occurs occasionally in Virgilian epic, and also in satirists. The rolling 'r's make it appropriate here to the professed agony of the speaker.

VII

(*p*.82). The existing Introductory note describes this elegy as a lament for Paetus, and so, with its emphasis on maternal grief and other pathetic features, it evidently in one sense is. But the point has well been made that in another and perhaps more essential sense the piece is a moralizing discourse, a warning against the pursuit of material gain; this appears from the opening sentiments (1-6) especially, and from the implications, in their context, of *auaris* (37 and *opes* (46). On this subject see F. Robertson, *TAPA* (1969) 377 ff.

13 (*p*.84). **Ōrithȳiae**: four syllables, the -*yi* being scanned as one, as in the Greek name which is being transliterated.

39ff. (*p*.86). It would appear from *auaris* (37) that the *exempla* are conceived as warning against sea-faring in quest of gain.

43-6 (*p*.86-7). It remains possible to suppose that something has fallen out between 42 and 43 which would provide a satisfactory conclusion to 37-42 and a satisfactory reintroduction of Paetus as subject of 43 ff.

45 (*p*.86). **dulcis conuiua**: as this is the man's own home (*suos*... *penates*) he is evidently host; so *conuiua* will = *conuiuator* = 'host' and *dulcis* no doubt will = 'genial'.

49 (*p*.87). **thȳio**: two syllables, cf. on 13 above.

60 (*p*.88-9). **attulimus longas in freta uestra manus**: the interpretation preferred in the existing note does not satisfy. But Smyth's alternative, *CQ* (1951) 78, gains in appeal when it is noted that Pliny in the passage cited says expressly that the superstition about long fingers prognosticating short life is *widespread*. Reference to widely familiar idea would make good sense here; better, perhaps in the form of a pathetic exclamation: *a ! tulimus longas in freta uestra manus!*

67 (*p*.89). **Nēreō**: two syllables, by synizesis; cf. on 3.7 above.

[Postscript. An explanation of the apparently dis-
jointed sequence of thought in the first part of the elegy is offered in
the Introductory note on p.83. It is observable however that an orderly
sequence can be procured by transposing 11-12 (*sed tua nunc...Carpathium
omne mare est*) to follow 18; and 13-16 (*infelix Aquilo...alueus ille uiros*)
to follow 24.]

VIII

4 (*p.*90). The objection made in the existing note to the recurrence
insanae(2)...*insana*(4) must be discounted, as too subjective.

IX

6 (*p.*94). **inflexo mox dare terga genu**: as it is a matter of
falling down under a weight, and not of being turned by pressure from the
front, one can infer that *dare terga* here means 'fall flat' (on one's
face).

7 (*p.*94). **omnia non pariter rerum sunt omnibus apta**: 'not
all pursuits suit all men's aptitudes'.

8 (*p.*94). [**palma...iugo**: an alternative line of interpretation
should have been mentioned, and perhaps preferred. This keeps, with one
small change only, to the MSS tradition's text, and reads: *Fama nec ex
aequo ducitur ulla iugo*. With this reading *iugo* is taken as 'yoke', and
a metaphor is supposed from the matching of draught animals paired to
pull evenly in harness. The metaphor is invoked sometimes to express
harmonious relationship, but sometimes also, as here would suit, exact
equivalence. The meaning will be: 'it is not by matched pairs in any
art that the Car of Fame is drawn', and this seems indeed to be the point
of the illustrative examples which follow in 9-16, where four pairs of
artists are cited, the members of each pair excelling in the same art
as one another but in different ways.]

58 (*p.*101). **dexteraque...da mihi signa**: in Ovid *Am.* 3.2.58
signa secunda dedit refers to a sign of encouragement or approval; and
in line 74 of the same elegy *signa* are actions by which spectators of
a race manifest their wishes and their excitement.

X

6 (*p.*102). [ponat...unda minax: the position of the adjective, at the end of the pentameter, is not contrary to the elegists' practice, since it is positive in value and not purely ornamental. But the positive value is perhaps too strong, obtruding the idea of *menacing* waves, where a picture of 'waves gently breaking' would be enough. The conjecture *minas* is attractive.]

XI

5 (*p.*105). uentorum melius praesagit nauita motus: the point being made is that sailor and soldier (and Propertius) have learned by hard experience not to be complacently confident of their own security. (The plural *motus* is a modification of Owen's *motum*, avoiding an echo with *metum* in the following line.)

17 (*p.*105). Omphalě in tantum: cf. among other examples Virg. *Georg.* 4.461 *flerunt Rhodopeīae arces; Aen.* 3.211 *insūlae Ionio in magno.*

27-28 (*p.*106). nam quid...domum: this brief reference to male addiction seems to be a perfunctory complement to the elaborate series of illustrations of female dynamism that has preceded through lines 9-26. Interest in the male, except in lines 19-20, has been subordinate since line 6, and in the story of Cleopatra which now follows Antony is noticed only in one indirect and inexplicit allusion (31).

28 (*p.*106). [Iuppiter infamat seque suamque domum: it has been suggested that *domum* refers to a temple, as in 2.20 above; the point then being that in Babylon (in mind as being Semiramis' city) there was a famous temple of Zeus Belos (Zeus = Jupiter) in which a concubine was provided nightly for the god: see M.E. Hubbard in *CR* (1968) 317; and Herodotus 1.181-2.]

XII

25 (*p.*113-4). [Ciconum mors Ismara capta: Wittig's conjecture *mox* (alternative to *mors*) for the tradition's *mons* has now been added to the app. crit. on p.33; it would read easily (with *capta*) and fit well stylistically with *mox* that follows in line 26.]

26 (*p.*114). genae: the extension of meaning from 'cheeks' to 'eyes' is not difficult, by way of the hollows in which eyes are set. Sometimes elsewhere the metonymy is startling, as at Ov. *Her.* 20.206 *fixis in tua membra genis,* said of gaze fixed on a person. (It will be noticed

that here Polyphemus is not assumed to be one-eyed: indeed in Homer he is never said so to be, though the story of his blinding as told in the Odyssey implies it.)

XIII

8 (*p*.116). Arabs: here Ărabs, but Ārabiae in 2.10.16.

15 (*p*.116). Eois: here Eŏīs but Ĕōo at 24.7 below.

32 (*p*.117). uersicoloris: the reference in the existing note to Lucretius 2.801-5 is misleading: that passage describes the irridescence of dove's plumage but does not apply *uersicolor* as epithet to it. Cicero *Fin.* 3.5.18 so applies it specifically.

35 (*p*.118). totos operibat amantes: the interpretation of *totos* in the existing note is far-fetched; it would be better to emend to *tectos* or *tutos* (both conjectured).

XIV

9 (*p*.122). ligat....gaudentia bracchia loris: *loris* can be construed with *ligat* as well as, or instead of, with *gaudentia*.

18 (*p*.123). equis: if after transposition of 15-16, as printed in the text on p.36, *equis* (18) is felt to jingle awkwardly with *aquis* (14), it would be possible to read *eques* ('as horseman') instead.

XV

3 (*p*.125). [In the app. crit. on p.37 *scripsi* is now corrected to *Fontein*.]

11 (*p*.126-7). testis erit Dirce: unfortunately the lay-out of the text on pp.38-9 obscures the fact that a pause is meant to be felt, and indicated by spacing, between 42 and 43, as between 10 and 11 earlier. And *testis erit Dirce* (= 'Dirce shall be my witness') should not indeed be *translated* 'think of Dirce' though the words have that value in the context.

33 (*p*.128). litore sub tacito: since the existing note was written L.D. Richardson (1977) has suggested *litore subtractae (sonitus rarescit harenae)*, a very probable correction which has now been included in the app. crit.

XVII

41 *(p.137)*. **seruitio uacuum me siste**: the reference in the existing note is not apposite; better would be *Aen.* 2.620 *tutum patrio te limine sistam*; better still the Plautine *saluum sistere* (e.g. Rudens 1049 *ego uos saluas sistam*) which brings out the special appropriateness of *sistere* to rescuing and putting in safety.

XIX

21-2 *(p.146)*. It seems best to keep *tuque* and transpose 15-16 to follow 20. (So Richardson and Hanslik, after Postgate.)

XX A and B

(pp.146-8). An alternative treatment makes no transposition and sees elegy 20 as one piece in two parts (or phases), 1-12 and 13-30 (= 13-24 + 25-30), which can be distinguished by a small spacing of the text between 12 and 13. In the first part the poet addresses the woman (in her presence or in imagination) urging her (10) to come quickly to his bed; and then (11-12) apostrophizes the Sun, who is urged not to dawdle but bring sunset (and bedtime with it) quickly. In the second part the poet, looking forward to (or welcoming) the promised night of love, apostrophizes the moon, who is urged to dawdle (as the sun was not to do) and so extend the night, in which long preliminaries are to precede the consummation of love. In line 13 the conjecture *da tempora nocti* (now included in the app. crit. on p.44) is preferred to *data tempora* accepted in text (p.44) and note (p.148), and seems indeed to be better both for sense and Latinity; it will mean 'add time to the night', extending its duration.

The argument that the woman is not supposed to be Cynthia is overstated: it is not clear that she is or that she is not.

XXI

6 *(p.151)*. **ex omni**: a simpler explanation takes *omni* as a substantive corresponding to *omnia* in 5, and renders 'but after every effort *(ex omni temptamento)* the god bears hard upon me still', *ex* referring, as often, to immediate sequence in time.

13 *(p.152)*. **iungiteque**: attachment of *-que* to a word ending in *-e* is rare; there is one other instance in Propertius *(taleque* 2.14.26), a few in Tibullus, and none in Ovid. (Platnauer, *Latin Elegiac Verse* 93).

18 (*p.152*). undisonos...deos: for the compound cf. Catull.
64.52 *fluentisono litore*. More remarkable than the form of the compound
adjective is its application to *deos*.

25 (*p.153*). stadiis: considering Cic. *Fin*. 5.1 *Academiae non
sine causa nobilitata spatia* (the Walks of the Academy) the alternative
conjecture *spatiis* is surely preferable here and it is now included in
the *app. crit.* on p.46. (So Hanslik.)

XXII

10-11 (*p.156*). It should be added that the poet's imagination is moving
into the real world; for the Argonauts' eastward voyage to Colchis took them
by way of Cyzicus, where Tullus is residing. Southward lie Ephesus and Egypt,
the latter as far distant as Colchis. Ephesus and Egypt had two of the
Seven Wonders of the World to show; respectively the temple of Diana and
the great tower on Pharos.

15 (*p.157*). et si qua Ortygie uisenda est...: the first
sentence of the existing note is confused and confusing. With the text as
printed *et si qua*... has to be parallel to the concessive constructions
begun in 7 and 11, and I think it means 'and if (i.e. though) Ortygie
(= Ephesus) has its wonders (for the traveller to admire)'.

ora Caystri: the Cayster was celebreated in its own right,
for the birds that abounded in its adjacent meadows (Hom. *Il*. 2.461; Virg.
Georg. 1.384). [It could be made a separate item here by reading *et*
between *Ortygie* and *uisenda*.]

[Postcript. In line 6 of this Elegy the MS tradition gives as first
word *et*, which cannot stand. In the text here printed on p.47 the
conjecture *at* is received, and *mouere* is 2nd person imperative passive,
making a main sentence which is apodosis to the conditional clauses of
1-5. Many editors prefer in 6 the reading of the emended manuscripts,
nec, with *mouere* as 2nd person indicative passive, and no main sentence
until line 17. With this reading (*nec* in 6) Housman wished to transpose
15-16 to stand between 6 and 7, as having a content more naturally related
to the content of 1-5 than to that of 7-14; also, there results as easily
intelligible construction of *et si qua*...(15) after *si te forte*...(5).
This suggestion recorded in *OCT* has now been included in the app. crit.:
see also CQ (1968) 319, where *serpentes* for *septenas* in 16 is proposed,
making that line refer to Maeander instead of to Nile.]